Be More Dog
Learning to Live in the Now

Rene Agredano & Jim Nelson

Enjoying Every Day to the Fullest
on the Road to Happiness

Many people dream of a magic reset button. With one touch, it would instantly change their circumstances and create a more fulfilling life. What they don't realize is that life provides plenty of opportunities to change direction, but few of us heed the signs showing us the way. For workaholic entrepreneurs Jim and Rene, their sign came as a cancer diagnosis. After growing their home-based business for ten years, their heart and soul dog, Jerry, had a front leg amputated because of bone cancer. Vets said their time together was running out. They decided to make the most of it. Acting quickly, they sold their home, their business, and nearly everything they owned. They bought a new RV and made Jerry a promise: "Stay with us long enough, and we'll take you on the road trip of a lifetime!"

By the time they hit the road to travel the country together as a pack, Jerry had already outlived his original prognosis. Their RV travels took them from northern California through the southwest desert, to the Atlantic coast in Maine, down to Florida and back to the top of the world in the Rocky Mountains. For two years they experienced many adventures, with Jerry leading the way and showing the world that it's better to hop on three legs than to limp on four. Their nomadic lifestyle breathed new life into the happy dog, who generously shared important life lessons along the way. Once they opened their eyes to how he lived each day to the fullest, everything looked different. Their reset button was pressed.

Be More Dog is more than a memoir about a three-legged dog on an epic road trip. This book is a heartwarming tale with deep meaning. Through his actions and attitude in the face of adversity, Jerry shows Jim and Rene how important it is to live in the now—to persevere when the going gets tough, to never give up, and that every day is a great day, no matter what life throws your way.

For Jerry.

Jerry, with Mooch and Earl
by Patrick McDonnell

BE MORE DOG

— FOREWORD —

By MUTTS Creator Patrick McDonnell

"Some people talk to animals. Not many listen though. That's the problem." — A.A. Milne, Winnie-the-Pooh

Rene Agredano and Jim Nelson listened. They listened with all their hearts.

They quit their jobs, sold their house, and bought an RV to go on a cross-country journey of compassion. All to listen to—and learn from—their three-legged miracle pup, Jerry G. Dawg.

Rene and Jim pursued the spiritual lessons our companion animals are trying to teach us—to be in the present moment, to accept what comes, to love everyone, and to Enjoy! Enjoy! Enjoy!

Rene and Jim didn't simply conceptualize these ideas. With Jerry's guidance, they learned to live them. A true love story, this book is a moving tribute to that special bond we share with our furry friends. It's a reminder of how deep they live in our hearts.

For me it was my Jack Russell Terrier, Earl, who lived for 19 years. He was everything you could want a dog to be and was the inspiration for my comic strip MUTTS. One of those MUTTS strips, printed here, found its way to Jim and Rene, where it spoke to them about their own Jerry.

March 4, 2008

MUTTS © 2019 Patrick McDonnell

Our work goes out to the universe and we never know how it might affect someone. Rene and Jim have helped thousands with their Tripawds charity, website, and blog. This powerful book is a love note to all who have had the honor and joy to share the companionship of a beloved dog. Embrace the message of reconnecting to our natural state.

Be more tree. Be more river. Be more mountain.

And, of course, *Be More Dog*.

The time is now.

Yesh!

— Patrick McDonnell

— CONTENTS —

BE MORE DOG

— INTRODUCTION —

Why We Love Cats and Dogs

This is a true story, more than twenty years in the making.

"Well, let's see, where to begin?" Jim sat on the rocks with Jerry's head in his lap. Rene took a spot next to them and stroked her tired dog's ears. The woman sitting cross-legged on the ground before the trio silently encouraged him to go on.

"This is Jerry, the Tripawds spokesdog! When he lost a leg to cancer, we sold everything and bought an RV to travel the country together. Now he's got followers all over the world, and we run the largest online community for three-legged dogs and their people, all from our mobile headquarters."

"Wait. Cut." It sounded like a commercial. The Emmy award-winning filmmaker and director of a new Nature episode for PBS didn't drag her crew across the country and up into the mountains outside Santa Fe to hear this. She needed some honest, heart-wrenching footage of the crazy couple who went to extreme lengths for their terminally ill dog. Her documentary would be titled, *Why We Love Cats and Dogs*. It was all about the unbreakable bonds created between people and their animals. She didn't want to hear about their website.

"Just be natural." From behind her dark sunglasses, the director encouraged the couple to just be themselves. "Tell me your story. Talk to me about Jerry. How did it all begin?"

Sure, Jim was nervous. The sun was beating down, and he was on the verge of tears. But not because of the cameraman standing behind the woman or the guy hanging the boom mic over his head. He'd done plenty of public speaking in his previous life. But he was a marketing guy at heart and he was proud of his pack. He had slipped into "commercial speak" because that was his comfort zone. But right now, he felt uncomfortable. Jim loved his dog more than anyone might ever believe. That morning, he was handed a reality check from his dog's veterinary oncologist. New tumors were growing in Jerry's lungs—the cancer had returned.

Distraught and now also embarrassed, Jim was noticeably shaken. He placed both hands on Jerry's body where his left leg once was, massaging the soft fur as his chest rose and fell with every panting breath.

"Let's start with you, Rene." The director signaled to the crew standing behind her. They shifted focus.

Rene began, "Jerry's been with us through the most important part of our lives…" The director kept the cameras rolling and started nodding with approval about what she was now hearing. What she was hearing was more authentic. It came from the heart. And that made for great TV.

"We got him soon after we got married, bought our first house, started a business…" She went on to detail how they "went whole hog" working from home 12 hours a day, for the past eight years, with Jerry always by their side.

Jim smiled as he joined in, now relaxed and reflecting on some of their favorite hiking trips together when Jerry was growing up. Then he got into details about the amputation. "The doctor told us he's already on three legs. Doing this will get rid of the pain. At that point, it was just a no-brainer.

"Amputate, and he'll have a bit longer to live, or medicate him for the short term." When Jerry's vet told them that even with the amputation he had less than a year to live, all the hours they'd dedicated to their business suddenly meant nothing. The dog alongside them was far more important than any profit and loss statement.

Jim went on. "The routine that Jerry did not like was waiting all day for us to play with him. So, we decided to take this road trip, to see new places, take him out into the wilderness where he loves to be. Our life just took this one-eighty, and it was all about Jerry."

Much later, he provided video footage of young Jerry romping in the snow and swimming in mountain lakes. The producers loved it, working in to paint the full picture of Jerry's journey. Even as a puppy, the dog was a ham for the camera—and always presenting a dramatic performance. His fur had the black and tan markings of a stereotypical German shepherd, but with another breed mixed in he had adorable white patches at the tip of his tail, a tiny dab between his soulful, brown eyes, and front feet that looked like he'd stepped in white paint.

"I figured he would let us know when he was sick. We know the signs..." Jim got choked up again. "You know, I want to see Jerry playing and enjoying life up until that happens. And when that time comes..." He reached out and scratched Jerry's head. "By all means, man..." Jim started sniffling and couldn't even form the words to go on. Jerry looked up right on cue, his eyes alight as he leaned into his dad's chest.

The director took off her sunglasses and paused while looking at Rene, encouraging her to pick up where Jim left off. She was pleased, knowing she had something to work with now, hoping for even more juicy material to illuminate the dynamic human-pet relationships she was trying to portray.

"A lot of people thought we were nuts when we sold our business and our house and said we were gonna travel for a while." Rene tried to explain just how much Jerry was part of their family, even though she noted, "He's not a kid. He's not human. But he means so much to us..."

Rene looked towards the camera. "How far do you go for a dog?"

"Cut." She had given the director precisely what she wanted to hear, and the filmmaker smiled. It was an ideal ending for one of the segments she crafted about Jerry and his people for *Why We Love Cats and Dogs*, which first aired on PBS in 2009.

"Perfect." She signaled for her crew to pack up the gear. "Let's go get some footage of you guys playing with Jerry in that snow over there."

Right on cue, Jerry hopped up and waited for direction. He was always ready to go places and he especially loved the snow—even if there was just a little remaining on the ground. Happy to oblige, he hopped over to the late spring snow patches and eagerly hammed it up for the camera. The newest medication to stall the cancer growing within him was working. Jerry romped without a worry.

❀　❀　❀

People need dogs. And not for the usual reasons one might imagine. They think they need a dog for love, or protection, or companionship.

Or maybe they think they need them to teach their kids responsibility, retrieve their ducks, guard the house, pull the sled, or win Best of Show. While most dogs can do these things quite well, life with a canine means so much more than that. People need dogs to feel grounded and to have a sense of purpose. A dog gives a person's life direction and meaning, if they pay attention to the clues. Dogs help humans understand there is more to life than striving for material goals and career achievements. This is why we really need a dog.

Big or small, mutt or purebred, dogs help people realize that their short lives are meant to be lived to the fullest, today. Not when they leave the office at night, when the kids fly the coop, or "someday" after retirement. Nearly every dog is born with the instinct to make the most of every minute. For anyone willing to learn, dogs demonstrate how to do that.

They do not stress themselves with destructive human emotions— like fear of the future, uncertainty, or doubt. Dogs do not become overwhelmed about jobs, family matters, or financial affairs. But people do. And when they get wrapped up in these emotions, they find that their problems manifest as pain. Many try to self-medicate with whatever drug du jour meets their needs. Or they get angry at tiny provocations, or worry, then take it out on loved ones. The more enlightened humans might turn to yoga, meditation, massage, or exercise to cope. But most people just bury their emotional pain deep in their hearts.

It's human instinct to turn to dogs when life gets tough. Humans and dogs don't speak the same language, but even without it, dogs know when hard times are coming long before the people realize it. Dogs understand when something is wrong and know how to give comfort without judgment. They may give a gentle nudge with a wet nose, a full body rub up against your leg, or they might even just walk out of the room. Whatever non-verbal action dogs choose to calm us down with, they are usually trying to say:

Stop, breathe. Your thoughts are killing you!

Not even the wisest dogs can speak in our language, but they don't need words to sense all the pointless worries exploding in the human mind. Look into that dog's eyes in times of distress, and you will see that all he or she wants is for you to be happy. Because when the person is happy, the dog is happy. The dog does not worry about today's decisions, nor regret the past, nor fret about the future. The dog does not try to be happy; the dog just is.

If only people would live their own life this way. If only they would learn how to Be More Dog.

Jim and Rene did—the hard way.

This is the story of a discarded dog who grew to become an impressive pack leader. Jerry taught a young, hardworking couple how to turn tragedy into a triumph when doctors said his leg needed to come off to save his life. They were warned that amputation would put an end to his pain, but it would not get rid of the cancer. The disease would return, and the dog they loved had less than a year to live.

Jerry was dying, and things had to change. Their steadfast companion deserved so much more than a long goodbye in the corner office. So, they made him a promise. They vowed to give him the one thing he wanted most: unlimited time with his favorite people, in the kinds of places he loved.

The situation demanded action. Instead of opting for chemotherapy treatments and vet visits, they made a plan for a one-year sabbatical. To pay for it, they sold their business, their home, and nearly all their possessions. Then they purchased a new RV to travel the country together as a pack, for however much time they had left together.

Jerry didn't seem to know why things changed so dramatically, and he didn't care. All that mattered to him was having fun with his people. He was their co-pilot on an ever-changing journey that just so happened to take them all around the United States. They waded in the Mississippi headwaters, chased waves on the Atlantic coast in Maine, swam in the Gulf of Mexico, and climbed to the top of the world in the Rocky Mountains. For the first time in their lives, every day was new and exciting. And in an ironic sort of way, cancer was the best thing that ever happened to the trio.

From Jerry's first stumble on three legs to his final hops under the big Montana sky, he taught them about acceptance, adaptation, tolerance, and the importance of living in a state of awareness. As his time on Earth came to a close, he left them knowing that no matter what happens, we have it within us to make every day a great day.

Jerry, like all dogs, demonstrated that being happy is about much more than the pursuit of possessions and money. Practicing compassion, gratitude, humility, and humor are the way to true joy. In other words, to find bliss, we must Be More Dog.

— 1 —

The Happy Threesome

"You got it pretty good, dawg." Jim caressed Jerry's soft, black-and-tan fur as he lay sprawled across the big, brown couch. The lean mutt rested his head in his dad's lap and let out a long, soft sigh, suggesting his agreement.

Upstairs in their 100-year-old Victorian home, they could finally relax in Jerry's dog den, a small corner room with an old television, a big basket of well-loved, crusty, slobber-matted dog toys, and not much else except an ugly, four-piece sectional sofa with well-worn cushions. A big ottoman fit perfectly under the windowsill to serve as a second-floor perch for Jerry to monitor the street below.

"Aww, Jer, you are such a love." Rene smiled as she entered the den with another box of work in her arms. "But I really wish you had thumbs!" She was wrapping up a graphics job that just hours earlier Jim had finished printing downstairs. From the first-floor office of their 3,700-square-foot home, he had designed and printed 1,000 small "shelf talker" cards that dangle from the edges of retail store shelves. Each had to be individually attached to a thin, plastic strip that would make them dangle and compete for customer attention. The job almost exceeded what their two-person business could produce, but in a recession, you don't say no.

Rene sat next to Jerry, peeling and sticking, peeling and sticking, occasionally stopping to pick off errant bits of fur that floated onto the sticky backs. Tiny, square pieces of adhesive backing lay strewn all over the floor. There would be cleaning to do, but not now. Now was the time to relax and be glad for the new—if brief—lease on life they got for Jerry.

She finished her project and sat back, giving Jim a smile as he massaged the spot where Jerry's front left leg used to be. It had been a few months since the amputation, and the peach fuzz on his left side was finally giving way to a full, thick coat that was softer than ever.

Jerry absorbed the attention. No words were necessary, just a sweet upward glance with gentle eyes reflecting pure gratitude.

Jerry had a dog's dream life—even after the cancer appeared. He may have lost one leg to the disease, but he still led his two-human pack on some wild adventures, with a few important life lessons tossed in for good measure. People might have pitied him and that funny hop of his, but he had more pressing concerns. After his amputation, Jerry persevered to keep Jim and Rene sane, as there were only the two of them to grow their small business. It was a big responsibility, but other dogs should have it so good. He got to be with his people all day, every day. And oh, how they treated their first dog.

Jerry was their baby. Not in a ribbons-in-the-hair kind of way, but rather how humans take pride in their first offspring. Only instead of driving a car with bumper stickers proclaiming, "My child is an Honor Student," the child-free couple proudly slapped an "I Love My Mutt" sticker on theirs. Jerry led the kind of picture-perfect life you see in dog food commercials. Not bad for a pound puppy.

Jerry's dream life almost ended in November 2006 when he was diagnosed with terminal bone cancer. Osteosarcoma, to be exact. The cancer that attacks the limbs of dogs and people alike was eating away his scapula. Science knows no cure for the disease that usually kills dogs within twelve months, but if the tumor—and the entire limb—is removed, patients can enjoy pain-free quality time until it does. Surgery would cost Jerry a leg, but not his life. At least not right away.

Amputation is a no-brainer for people with osteosarcoma, but it's not like that for dogs. Many family dogs with osteosarcoma will die an early death because their guardians are under the impression that dogs can't be happy without all four legs. Even some of the biggest dog lovers out there recoil at the very idea of amputating. They think it's cruel, and refuse to believe a dog can have a good, high quality life as an amputee. "Dogs aren't meant to live like that," they say.

But Jerry lucked out. When he got sick, his people stopped to ask themselves: "What would Jerry want?"

They had their doubts, like anyone else. They agonized over the ethics. Was amputation for the dog or for them? Neither had ever seen a dog with a missing limb and wondered how any active canine could be happy on three legs. But the thought of euthanizing him before he had a chance to prove it was unbearable. Two days after the diagnosis, Jim and Rene followed their hearts and listened to the experts. Vets know. They see three-legged animals all the time. "Dogs don't care if they're missing a leg. They don't get depressed about it the way we do. They adapt."

On Thanksgiving Day 2006, this trio had much to be thankful for. When Jerry triumphantly hopped down the white, sterile hallway with his surgeon to greet Jim and Rene, their eyes filled with tears. Their handsome dog with rugged German shepherd looks and the heart of a collie now resembled a carved-up turkey. His body was shaved on one side where a gruesome incision snaked around the void where his leg had been. Rene had promised she wouldn't cry, but that didn't last long as she wept, "Oh, Jerry, please don't hate us! I'm so sorry!"

But Jerry wasn't sorry. He wasn't mad because the young university surgeon lopped off his diseased limb. Wagging his tail wildly with enthusiasm, he seemed to say, "Look at me, not my missing leg. I am still me, and I don't hurt anymore!" His long, fluffy tail swished to and fro and his bright eyes sparkled with the sheer joy of a new day without pain. The unforgettable morning started with sadness but ended with a joyful Jerry hopping out of the clinic and on with his mission. He was alive, and he would show people it really is better to hop on three strong legs than to painfully limp along on four.

That dog had already given Jim and Rene so much in his eight years. "You wouldn't tell a person they should be put down if they had bone cancer, would you?" Rene asked well-meaning people who questioned their decision to amputate. "We owe it to him. He keeps us sane." They would face the unknown with the same fortitude Jerry showed every time they took him on another crazy adventure—or into a surgery ward. She and Jim would go the distance for this dog, which ended up being about 150,000 miles—and counting. In life and beyond, Jerry was their spiritual navigator who steered them toward the happier life they craved.

But let's not get ahead of ourselves here. Like any epic journey, this one is best told from the beginning.

※ ※ ※

Jerry was an extraordinary dog who adopted two people that were just as out of the ordinary as he was. They were an intrepid couple from the beginning. She rode a motorcycle, he had long hair, and together they found their way to Burning Man when only a couple hundred San Franciscans knew about it. By day they worked to pay the bills, but after five, they clocked out in search of outdoorsy adventure.

Pedal across the Golden Gate Bridge to Marin? No problem. Take a Sunday morning motorcycle ride to the Sonoma Coast? Count them in. When friends invited them to hike across the Sierra Nevadas, they said, "Why not?" Nature satisfied their souls like nothing else could.

Hardly a month had passed from their first date when they and two friends set out together on a springtime trek into the Sierras. The cool air felt nice on their overheated bodies as they gingerly treaded atop the granite rocks, slippery and wet from snowmelt. After six or so miles, the perfect campsite appeared beyond the glistening snowbanks. For the next four days, they would live in the little clearing and dream about the ways in which they could escape city life for good.

Jim gave a not-so-subtle hint that he wanted some private time with Rene. "Let's go take a look around." It was the early part of their dating days, filled with spontaneous make-outs and googly-eyed affection. Hand in hand, they went in search of some privacy. But just as he leaned in to make his move under the quiet shade of pine branches, a chorus of ear-splitting shrieks and high-pitched chatter interrupted the rendezvous. Several kids and two couples had decided to camp nearby. "Well, so much for that."

Both gazed toward the rambunctious kids, neither looking at the other. Rene finally blurted out, "I don't want kids. Do you?" She looked into his eyes dead-on, expecting an answer.

Jim blinked in surprise—and relief. "You have no idea how happy I am you said that!" Score! This girl didn't waste time. She had just lifted a burden the size of his ridiculously heavy backpack lying 100 yards away. He was the youngest of six kids; she, the last of five. Neither had any desire to clone their DNA or share their toys.

"There's already enough of us," Rene liked to say about her sizeable Mexican family.

Nearing 30, Jim was ready for his dating days to end, and her attitude indicated he may have finally found The One.

Always logical, always careful, he immediately put his eighteen-month plan into effect:

Date for six months. Live together for six months. Get married six months after that.

He was logical that way, and figured his plan would work perfectly.

Once they returned to the city, Jim knew their next getaway would be a special one. A couple months later, Rene made it happen by planning an epic road trip. When they were halfway through the 1,200-mile motorcycle tour to Utah's Capitol Reef National Park, he made his move. On a long hike through the secluded Cohab Canyon he started to talk, fumbled his words, held her hand, then dropped the ball again. Finally, he just looked her in the eyes, and when he couldn't find the right thing to say, he just waited for her to talk.

"Do you have something to say?" She knew he was up to something. Women always know.

He reached into his pocket and retrieved what he had been holding onto. The perfect moment had arrived.

Her eyes met his, and she broke into a huge smile that lit up the sandstone canyon. He placed a dainty silver ring in her sweaty palm and smiled. A few days earlier, he'd made the surprise acquisition at a Death Valley gift shop, along with a six-pack of Bud for liquid courage. In his other hand, he clutched a tattered, yellowing comic strip that he passed to her with a sheepish grin. The black-and-white sketch fluttered in the breeze of an oncoming thunderstorm as she held it in her hand. It showed an astonished girl with hair standing on end, shocked over her suitor's wedding proposal. The comic simply read: "Surprised?"

Sunburned and road-weary from their long trip, at this point, he figured she was stuck with him and there was no way she could turn down the proposal. His guts turned in knots as she stared at him, smiling but mute. He needed her answer before it started raining or he threw up, whichever came first. Finally, he had to know. "Well?"

"You haven't asked me."

Somewhere deep inside he found the courage, took a deep breath, and said the four scariest words of his life.

"Will you marry me?"

"Yes! Duh, you goof!"

With perfect timing, lightning struck and rain gently sprinkled down from the stormy clouds churning overhead. The kiss that sealed the deal lasted forever. The sun broke through, and they were on their way to living happily ever after.

🐾 🐾 🐾

Always the oddballs of their family tribe, as no surprise to anyone when the newlyweds announced they were walking away from good-paying Silicon Valley jobs to move to the remote coastal town of Eureka, California. Yet, everyone was still skeptical. And who could blame them? In the prime of their lives, Jim and Rene were fleeing behind "The Redwood Curtain." It was a region deep in the heart of Northern California, famous for giant trees, marijuana farming, and not much else.

"How are you going to live?"

"Are you growing dope?"

"Are you out of your mind!?"

Rene and Jim laughed at the assumptions and casually waved away others' doubts. They knew that on the North Coast they could afford a house with acreage and extra rooms. And in all that cheap space they could start a business and call their own shots. Jim crunched the numbers to make sure his freelance graphic design work and a large format printer would be their ticket away from convention.

It all looked great on paper, but after the move, they had more time on their hands than actual business. Locals weren't after the big-city marketing and printing services the couple was selling. "Wow, that's really expensive," they would say after Jim told them his hourly consulting rate, a bargain down south. "I can get it at the Copy Shop."

"So let them," Jim told himself. The business he wanted was the tech-savvy clientele in faraway places where money flowed from the dot-com boom. Carefully and slowly, he built their Internet presence while Rene earned a steady paycheck at the local hospital. Each day he sat alone in his home office designing marketing materials and trade show displays for a small but growing client base. Eventually, his plan fell into place. In less than a year, the business was bringing in cash and along with it, a new problem: he couldn't keep up with the workload. He turned to Rene. "I need your help. Please quit your job and come to work at home with me."

It took her less than two seconds to decide.

❁　❁　❁

They soon had a good thing going with the new lifestyle. It was 1998, and unlike their city friends who capped off long workdays in bars, theirs usually ended with a hot tub soak under the tall redwood trees towering over their home. Rural life was an easy adjustment; the business was thriving, and weekends were filled with wild treks to the rugged coast or into the nearby mountains. But something was missing.

"Hey, let's go look at dogs." Rene liked to throw that in during their Saturday morning errands. The animal shelter was just down the road, and her heart ached every time they passed it. She wanted a dog in her life, but Jim wasn't ready. Not yet anyway.

"I've told you, I don't want to get a dog until we have the time to spend with it. We're so focused on work all the time, it just wouldn't be fair to the dog."

"That's just it, though, we're always home!" It was an ongoing argument. And lately, she was pleading her case more than ever. "We have the perfect yard, and it's just a few minutes to the beach. We could go hiking whenever we want." She made it sound like any dog's dream, which it was.

"Come on. When are we going to find the time to train a puppy?" He just couldn't commit to the responsibility.

"We'll make time." Now she was starting to pout.

It was time to change the subject. "Let's go for a bike ride instead. You can't do that with a dog!" He tried to convince himself they couldn't devote enough time and attention to keep a dog happy. What he didn't want to admit was that the perfect time never exists.

❖   ❖   ❖

Midnight car alarms are the soundtrack to city life. Most people ignore them. But this time, one guy didn't. During another late night in San Francisco, one South of Market resident was pissed off. His sleep got interrupted by the alarm on a green Ford Ranger parked outside his bedroom window. He almost threw a brick at the offender, but noticed a phone number on the truck's window decals.

A few blocks away, Jim was enjoying a late-night dinner with clients. "To Macworld!" they cheered, pint glasses clanging together. Jim had spent the day with his clients installing exhibit graphics he made for the big tech conference that started in the morning. The next day, he would make a big ad campaign presentation to them to drum up more business.

Back in Eureka, Rene tried to get used to being alone in their quiet country home. The whir of the computer network and an occasional dog bark in the neighbor's yard were the only sounds interrupting the dozens of random thoughts keeping her awake. After living among the chaos of the city and roommates for many years, silence made her feel uneasy. When she finally started dozing off at 1:00 a.m., the phone rang. She jumped to answer, thinking it was Jim.

"Hey, your car alarm is going off! Come turn it off now or I'm having it towed!"

She rubbed her eyes and tried to make sense of the threatening voice. "Who is this? How did you get my number?"

"I'm looking at your phone number!"

In a split second, she knew what he meant. The windows on their truck had decals with their business name and phone number. "Oh, that number!" He didn't bother to tell her about the smashed-in passenger-side window. All he cared about was getting someone to stop the noise.

"I'm so sorry, it's my husband's truck. I'll try to find him." She hung up the phone before the angry man could continue. Now she really wasn't going to sleep.

She unsuccessfully tried to reach Jim at the friend's house where he was staying. Anger and fear surged through her. Where is he? What happened to the truck? What would make the alarm go off? Then she remembered how he always left his house keys in the glove box and grew fearful. What if someone was on their way up to rob them?

Oblivious to the crime, Jim wrapped up dinner and headed back to his parking spot, happy and confident. But when he arrived at his truck and saw the pile of broken glass, his emotions crashed to the gutter. That fabulous meal he just ate rose in his throat as he peered into the cab and saw that his design portfolio was gone. The artwork it held was utterly worthless to anyone else. But for him, it was the ticket to good-paying work in the competitive Silicon Valley.

"Oh my God…oh my gawd!" he yelled as he opened the door to a seat full of broken glass. Hot tears stung his eyes as he tore apart the crime scene looking for any sign of the black case. A quick look up and down the street, and he knew it was gone for good.

Nauseated from having his life's passion stolen and probably tossed into a dumpster, he drove away. There was nothing more to do. Back at his friend's home, a short note was waiting. The hasty scrawl on a small scrap of paper simply read, "Call your wife!"

The 2:00 a.m. call didn't go so well. Rene was pissed, and with reason. She was scared, alone, and six hours away. After he reassured her that he was okay and nobody was coming to rob her, she calmed down, then addressed his problem. "What are you going to do about tomorrow?" His big presentation could pay the bills for months. Everything relied on the artwork.

"Don't worry. I got back here and remembered the ad comps are in my suitcase." The broken window was still a problem, but he had what he needed for the meeting—as long as he could control his emotions about the incident.

The next day, he presented without skipping a beat. The clients loved his ideas and gave the go-ahead for a major project. While he should have been elated, he felt miserable on the chilly, six-hour drive back to Eureka, knowing that his truck needed repair and his wife needed reassurance.

❈   ❈   ❈

"We need a dog," Rene said with a serious look. Just three days after the break-in, Jim wasn't about to disagree. "I want a dog here when you're gone. If someone is going to break into our house, I want protection." She would never admit that what she really wanted was a calm soul to keep her company.

"All right, we'll go to the shelter this weekend." He shrugged and sighed, knowing he was finally caving in. "Just remember, this was your idea!" Deep down he could hear a voice telling him he was also ready for a dog, but he wasn't about to admit it.

On Saturday morning, they walked through the doors of the nearby humane society. Life as they knew it would never be the same.

❈   ❈   ❈

People kid themselves into thinking that they pick out the family dog. The truth is, dogs pick them. It often unfolds like a sappy TV show. A rambunctious puppy runs across a field and into the arms of a happy little boy. He gets smothered with sloppy, wet kisses by the puppy, the parents nod in agreement, and everyone lives happily ever after.

On the day Jim and Rene walked into the Humboldt County

Humane Society shelter, one puppy was ready to turn on the charm. He was one of a dozen other dogs, all desperately waiting to break out. The most anxious ones fought for their attention, barking loudly to catch the eye of the hopeful couple. Their loud barks all screamed, "Look at me! Look at me!"

Pine-Sol and urine odors filled the air as they took their first steps into the world of pet parenting. Chain-link fences clanked as burly dogs hurled their bodies against the barriers that separated them from death row. Those dogs hadn't yet given up, unlike the overlooked misfits who had seen it all before. Always passed up for inmates who resembled golden retrievers and Labs, the defeated dogs lay against the cinder block walls without trying to impress.

Jim and Rene couldn't imagine picking just one. They walked past the kennels, hearts shattering with each glimpse of their pleading eyes. Good thing most of them didn't fit the "guard dog" vision that Rene wanted. They stopped at the last run. There he was.

A gangly, black-and-tan puppy sprang to his feet. It was his turn to plead his case, but the jury wouldn't need much convincing. His huge paws and markings gave him the appearance of a big German shepherd in the making. Some other breed was in his makeup too. He had one white front paw, and a big, pointy ear irresistibly flopping forward. She walked over, and he barked a head-turning yap for her attention.

When Jim approached, the lonely pup behaved as if he had to act quickly. He barked once, then galloped to the back of his kennel to further demonstrate his demolition skills; a plastic laundry basket slowly being torn to bits. Using his sharp, white puppy teeth, the dog clenched one end of the basket in his mouth and dragged it around to impress his audience. The makeshift toy was larger than him, but it wasn't going to stop him from showing what he could do with those teeth. For a final act, he scrunched up his face and bit down as hard as he could on the basket, then shook it side to side with every ounce of his thirty-pound puppy body.

Their eyes connected. The other dogs' barking faded away. "You are adorable!" Rene squealed as Jim laughed loudly at the spectacle. They were easily impressed. A kennel attendant was coiling up a hose at the other end of the wet concrete aisle, so Jim waved to get her attention. "We want to meet him!"

They headed outside to a fence corral where the puppy waited. He was exuberant, and clearly destructive. Most people wouldn't want a dog like that, but Jim and Rene weren't like most people. The dog seemed to know he had them hooked, but still couldn't resist showing off. He raced to one end of the run, then back to the two smiling people, then over to the other end. For his finale, he galloped back at full speed and barreled right into Jim. Next, he—you guessed it—jumped into Jim's lap and washed his face with dog drool and the sweet, milky scent of puppy breath.

The awkward inmate teetering on the edge of German shepherd adolescence finally found his people. His sentence was over. This puppy was going home.

        ❀   ❀   ❀

Jim and Rene waited in the shelter lobby. She wore a wide grin and Jim looked as nervous as a new dad waiting in the maternity ward. "Here you go, he's all yours." The kennel worker handed Jim a flimsy chain leash with a red leather handle and a shopping list of pet supplies. The dog pushed his body between their legs and leaned hard with an implied sense of gratitude. Rene knelt down and planted a huge kiss on top of his head. He smelled like heaven.

The new parents had a lot to learn, but first the dog known as SH100198 needed a name. Back then, all shelter dogs were only known by the number posted to their kennel. "We don't name the dogs, because we don't want to become too attached," one volunteer explained. Most of the dogs who ended up in this overburdened shelter were put down long before they could learn a new name.

But this lucky dog was an exception. He was theirs now, and needed a name. Not just any moniker would do. The people holding his leash liked to camp, hike, and swim in cold mountain lakes. This dog needed a name that captured the essence of the life he was about to inherit. "What are we going to name him? I don't want a boring one," Rene said as Jim drove them home with the dog on her lap.

Looking at the grateful dog sitting next to him, Jim wondered what it would be. "How about Sport? Or Rex?"

"Nah, those are all too...doggy. We need something more meaningful, more unique. Like him."

They headed for home in the giant redwood trees that stood like ancient sentinels of the Humboldt County countryside. It was the chosen land of old hippies, and although Jerry Garcia had recently died, the movement lived on.

Jim was too young to be a real Dead Head hippie, but he had been to his share of Grateful Dead concerts. As they bantered over masculine dog names, the only thing Jim knew for sure was that it had to sound cool if he ever had to run down the street shouting after him.

"What about Jerry?"

The proud new pet parents smiled and looked at each other, knowing nothing more needed to be said. The name stuck. Jerry G. Dawg. Neither of them ever had to run down the road shouting his name. But that dog definitely led them on a long, strange trip through the best days of their lives.

— 2 —

Who Is Raising Whom?

"Hey! Come play with us." Jim wanted her to join in the fun he was having with their new little buddy in the living room. She muttered something about being busy, so the hallway ball game continued without her. "Hah!" Jim grabbed the rubber ball away from the excited puppy and hid it behind his back. Wide-eyed and bewildered, the dog looked around, then darted back down the hall to retrieve his prize.

"Here it is, Jerry!" Jim tossed the ball across the living room. The spry puppy leaped up and twirled around on his paws to nab the bouncy prey, his young, pliable body bending and turning in every direction the ball bounced. Now wise to Jim's tactics, he was on to the game and wasn't about to let the ball get by him this time.

"Go get it, Jerry!" Grabbing the ball again, Jim tossed it down the long, narrow hall. He read somewhere it was good to say a new dog's name whenever possible.

"Whoa! Hey, dog, look out!" Rene squealed as she stepped out of the bathroom and into the path of the flying rubber projectile. It nearly bonked her in the nose as Jerry ran to get it, almost tripping her when his oversized paws ran over her bare feet. He ran so fast he missed seeing the tiny space Rene had just set up for his first night at home.

"Whatchya doing?" Jim walked over and poked his head in the bathroom. She had placed blankets in the shower stall, bowls by the toilet, and newspapers spread out in front of the sink. Joyfully oblivious, Jerry lay at the end of the dark hallway chomping on his chewy trophy.

"I read that young puppies need to sleep in a small space for a while. That way, they don't pee all over the house."

"Huh. You think he's going to sleep in there?"

"It's the best thing for him," she explained in that tone reserved for decisions she made regardless of what he thought.

It seemed like a bad idea, but he knew how to pick his battles. This wasn't one worth fighting. "Whatever." He crouched down and army-crawled on all fours toward Jerry, who cautiously peered up from the toy he was slowly destroying. "Gimme that ball, Jerry!"

"Time for bed, Jerry!" Rene interrupted. "Come on, come inside!" It was game over when she lured him into the bathroom with some kibble, then knelt down on one knee as he eagerly gobbled the food. "Good boy…" Petting his soft fur as he sat next to the toilet, she tried to lessen the blow of his nighttime quarters. "This is where you'll sleep tonight, Jerry; we'll just be in the next room."

Jerry studied the expression on her face, but the sounds spilling from her mouth sounded like gibberish. He couldn't figure out her intentions; then she got up to leave.

"Okay, Jerry, I'll leave the nightlight on for you. Goodnight." Then she turned and left, closing the door behind her.

At the end of their long first day together, Jim and Rene crawled into bed while less than ten feet away, the young puppy serenaded them with an endless, lonesome-sounding song. *Aaaaroooooooooo… Wowwoorooroorooo…*

Trying to decipher his howls, Rene immediately thought about Jerry's nights in the kennel. What was he thinking? *Why did you leave me here? All alone!*

"Do we really have to leave him in there all night? The poor guy. Let's just let him sleep in here." Jim just wanted to get some rest and tried multiple times to plead his case. "If he has to go, I'll take him out." He didn't like her tough-love approach, and hoped she might cave in once he pleaded his case with love-filled eyes.

Feeling his stare, she lifted the pillow covering her ears and peered into his eyes through the darkness. "He has to know we're in charge. He needs to stay there. Puppies need strong leadership," she explained. "Dogs need people to make decisions and stick to them, not be wishy-washy softies."

It's what the TV trainers taught, but the dog howling from the next room made her feel like a jerk.

The cries continued and nobody slept. Finally, after several hours of trying to ignore it, she got out of bed and opened the bathroom door. Jerry shook his head and ran into the hallway. He jumped up on his rear legs and tried licking her face, whether from the joy that he hadn't been forgotten or to show how proud he was for not peeing, Rene didn't know.

The sweet, milky scent of puppy breath melted her heart. "Awww, Jerry. I'm so sorry for leaving you in there. I don't think that was such a good idea after all, was it? Do you promise to be good if I let you sleep in the bedroom with us?" Those TV dog trainers didn't seem so smart after all. Maybe Jerry didn't need tough love, or so she hoped while bending over to kiss the small white spot on top of his head. "Can you forgive me?"

All he heard were unintelligible sounds, but Jerry sensed that she spoke from the heart. Blame or anger just isn't part of a dog's nature.

❀   ❀   ❀

Their mutual trust and respect grew almost as fast as Jerry's spindly, deer-like legs, until a playful game of tug-of-war with his rope toy got ugly. "You get it, Jerry!" Jim tightly grasped one end of the thick rope and pulled hard while sharp puppy teeth clamped down on the other. Back and forth, dog and man pulled in opposite directions with nobody ever really gaining ground. Jim would pull him across the rug, then let him regain some ground.

Grrrrr...Arrrrrrgh! Grunt! Grunt! Grunt! The noises grew louder and spilled into the kitchen where Rene was making dinner. She heard gnashing, growling, and laughter until it ended in a snap with Jim's ear-splitting shout:

"Ouch! Dammit. He bit me!"

Horrified at what she might see, Rene ran out to find Jerry pinned to the ground on his back with all four legs flinging wildly in the air. "NEVER. BITE. ANYONE!" Jim's voice boomed as he held the stunned puppy down by his scruff.

Jerry laid limp, crying and whimpering in surprise.

"What are you doing to him?" Rene yelled at Jim. It looked like abuse; she couldn't believe their innocent little dog had done anything that bad. "Come on...are you sure he bit you?"

"It hurts! Look!" He released his grip on Jerry's neck and held out one hand, keeping the dog pinned down with the other. Two tiny droplets of blood dripped from his hand. "You're the one reading that book...about being the alpha and all that."

She said nothing, stunned that he would be so upset over a tiny puncture.

"You're the one who told me, remember? About how it's not being mean, it's just showing a dog who's boss." But then he stopped, a bit ashamed for mocking her. He looked back at Jerry, pathetically miserable on one side, his oversized paws limp on the floor with all four toes outstretched, surrendering to the alpha. A single toe lightly brushed Jim's kneecap, prompting a realization that would turn his puppy-training tactics upside down: *He has no thumbs!*

It should have been evident to Jim from the day they brought Jerry home. Sickening waves of shame rippled through his stomach as he began to hate himself for being so clueless. *He has to use his teeth. That's all he's got. Four paws, four toes....*

Who could blame that dog for sinking his teeth into the hand that held his prize? It wasn't a fair match. He was only trying to win back the toy he was peacefully playing with on his bed just a few minutes earlier. The rollover trick looked so easy when the trainers did it. But when Jim did it on his own dog, it made him feel sick. Maybe it works for some dogs, he thought, but this happy puppy was only acting in self-defense.

"Come here, little buddy. It's okay..." Jim held out his hands, trying to make amends.

Jerry got up, then corkscrewed his long, lean body into a shake from head to tail and back again. Confused and uncertain, he tried to make sense of Jim's sudden aggression and unexplained surrender. He walked away, but not before giving Jim a quick sniff and good, long stare. When he turned away and walked to his bed, Jim knew in his heart that his dog didn't have an aggressive bone in his body. From that day on, the "As Seen on TV" training tactics were over.

* * *

German shepherds scare lots of people, but even when he was a puppy, anyone could see that Jerry was a lover, not a fighter. Big dogs or small dogs, it didn't matter, he always got along with other canines. Being abandoned and stuffed into a dark drop box at the county shelter never damaged his gentle temperament. Neighborhood dogs who approached his yard were greeted with a deep, joyful welcoming bark, not the usual angry warnings fired off by more paranoid watchdogs.

All creatures were his friends until they proved otherwise. Each day he could morph from a loving lap dog at breakfast, to a rowdy backyard barker at lunch, and back to a couch potato before dinner, never once pushing the limits of bad behavior. Jerry could calmly walk into any situation and be the well-behaved calendar dog of every pet parent's dreams.

Obedience school was a breeze. The dog trainer woman with the booming voice and giant bag of treats was easily pleased. "Sit." Jerry sat. That was easy. "Stand." Easy, no problem there. "Come." Jerry happily came when called. The young dog caught on quickly and tolerated her patronizing commands. Anything for the treats. For two months, he put up with the classes to score more goodies and praise. But maybe the real reason he tolerated the repetitive commands was that he saw his humans making progress. The gruff lady taught them what to do at their end of the leash, without using strong-arm tactics. Jerry was no dummy. He knew that obedience lessons are really for the humans.

All the while, Jim and Rene were clueless of their good fortune. Nobody told them they had won the Doggy Lotto when Jerry picked them as parents. They foolishly assumed all dogs turned out this way with a little training and effort.

❄   ❄   ❄

Gangly, lanky, and adorably awkward, Jerry gradually grew into those giant, wolf-like paws, but his personality never matched the black-and-tan German shepherd markings on his coat. Whenever Jim and Rene stepped back to admire their handsome puppy, they sensed that he *looked* more like a German shepherd—but never quite *acted* like one. On the outside, he appeared to be an effective guard dog with his big, pointy ears, long, dark muzzle, visibly large and sharp white teeth, and deep, booming bark. But his welcoming nature, innocent eyes, and wagging tail told a different story.

Jerry wouldn't harm a flea, but worked hard to protect his pack from the two most prevalent evils of suburbia: squirrels, and the errant cats who teased him from outside the window. His sudden loud barks at front-yard invaders were intimidating to all but harmful to no one. Each day he sounded the alarm from the comfy spot on his fluffy, round bed placed in front of the full-length living room windows. The angry outdoor cat Jim and Rene had inherited with the house was the worst, knowing their protector couldn't fight back from his shielded perch. Despite Jerry's fierce demands for her to leave, that feline never budged from her favorite spot on the other side of the glass.

"Well, so much for thinking we were getting a guard dog. Even the old alley cat knows there is no bite behind that bark!" Rene said with joy instead of disappointment. If that window wasn't in the way, she suspected the fat, gray cat would likely chase gentle Jerry into hiding.

❧ ❧ ❧

Most dogs sit alone in quiet houses all afternoon waiting for their people to leave the office and walk through the front door, but not Jerry. His humans never left. They worked at home. But it wasn't always fun and games for all of them. Each day the young dog lay patiently snoozing between their spare bedroom offices, waiting to see who would stand first to take a break. It was always the same, with both sitting and staring into the glowing computer screens two feet from their faces. Occasionally Jerry would get up to investigate by sniffing around Rene's desk or nudging the plastic board Jim continuously tapped—as if wondering when they might ever get up and go do something fun. But mostly he just sat around waiting for them to stop gazing into the big, bright boxes.

Rene was often out running errands or delivering projects, while Jim worked alone creating artwork. He rarely moved. Aside from the constant hum of the computers in the closet, the only sounds Jerry heard were the *click, click...tap, tap, tap...click* of the keyboard and mouse, while Jim sat transfixed on projects for businesses in faraway places.

With a small but growing list of tech industry clients impressed by his marketing and design talent, Jim didn't let anything slow down his creative process. Well, almost anything. Whenever he spun his chair around, the creak caused Jerry to sit up and prepare for whatever excitement was about to begin. "Not right now, buddy." Instead, Jim grabbed the sheet of paper spilling from his tabloid printer and reached for an X-ACTO blade knife. Then he hunched over his cutting mat for the next fifteen minutes without looking up.

Disappointed, Jerry eyed him with his usual forlorn look. A deep stare, with his head cocked, waiting for a reaction. He had no concept of why that piece of paper was so important.

Day after day, the exchange continued. Each time, Jim felt Jerry's unbreakable glare on his back. "Not. Yet. I need to get this done." Sometimes he would get irritated with his persistent puppy demanding a break time. "You've already gone out. We'll play at lunch, I promise." The words were meaningless to Jerry, and it didn't take long for Jim's conscience to remind him that he was neglecting the dog he was learning to love so deeply. "Okay, you win, let's go."

"Go!" It was a word that Jerry came to learn and love, the signal to get up and run to the door for a "Jerry Break" in the big backyard behind the house. The grassy, half-acre parcel had three tall redwood trees standing as sentinels over the modest little house. Beneath them grew a large shrub Jim was crudely trimming to look like an ostrich. In the rear, Rene's garden was coming alive with zucchini, peas, and lettuce starts. The green oasis was Jerry's entire world, and it was everything Jim and Rene wanted when they fled San Francisco to move into the country in 1998. It was why they crossed the Golden Gate and headed six hours north, for open space all their own where they could grow vegetables, play with their dog, and sit in their redwood hot tub underneath the stars.

Free from the glow of his computer monitor, Jim looked upon the yard to survey his kingdom. Standing in the shade of the tall, green trees under the bright-blue sky, he felt grateful to be outside in his own quiet space, with unpolluted air and a patient dog with energy to spare. Those Jerry Breaks gave Jim a brisk burst of fresh air every time.

"Okay, but we're only going to kick it a few times." Jim loved their new life, but the need to pay for it nagged at him while Jerry tugged at his heartstrings.

Jerry crouched and froze as Jim stepped toward the tattered soccer ball sitting on the brick patio. He tried to fake him out with a false kick in one direction, but the dog didn't flinch. So, he punted the ball in the other direction across the large, grassy yard. "Go get it, Jer!"

Determined and focused, Jerry ran toward the flying prize and jumped high into the air. He nabbed the partially deflated ball with his teeth and came down hard on all fours. He rarely missed, and in hardly any time became an excellent goalie. The position suited him well, since he was clearly no retriever. Clutching the ball firmly in his strong jaws, he always ran away with his prize, ignoring Jim's demands. "Jerry, come! Bring it back!"

Soccer was always a one-sided game with Jerry. If he wanted the ball, Jim would have to chase after him. Running around the ostrich shrub with his prize clenched in his teeth, the intelligent dog quickly learned that Jerry Breaks always lasted longer if Jim wasn't able to catch him.

"Drop it!"

Jerry obeyed and released his grip on the ball, only to snatch it back up and run away as Jim stepped closer. If he gave up the ball, he knew they would go back inside. Smart dog. It didn't take much to lure his human into a few more laps around the yard.

"Gotcha!" Jim smiled and grabbed the ball. It was game over when he walked back into the garage to stow the ball high on a shelf. Panting and satisfied, Jerry trotted back into the house and appeared satisfied with the few sacred minutes of Jim's time. Then he curled back up to nap while Jim returned to work for several more hours.

Devoted to showing his people how to make the most of each day, Jerry always made sure they put fun before profits. Thus, he was quickly promoted to the most important role in the pack: Chief Fun Officer.

꙳   ꙳   ꙳

For nearly a year, every day was a repeat of the last. Walk. Sleep. Watch Jim. Spy on the evil cat. Wait for a Jerry Break. Eventually, the sound that signaled day's end could be heard, usually around six o'clock. Sometimes it was as late as midnight. But even if sound asleep, Jerry would always open an eye upon hearing that familiar crinkling paper sound of Jim emptying the trash on his Mac's desktop, followed by the large hard drives spinning down and then the distinct *fwump, fump* of both big computer monitors being turned off.

Sshhhhck, clack... By the time Jim slid in the keyboard tray and pushed his big chair back from his desk, Jerry would be standing tall, shaking off any sleep, and giving a good Downward Dog stretch—the sign that he was ready to go and do the next activity of the day.

Like most people, Jim and Rene assumed all dogs needed long walks to be happy, so their catch-up times often turned into mile-long treks with their growing puppy. One evening, they went on a longer than usual walk, when Jerry stopped mid-stride. He stood in place and looked up at Rene, then plopped his body down on the sidewalk. Lying prone on his little round belly, he panted and looked up with tired but happy eyes. It was the only way he could tell her he was too exhausted to continue. But she didn't understand his clues.

"Come on, Jerry, don't be so stubborn!" He didn't budge. "Really? Do I need to carry you?"

When the dog didn't get up, she put him in her arms for the long trek home.

He did this a few more times over the next month. Rene couldn't figure out the behavior. "Maybe he just wants to play ball?" She didn't know of any dog who hated walks, but it seemed Jerry would rather play soccer. "I think he's messing with us."

"Jerry! Really? Are you going to do that again? I know you want to play soccer, but walks are just as good for you!" He did it again on their nightly walk, just decided to plop down and lay there while looking up at her, with a heavy tongue hanging from his slack-jawed mouth. His tail swept across the concrete sidewalk in a prone wag, and Rene's instinct finally spoke up. This was not normal puppy behavior. She made a mental note to schedule a vet appointment and waited for him to get up.

He was still resting when an old man approached and stopped to assess the situation. He walked with a cane and wore a big Navy-style peacoat, with a black woven beanie pulled down over his ears. Steve was frail, but daily neighborhood walks livened up his otherwise humdrum days. He hobbled along with an awkward limp and spoke with a slur, but he never missed a chance to get outside, even in foul weather. He would talk to anyone who stopped long enough to chat and decipher his jumbled words, but hardly anyone ever did. They were always in too much of a hurry. Few of his neighbors realized the gruff-looking character was not the angry old man he appeared to be.

The first time Steve saw Jerry, he stooped over to give the lazy dog a long, discerning look. In an ornery tone with a *get up* gesture of his swinging fist, he barked his first order. "Come on, dawwwg, get with the program!" The long, drawn-out command bordered on cranky, but Jerry didn't seem to mind the man's gravelly voice and gritty demeanor. He looked up to study Steve's hollow cheeks, sunken eyes and long, gray stubble. The old man wasn't mad, he was actually cracking a subtle smile. When Rene spied Jerry's reaction, she noticed Steve's thin smile. The order wasn't meant to be taken seriously, and her astute puppy knew it before she did. Jerry rose to his feet, leaned in and rubbed his long, lean body against Steve's pant leg. With one swoosh of his fluffy tail, their friendship was sealed. Steve and Jerry became instant buddies.

❧   ❧   ❧

Each time he spied Steve coming down the street, Jerry pulled hard on his leash and ran toward the old man with the funny walk. Though misunderstood by most people, they clearly comprehended each other. Lacking any real vocabulary, each used eye contact and body language to communicate.

"Come on, dawwwg, get with the prooograaam!" Steve always hollered out to Jerry without fail. From half a block away, you could catch a glimpse of the man's grin and know the lanky little dog was making his day. Steve's health was poor, but Jerry could always count on him for a daily round of affectionate pats on the head. Maybe they bonded because Steve had the soul of an old salty dog himself, but deep down, they had much more in common. Despite the physical challenges nature threw at him, Steve lived every day as best he could. His health wasn't going to keep him from exploring the world outside his front door.

— 3 —

The CFO Years

Jerry worked hard as Chief Fun Officer, and he did his job well. As CFO he took on the role of convincing Jim and Rene to stop banging away on their keyboards for ten hours at a stretch. Jerry patiently waited each morning, but after a couple hours, he encouraged them to get off their butts. At least twice a day they obliged, and Jerry got to play soccer. If not for him, they may have never taken any breaks, but the growing puppy at their feet couldn't wait until 5:00 p.m. to have fun. Without words, he used his best dog language to tell his team members about their most important task: to enjoy life.

Once in a while, they complied. More often, they did not. When his pouting eyes failed to get them away from their desks, Jerry resorted to the power of the paw. Using his big, wet nose as a projectile, he repeatedly nudged Rene's elbow while she worked away at something not nearly as important as a bathroom break. If that didn't work, a loud *thwack*! with his forepaw on the kitchen door usually did the trick.

Sometimes he resorted to plopping down between their two doors and letting out a loud, sad surrender. *Hmmmmfh...* Jerry would sigh, sprawling out in the hallway between their two offices. They knew he'd retreated, but only for a while.

One evening, they were both working late and neither had even mentioned dinner. "You gonna be much longer?" Jim was getting hungry, and he knew Jerry wanted to eat too. They hadn't had any playtime yet, and it was already dark out.

Jerry strolled to the next room to check on Rene's answer. "Just a little longer!"

Jim had come to understand what that meant—no time soon. He usually heard it at least a few times before she actually quit. Another project needed his attention, so he kept working.

But Jerry wanted attention any way he could get it. He paced back into Jim's office to find his ally staring closely at the screen. Way too close. Jim didn't even look away from the glowing screen after Jerry gave him a good whimper.

"Almost done..." Rene called from the other room. Jerry padded back into her office to see if she meant it. Nothing. She wasn't budging. This called for more assertive hints.

He walked back to Jim's desk and sat by his side. Jim felt his stare but stayed silent while continuing to fine-tune the design on his screen.

WHAM!

Jerry crashed his paw down on the keyboard. Jim jerked his hand in surprise and stared in shock at the big streak he'd made across the photo he was retouching. "What the...?" He turned to scold his dog but saw those brown eyes zeroed in on him, intense and serious. No cajoling or pleading in those doggie eyes this time—the dog meant business. Jim let out his breath and shook his head. All he could do was smile at the boss and rub his furry head. "Okay! I get it! Okay..." He clicked Undo and saved his work, emptied the trash, and shut down his machine.

Jerry thumped his tail, knowing those sounds meant he had done his duty. He led Jim into Rene's office and together, they dragged her away for the night.

❧　❧　❧

The work from Silicon Valley clients never stopped coming, which was good because in their remote part of Northern California, small business owners weren't spending big bucks on the full-service marketing solutions Jim and Rene had to offer. Costs didn't matter to their customers down south, but they always expected the impossible. Rene and Jim did their best to meet their expectations, but Jerry sensed the tension it created. He cringed when the loud voices on the other end of the phone boomed, "I need this done ASAP!"

"No problem." Jim knew which side his bread was buttered on. "Do you need that today or yesterday?"

Meeting big-city customer demands was tricky in their laid-back hippie town. Eureka was the commercial center of Humboldt County, but even in business, vendors and people just acted slower. Life was slower. Even the man who brought the packages—and dog treats—in the brown truck was never in much of a hurry. Locals called it Humboldt Time and at first, Jim had a hard time dealing with it. His fast-talking city ways scared off the first few locals he approached for new business.

Jerry quickly picked up on the growing confusion around their new lifestyle. He sensed the schizophrenia in the air. Every day his people worked long hours for the big-city income while trying to get jobs done on Humboldt Time.

As a dog, he never understood why his people worked so hard. After all, they moved north to get away from all that. If only he could have called them into his office—the backyard—to sit them down for a serious talk. He'd likely explain how they can't have it all, at least not the way most people define "all."

"Stop working so hard and start enjoying this beautiful day," he seemed to say each time he ran to the door, expecting them to follow. That's all that matters in this world, but with only puppy breath and body language to communicate, his message wasn't coming across to the oblivious workaholics. Constant work, deadlines, bills—the pressure was building.

The busier they got, the more upset they became over things that threatened their precarious livelihood. Attempting to balance their ideal of a laid-back lifestyle with ever-increasing work demands was stressing them out. Rather than stop and breathe, each of them tended to explode when the going got tough. The smart CFO puppy quickly learned when a daily outburst brewed—and where to hide from the aftermath. He knew when he might be able to lighten the mood and when to walk away.

"Oh, give me a break!" Jim would yell into the phone as he slammed it down. Jerry would get up and silently sneak out of his office to go sit at Rene's feet. He knew better than to stick around whenever it sounded that bad.

Moments later, Rene might lose her cool over an email. "Oh, hell! There's no way! How can they expect us to do that?" She had no sooner finished cursing at her screen when Jim would notice Jerry silently pad back into the corner of his room.

Then his ears perked up at the sound of her crying and he returned to her side, searching her face. In less than sixty seconds, Jerry went from a blissful snooze to confusion and fear. Were they yelling at him or something else? Was she crying because he'd done something wrong or was she hurt? Confused and tensing up for something terrible, he put his ears back and dropped his head.

"Oh, Jerry, it's not you. Nothing you did, I promise." Rene swiped at her tears and gave him a big hug. Jerry's reaction was like the bell in a boxing match. His pitiful cowering posture knocked Rene and Jim to their senses, if only temporarily. Those tense situations played out almost weekly. And each time, Jerry fulfilled his CFO duties by diffusing the bad energy with his calm sensibility. It was the only thing that grounded them. One look into his worried eyes brought them back to reality with a reminder of what matters most. He was perfect for the job of Chief Fun Officer because dogs see the world so much clearer, without complicated emotions, worry, or ego getting in the way. Whether he was smart enough to know what he was doing or not, Jerry's reaction to their outbursts proved that no amount of work or money was more important than making sure everyone was happy and felt loved.

As the Jerry Breaks became more frequent, they had fewer frustrating arguments about work. Jim and Rene slowly learned to follow his lead, and readily agreed that was a good thing.

🐾　🐾　🐾

When they weren't typing, or drawing, or printing, or packaging, or wrapped up in other work, CFO Jerry always made sure his busy people took the time to stop and smell the roses in their yard and the sea breeze at the beach. His most favorite playtimes had to wait until Friday afternoon, but he didn't mind. He always knew when a trip to Samoa Beach was coming soon. All it took was those two magic words, "You wanna…" But before they finished the question, he was waiting at the door with a big, panting breath. "…go to the beach?"

The foggy shoreline of the Lost Coast isn't all that great for sunbathing, but it's a paradise for dogs. Nobody makes them wear leashes, and dogs can just be dogs. They splash in the waves, dig up old driftwood, or retrieve kelp from crashing waves. At the end of a long workweek, Jerry never felt so free as he searched the shoreline for the freshest strands of that salty ocean plant.

"Get it, dawg!" Jim yelled as he teased Jerry with the longest, thickest stem of beached kelp he could find. The two ran along the shore with Jim in the lead and Jerry in close pursuit of the kelp's juicy bulb. "Bet you can't reach it!" Jim teased by tossing the kelp into the air like a lasso and then down onto the sand. He spun it round and round at his feet as the bulb bounced on the sand and Jerry ran in circles to get it.

Most dogs would keep chasing the vine, but Jerry was smarter than that. He quickly caught on to the game and stopped, turned around, and prepared to land his prize. Before Jim could change direction, he swung the ropey string right into his smart dog's open mouth. Snap! With one bone-crushing bite, Jerry broke the thick seaweed and shredded the long stalk into small bits. Panting with pride, with salty, brown seaweed strands spilling from his mouth, he looked at his smiling partner and knew he had performed another fine job as CFO.

※　※　※

In Humboldt County, the land of tall redwood tree forests, remote rivers, and empty beaches, there is always another creek to explore or long, epic trail to hike. Camping and hiking was a way of life for Jim and Rene, even before Jerry came along. So it wasn't long after Jerry's adoption day that they decided it was time for Jerry's first tent camping trip. Those silly humans. Like most people, they just assumed that all dogs knew how to swim and hike. They had no idea that their young, inexperienced pack mate had a lot to learn about the great outdoors.

One afternoon, there was a ruckus in the garage. Jim was pulling stuffed nylon bags down from the rafters, going through sacks, and loading his selections into the truck. Rene was creating a stir, too, but she was in the kitchen, choosing boxes and bags from the pantry and laying them on the counter. Jerry spied a bag of his kibble sitting by the broom closet, looked over at her, then back at the garage door. Something was up, and he seemed to know it. When Jim walked down the hall toward the kitchen, the curious dog leapt to his feet.

"Tent, bags, stove…" Jim smiled at Jerry, then took a verbal inventory to make sure they didn't forget anything. Their last trip was an entire season ago, and he was eager to get going. "The packs are ready, let's get with the program!"

Jerry tilted his head, probably wondering why Jim sounded like Steve.

"I've got the food, pans, and plates. What else?" Rene studied the meal portions. It never seemed like enough food when she packed for camping trips.

"Oh, his bed!" Jim darted back into the living room to grab the big, fluffy dog bed from the corner window. Jerry took it as a sign to play tug-of-war. He sprang up and snatched the other end of the bed with his teeth, then flung it back and forth without letting go.

"Ha! Wanna help, Jerry?" Rene laughed while Jim tugged at the bed as the determined dog down-slid across the wood floor. When they got to the back door, his jaws were still clamped onto the bedding. "Okay, Jerry, let go. Drop it!"

The young puppy opened his mouth and obliged, apparently remembering the "Drop it!" command he'd recently learned. Jim flung the big bed into the back of the truck with a single toss, then bent over and hoisted Jerry onto it. *Slam!* Jim shut the tailgate and closed the camper shell window while Jerry watched with some confusion. The staff retreat was on. It was time for Jerry's first camping trip.

❉ ❉ ❉

He stood at attention, tethered to the picnic table, and watched them fuss with the little shelter. Rene put the last long tent pole through the fabric and then called to the curious canine, "Hey, Jerry, check it out! This is where we'll sleep." She walked over and untethered him from the picnic table, but he approached the blue dome with more caution than she expected. Jerry stood at the opening and peered inside the nylon cave, clearly reluctant to enter. He refused to step inside until she tossed a few kibbles onto his bed.

Once inside the contraption, he padded around and planted his butt on a sleeping bag. With nose down, he snarfed around for more kibble while the redwood forest grew dark overhead. Then he went outside to nibble at the remaining food in his bowl placed under the wooden picnic table. He devoured every last kibble, and when he finally looked up, the inky-black sky and dark tree shadows seemed to catch him by surprise. Darkness had smothered the campsite. The two-foot-tall puppy could hardly see beyond his long snout. Bewildered, he sprinted to Jim in a nervous panic.

"Whoa, you're shaking, dude. Awww...what's the matter? Are you scared?"

Jerry replied with a barely audible puppy whine. He was trembling from confusion over his new sleeping arrangement. Acutely aware of the dog's anxiety, Jim picked up the pup to comfort him. He placed all 30 pounds of him atop the picnic table, then put his arm around the dog's quivering shoulders. It was time for a muzzle-to-nose chat.

"You silly dog, look. There's nothing out there. See?" He used his best soothing voice for reassurance. "It's just us; you don't have to be afraid. We would never let anything happen to you." The new moon night grew darker, which made Jim feel as exposed and spooked as his young dog. Outside, underneath the redwood forest canopy, they both needed a confidence boost.

"Awww, look at that scaredy-dog of ours, poor thing..." Rene came over to join the circle and chuckled at the sight of her quivering puppy. "Some guard dog he's going to be!"

❧   ❧   ❧

"All right, Jer, let's go!" Jim called out the moment orange and purple hues painted the sky. After a long night trying to sleep through Jerry's whining and pacing, he was ready for Jerry's first hike in the woods.

Jerry's confidence returned at sunrise. With plenty of water, granola, and kibble packed, he, Rene, and Jim set out on a four-mile trail that meandered through lush redwood groves and along clear streams. To Jim and Rene, it was the perfect hike. But these first-time dog parents didn't know that for a six-month-old puppy, any walks over a mile were too much. Fifteen minutes into their hike, Jerry's young limbs just couldn't keep up. He fell back, laid down, and looked up at Jim.

"Oh, he needs some water." Jim reached for the water bottle clipped to his belt. He poured some into Jerry's collapsible water bowl, and the thirsty dog lapped it up while lying on his belly. But when he finished, he didn't get up; he just lay there, panting.

"All right, Jerry, break's over, let's go!" Rene walked along, with Jerry trotting at her heels, but within five minutes, he was back on the ground.

"More water? Already?" Surprised, Rene reached into her day pack and poured more into Jerry's bowl. This time, he didn't make a move when she placed it on the ground. He just looked up at her again and stared.

"Maybe he's hungry." Jim opened a small baggie and dumped

— 35 —

some kibble into his hand. Reaching down, he offered it to Jerry. It smelled tasty to the tired dog, but not exciting enough to eat. Jerry just turned away and sighed, resting his chin on his paws.

"Wow, that's weird. I wonder what's wrong?" It wasn't hot under the forest canopy. Gently, Rene tugged the leash and encouraged him to stand by gently pulling up. He followed her signal and slowly got to his feet, but didn't step forward. He just stood there looking at them both.

They tried all kinds of silly gestures and voices to get him moving forward. Jim walked ahead at one point and called out in his best Steve impression, "Come on, daaawg, get with the prooograaam!" Rene cheered him on and said, "Jerry! Look at Jim! Let's go get him!"

Their goofy enthusiasm gave him the strength to forge on, but when he sat down one more time, his soft puppy tongue flopped out one side of his mouth. Tired and defeated, he laid down and sprawled out on the cold, damp earth.

Finally, his people caught on. "We must have walked too far. I'll carry him home." Jim reached down and hoisted his exhausted dog into his arms. With Jerry's long legs dangling and head resting on Jim's shoulder, they made it back to the campsite.

Rene felt awful, stroking Jerry's head as she walked alongside them. "Awww, Jerry, I'm so sorry. We're so dumb."

The next day after breakfast, the tent came down, bags and stove got stashed in the truck, and Jerry was lovingly placed on his bed in the back. The worn-out pooch snoozed the entire way home. He had survived his first great outdoor adventure, exhausted but happy.

❅　❅　❅

Soon after that first camping trip, Jerry went on another new adventure of sorts—his first vet visit. It was time for his checkup with the local country vet, a brusque man lacking in bedside manner. He poked and prodded while Jerry's eyes pleaded with Rene for a fast exit.

While the vet did his thing, Jim remembered how Jerry often sat down on longer walks. "He's pretty active, but sometimes he'll just sit down when we're going around the block. We've even had to carry him home a few times."

The vet had no immediate explanation. "We could take x-rays to see if anything is going on."

Ca-ching! Dollar signs flashed in Jim's mind. But he looked at Rene, and they knew it had to be done. "I knew this was going to be expensive," he muttered as the vet whisked Jerry away.

Twenty minutes later, the vet returned. "Your dog did good; didn't even need sedation." Then he clipped the giant x-ray films up on the light box and pointed to Jerry's hips. "There's no injury, but it does look like he has some early signs of hip dysplasia on the right." He took his pen and circled where Jerry's hip bone met the socket. "See it right here?"

Jim and Rene were new to this dog thing, but because they loved German shepherds, they already knew that phrase. "Hip dysplasia" was something they hoped they would never hear. "Is it serious?"

"Not now. He has a touch, but only time will tell how bad it gets."

"Can we still take him hiking and swimming?"

The vet turned and gave advice they would never forget. "Oh sure, he can do that. Just have fun now…and run him while he's young."

And run him they did.

❀   ❀   ❀

Jerry blossomed into a handsome, lean, and tall dog. One day after a long afternoon working, Rene looked up and noticed that his large and cumbersome front feet finally fit his larger frame. Those white paws proved his German shepherd mama had dated another breed. The toes on his left paw were dappled in white, but his right foot was solid white all the way up past the wrist. From afar, the dog appeared to be wearing a sock or a cast.

Jerry inherited the rugged looks of a hardworking German shepherd, but was gifted with a more affectionate personality, like a collie's. He loved corralling his people and keeping an eye on the pack, but when push came to shove, Jerry demonstrated that he was a lover, not a fighter. The "guard dog" with the soft heart could always be counted on for a friendly encounter with people or pets, even when a random rowdy animal tried to take him down.

One evening after work during their nightly neighborhood stroll, a fat cat ran out of a house. She sprinted all the way to the curb, then flung herself at Jerry with extended claws and a look to kill. The crazed feline latched onto his rear end and hung on hard, loudly hissing, as if Jerry had just tried to kidnap her young.

"Aaaack!" Rene screamed and swatted at the cat with the end of Jerry's leash. "Get off him! Get off!" Jerry spun around in surprise and vigorously tried to fling the angry cat from his haunches. He ran for cover behind Jim's legs with the cat still hanging on. Rene ran interference and with one final leash thwack on her rear, the cat loosened her grip and bolted.

"Oh my God, Jerry, are you okay?" Rene rubbed his haunches, checking for blood.

"What the hell, man!?" Jim yelled toward the open door of the cat's house. Jim's shock turned to embarrassment about his timid dog's reaction to the attack. His dog just got beat up by a cat. Wasn't it supposed to be the other way around? "Hey, man, get your damn cat!"

"Oh, sorry..." came a voice from inside. "She just had kittens." Whoever it was didn't even bother to step onto the porch. Rene and Jim's emotions ran high, their breathing hard and loud from anxiety that interrupted their peaceful stroll. Jerry seemed to read their signals as his body language deteriorated into a slight cower. But instead of standing his ground at the crime scene, he apparently wanted to put those stressful emotions behind him. He walked on ahead and leaned into the end of his leash with all seventy pounds, pulling everyone forward and away.

He showed no aggression in response to the momma cat, but her ferocious attack left him with a lifelong aversion to all cats. Whenever he spied one on walks, he tried walking the opposite way. Each time, the young CFO shared a lesson about nonresistance in the face of aggression. It was the first clue to Jerry's pacifist tendencies.

※   ※   ※

Two more years of the same routine went on around the home office each day. Walk, work, play, work some more, and wait. The weekends were always worth waiting for.

"Yard sale-ing is not a verb!" Jim shook his head as Rene pulled out the newspaper, turning to the classified ads. It was Friday night, and she was mapping her yard sale route for the next day.

Spring and summer garage sales seem to be a way of life in rural America, and their town was no different. Always happy for the cheap entertainment of hunting for secondhand treasures, their love affair with pre-owned merchandise started when the old man across the street explained the art of "yard sale-ing" to Rene. "Always have lots of singles with you, but pay with change first!" he advised. "Oh, and wear your dirty jeans. If you tell 'em where you live, they'll think you can pay more."

At first, Jim grumbled about "digging through other people's crap," but he always enjoyed tagging along—if only to keep her from coming home with junk they didn't need. On Saturday mornings, both of them could be found rooting through piles tossed onto lawns or nosing around inside someone's dusty garage. If a cute, floppy old hat or a semi-new cookie tray was looking for a new home, Rene could always justify the small expense with, "But we *need* it!"

"Careful, or you'll turn into a hoarder!" Jim objected over most of her frivolous finds, so she promised only to buy what they could carry on her bike or on foot. Jerry always tagged along and although he enjoyed those longer walks, he didn't find their version of entertainment too interesting. That is, until they stumbled onto a sprawling pile of discarded stuffed animals.

"Pick a toy, Jerry!" Jim pointed to the heap of grungy toys strewn across the lawn.

"Toy?" Jerry tilted his head at the sound of the word he knew all too well. With permission to dive in, he bent down and burrowed his snout deep into the mound of ratty-haired dolls and crusty, old plush toys. The heavenly aroma of dried baby food and saliva wafted into his nostrils. When a fuzzy purple plush toy poked through the playschool detritus, he froze.

The soft fabric carried an enticing scent that compelled him to claim it with one hungry *Chomp!* His choice was clear. Jerry lifted his head and a fat little dinosaur with a green belly hung from his clenched jaws. He looked up to see Jim and Rene hysterically laughing at his attraction to what they thought was the most obnoxious kid's plaything that ever existed.

"Barney? Seriously?" Jim shook his head in disgust. "You want that one, really?"

Rene laughed at the sing-song beast's resurrection.

Young kids adored the purple dinosaur and its moral lessons, but Jerry's interest was more visceral.

"You go, Jerry, get him!" Jim cheered as he grabbed for the purple toy, setting the first Purple Dinosaur Tug-of-War game into motion. Back and forth, they pulled in opposite directions until Jim released his grip. Jerry stumbled backward with his plush prey clutched tightly in his jaws. Then he shook it hard like a limp rabbit. Jerry liked his new toy, which would quickly become his new obsession.

"You're buyin' that now!" a large lady hollered from the porch.

Fifty cents later, the war to obliterate purple dinosaurs from the planet had begun. Each weekend, they hunted for more replicas. One led to another and before long, Jerry was codependent on that purple posse. He corralled them up in the dog den and had his choice of daily favorites. His collection included Big Barney, Travel Barney, and all sizes in between. His arch nemeses were the ones he hated most: the Singing Barneys, those that sang a sickeningly sweet song when squeezed. Every so often, a perfectly good Barney would bite the dust in Jerry's jaws, but for the most part, the gentle dog kept them all around far longer than any average dog would tolerate. Over time he liberated more purple dinosaurs from yard sales and thrift store shelves, until his toy basket could no longer contain them.

— 4 —

Life Takes a Turn

Three years after Jerry became CFO, he had proven his worth. He helped his people stay sane through the death of family members, cope with the horrors of 9/11, and nursed Rene out of a motorcycle crash that almost took her life. When their little business got too big for their small home office, he helped them though the hardest workdays of their lives.

"We'll take it!" Rene said almost as soon as they entered the abandoned house in downtown Eureka. She had always wanted to restore an old Victorian, ever since living in San Francisco's Haight-Ashbury neighborhood. Jim was happy to find one they could afford to tackle in a city that wasn't nearly as chaotic. Affordability was one thing. Feasibility was another they didn't consider.

"What about parking?" Jim asked the realtor as they gingerly stepped through a decade of overgrown weeds and backyard debris. He thought he was being smart by asking, and hoped they could turn the big, two-level building into a commercial property. "We could run our business downstairs and rent out the top, right?" He peered into the old stucco-sided garage that was listing to one side, ready to fall down.

"No problem, it just takes some re-zoning." The eager realtor took out a notebook and drew a rough sketch of the lot. Where the garage was, he showed cars. "See, plenty of room for parking here. We do it all the time."

Flecks of sunlight bounced off broken glass scattered around the driveway where Jerry was exploring. "Look out, Jerry! No! No! No!" Rene ran to pull him away from the shards before any sliced open his paws. It was the first of many times she would deter him from the remnants of vandals and vagrants living in the heart of their future neighborhood.

For over a year, their printing jobs had been overflowing into every spare inch of their tiny home. This fixer-upper was an attractive way out of that mess, and Jim and Rene were ready to believe—and overlook—anything. They didn't care that the 1908 redwood building had homeless people living underneath it. At the time, they also didn't know that it would need a foundation, all new plumbing and electrical, not to mention a roof, and a great fight with bureaucrats to tear down the dilapidated garage some local historical buffs called, "a charming example of 1930s architecture." No wonder it sat vacant for nearly a decade.

Most of the building's original woodwork was gone, the single-pane windows were cracked, and plywood had replaced one of the front doors. Ferns flourished in the rotting wooden rain gutters. Any sane investor would have run away, but not those two dreamers. By the time their first visit was over, they were so starry-eyed that they couldn't even see how the realtor was lying through his teeth to get the deal done. Before ink ever hit paper, they were dedicated to saving the old house.

But as any fan of the old public television show *This Old House* knows, one expensive repair leads to another as the costs skyrocket. Rene and Jim's awakening came swiftly. Nearly a dozen times in the first year, they considered bailing out and putting the property back up for sale. Each time they argued about the latest construction problem, Jerry refereed the fight with a soothing walk on the beach. Three years, two mortgage lenders, and hundreds of thousands of dollars later, the battle with contractors, bureaucrats, and bankers ended. Jim and Rene moved their belongings into their halfway-finished Victorian home in the summer of 2003. The business now had plenty of room to grow in the finished downstairs office space, and with wet plaster drying on the upstairs walls, they called the top half home.

Even Jerry sacrificed for the good of the pack. After the move, he lost his big backyard and no longer saw his buddy Steve on walks through the quiet neighborhood. While Rene and Jim enjoyed a larger facility and the ability to close their office doors at night, the days of Jerry's lunchtime soccer matches were over. His new outdoor play area had a postage-stamp footprint that was mostly consumed by the new garage. Jerry's only earthy spot to relieve himself was on a small patch of grass not much bigger than the 10x10 trade show booths Jim designed. Far from his sunny paradise a few miles up the road, Jerry now spent most of his days inside the boardroom.

Still, he maintained his CFO duties without complaint. From his corner bed in Rene's office, he had to sit up to look outside onto the front porch. More visitors came and went, each receiving a welcoming bark from the friendly greeter. The man in the brown shorts was the highlight of his day. He brought packages out of the big, brown truck for them, but even better, he always carried treats.

One morning, Jerry heard someone climbing the steps up to the front porch. Hoping it was Mr. Brown Shorts, he sat up to investigate with his ears perked. He immediately started barking—but not with his usual welcoming bark. It was louder, with a sharp and warning edge. Then the doorbell rang.

"Uhh, Jim...will you get the door?" Rene looked out the window and didn't like what she saw.

"Can I help you?" Jim cracked the door, blocking it with his foot.

"Yeah. Is Dave here?" The man appeared nervous, hopped-up on drugs, or desperately looking for some. Jim figured at least two out of the three. "Sorry, no Dave here." He started to close the door.

"Oh. Then Debbie; how 'bout Debbie? Debbie home?" The drifter scratched his dirty neck as he peered over Jim's shoulder, attempting to look around the office.

Jim's growing tension and Rene's wide-eyed fear set off Jerry's alarm bells. On cue, he leaped at the cracked door and let loose with his most ferocious guard dog barking. *GRRROWWOOF! WOOF! WOOF! WOOF!*

The scrawny punk jumped backward. Jim pushed the door shut and latched the deadbolt. They watched as he skirted by the open window with Jerry standing guard, still going off like a car alarm.

Jim and Rene looked at each other, then at Jerry, and smiled. The rough and unpredictable city life finally brought out the guard dog in him. He was an excellent judge of character.

❧   ❧   ❧

Time moved fast as the business grew, and the workdays just seemed to get longer. It wasn't uncommon for them to head back downstairs after dinner and work until 10:00 p.m. The dot-com industry was booming, and they took full advantage of the good times to pay for their expensive new headquarters. The more intense life got, the harder

Jerry worked to remind his people to look up from their computers and enjoy their latest achievements. Rain or shine, he always got them outside for some fun, even if it was just for a short, sweet escape.

Jerry didn't find many friends in the new neighborhood. Not because nobody liked him, but because they were the only residents living downtown at the time. But one afternoon shortly after Jerry claimed his turf, a tall Weimaraner trotted up to their driveway's four-foot-tall lattice fence. He stuck his long, gray snout through an opening but didn't bark or snarl as Jerry investigated the protruding proboscis.

"Hi there, guy. That's Winston!" The young woman was talking to Jerry with a happy southern drawl. Rene looked out the window and observed Winston and Jerry's relaxed stance and loose, wagging tails. Anyone could see that the dogs might get along.

Hopeful that Jerry might have made a new friend, Rene hollered from inside and walked outside to meet their guests. "Want to come in, Winston?" Finally, she was happy to encounter someone on their block who didn't appear to be homeless.

"Sure! Why not?!" The Texan had just moved to town with her boyfriend and Winston. The only dogs she had met in the area were behind chain-link fences, always aggressive and territorial. Jerry was clearly a dog she could trust.

Jim walked out and opened the gate for Winston as he confidently trotted into the yard with his mom holding onto his leash. Several butt sniffs and muzzle nudges later, Jerry and Winston's new pack was in order. By the end of that first playdate, Jerry and Winston were best buddies.

※　　※　　※

Rene didn't care for Eureka's cool, foggy summers. Every few weeks, she would plan a new hiking adventure away from the drizzly weather. It was as easy as driving a couple hours and heading to some small lake in the Trinity Alps, or out on the Pacific Crest Trail that zig-zagged across the Marble Mountains' backbone. Jim was always happy to oblige and load up the backpacking gear.

By now, Jerry was a dog in the prime of his life. At nearly eight years old, he was healthy and happy, lean and large, with a slight touch of gray on his muzzle. He was entirely at ease in the woods, and not at all like the fearful pooch from eight years prior, cowering in the dark unknown of an overnight campout. The eager trail dog was always up for strenuous, high-altitude hikes, and even carried his own doggy backpack filled with kibble. If the vet's diagnosis of hip dysplasia was affecting him, it was not at all obvious.

Rene and Jim were also in pretty decent shape for two thirty-something workaholics who sat on their butts all day. All three of them loved the outdoors. If they could have camped out in the wilderness all year long, they would have. But their business kept them away more than they would have liked. Unfortunately, one year after moving downtown, they got their wish for more free time. Northern California's tech industry was in a meltdown, and the big-bucks jobs came to a crawl. Their clients were closing shop, and the phone rang much less than in the old days. Despite fewer paying jobs, they worked even longer hours to launch a new online storefront that would grow their client base beyond the tech sector.

The future of their company was uncertain but in September of 2006, Rene knew if they didn't get away from the office and squeeze in one more backpacking trip that season, they would go crazy. She was laser-focused on tackling a particular section of the Pacific Crest Trail for the finale. An oasis called Waterdog Lake was her target, and with only a couple jobs on the production schedule, the timing was perfect for a last hurrah. They had no idea it would be their last overnight hike with Jerry.

❧   ❧   ❧

That Friday-evening walk into the woods was easy and relaxing, even at the 8,000-foot altitude. Warm, golden sunlight painted the narrow dirt path as they took their time forging ahead to their destination: a deep-blue lake tucked in among cool granite canyons. With Jerry out front, two cold beers tucked into their packs and hardly anyone on the trail, the trip began perfectly.

Returning to nature soothed their souls and gave them renewed faith that business would pick up. On their last night, they'd just settled into their sleeping bags when without warning, a lightning storm thundered through the canyon. *Boom! Craaaaaackackckkkk!* The turbulent cloud cover shattered the dark silence. Jerry instantly awakened and leaped to his feet inside the small tent. Fear filled his wide, panicked eyes as he hovered over Rene and Jim, pressing his head into the tent ceiling. He stood guard and paced around the small tent all night long, robbing everyone of sleep.

The storm passed sometime during the early morning hours. But when they finally opened their eyes, they could smell the wisps of smoke drifting into the glacial valley. While unpeeling from their sleeping bags, the clatter of approaching helicopters floated in from the west. *Thwap! Thwap! Thwap!* That's when Jim realized the smoke was not from a nearby campfire. He knew there was a fire nearby, and with eight long miles to the trailhead, they had to get out fast. Rene tried to stay cool while she and Jim broke camp.

"Come on, Jer, we gotta go!" Jim took the lead and quickly headed out while munching on granola bars for breakfast. Jerry kept his nose in the air most of the way, sniffing for the telltale signs of danger. Few words were exchanged during the frantic hike out, and they only stopped for one short break before safely getting to the trailhead parking lot. That's where they saw the flames. The forest was on fire, and a squadron of fire trucks and people with chain saws were scampering around trying to contain the burn.

Jim turned back to make sure they were together. "Step on it! Come on, Jerry, let's go!"

"I am, I am!" Rene walked as fast as she had ever done with 20 pounds strapped on her back. She had never felt more relieved than the moment Jim pulled his keys from his pack and opened the truck door.

❧　❧　❧

Three hours later, they were grateful to be back in the cool coastal fog. Jim parked the green pickup curbside and opened the back to let Jerry out. He dropped the tailgate as usual, then stepped away to open the driveway gate. But Jerry didn't budge. Normally he would have jumped onto the sidewalk, eager to be in familiar territory. Not today. The tired dog just lay there on his bed, clearly content to stay put. He let out a heavy sigh. *Hmmph...*

"We're home, Jerry!" Rene went around back to unload gear. When she started piling it on the sidewalk, she noticed Jerry's unusual malaise.

"He won't get out!" she yelled to Jim, and moved in closer to check for a cause.

"He'll get out when he's ready." Jim was unconcerned, and took another load into the garage.

"Come on, Jerry, let's go inside!" His eyes looked up at hers, but not even her best, high-pitched dog mom voice could make him stir. After a minute he slowly got to his feet and stretched, looking at her, then at Jim, then right through both of them, lost in thought.

"Hmmm...I'm sure he's just tired." Jim was too. "We got out of there so fast. I'm whupped."

"Maybe it's his hips?" She was free-falling into worry, thinking about her eight-year-old dog slowing down. The country vet's words from long ago echoed through her mind: "Run him while he's young."

"Come on, buddy, we're going inside." Jim thumped the tailgate and gently tugged at the exhausted dog's collar until he finally stepped to the edge. "Come, Jerry, let's go!" Like always, Jerry did what was asked of him and jumped out. Only this time, the moment his paws hit the sidewalk, he let out a loud, ear-splitting, heart-wrenching *Yelp!*

BE MORE DOG

— 5 —

The Persistent Limp

Humans think they're so smart. But dogs know the truth. Those big brains and stumpy thumbs can hold tools, but they can't help people transcend the limitations of spoken language. Jim and Rene spent 24 hours a day with Jerry, but they still didn't grasp everything he was telling them. Sure, they understood on a basic level, like when he wanted to go out or if he needed a drink of water. But they never guessed that his lack of appetite after a long summer hike was dog speak for, "I hurt."

❀ ❀ ❀

Rays of sunlight penetrated the fog just before noon. Rene paused in the kitchen to bask in the warmth beaming inside the little room. Those rare sunny days were few and far between, and she cherished them in her love/hate relationship with coastal living. Just two days earlier when they'd returned from their hike in the Trinity Alps, she'd found herself wishing they never had to leave those rugged mountains. Lost in thoughts of wanderlust, she slowly stirred Jerry's meal of kibble and chicken scraps, then placed his bowl on the floor.

"Jerry, come and get it!" She heard nothing. "Jerrrrrrrrry, breakfast!"

Dog tags jingled from the other room, a signal that Jerry was getting closer. She could hear his paws delicately shuffle along the smooth oak floors as he approached the kitchen. "There you are, Jerry!"

But he had no tail wag that said, "Yum!" and no happy dances around the table. It was already past eight, but Jerry seemed a little sleepy as he walked to his meal, sniffed, and nibbled a few bites. He stopped with more than half left in the bowl, something he never did anymore now that Rene was feeding him better food.

— 49 —

"Come on, Jerry, you know you love it!" She watched his long nose push around the mixture of kibble and chicken. "Don't be such a picky eater. Remember the starving dogs in Africa? Eat something, buddy!"

He looked up and through her with a faraway stare, then stood in place, waiting for any command except "eat something." But that's precisely what she told him. Again.

If Rene knew how animals communicated pain, she would have understood the meaning of his scrunched facial expression and hunched posture. Those big ears that lay flat on his head were also trying to say something. But she was too inexperienced as a dog parent to know he was screaming, "I hurt, Mom!"

The following morning's breakfast was a repeat of the day before. "Oh, Jerry, are you being picky?" she asked, as if a dog could answer in English. She wondered if he was bored with the same old food. And why shouldn't he grow tired of it? People didn't eat the same thing every day, why should he? But deep down, her intuition screamed something was wrong.

One night during their usual evening walk, he sat down after a few minutes. The way he plopped his butt on the sidewalk was reminiscent of those puppy days when they unknowingly walked him to the point of exhaustion.

"What the...?" Jim looked down at a dog who wasn't going anywhere. Jerry looked up with big, saucer eyes and flat ears. "Well, that's weird. Jerry, what's up? You just want to eat?" Jim tugged on his leash, but the dog didn't move. "Come on, daaaawwg...get with the program!" He gave his best Steve imitation, hoping to motivate the disinterested canine. Then he looked Jerry straight in the eyes and with a more stern tone, ordered him to move. "Let's GO, Jerry!"

Slowly, gingerly, he obeyed. But as he passed them and slowly moved ahead, Jim could see there was something different about the dog's gait. It was off. Trot. Limp. Trot. Limp. His natural, smooth stride was gone. There was more hopping than trotting, and his head bucked with each forward motion. Rene was walking a few paces behind and also noticed his odd movement. "He's not putting weight on all of his paws, look."

With each forward motion, Jerry's left paw rose slightly during mid-stride. Then, after a few more steps, he did the same with his right. They could see something was wrong, but found it hard to tell which foot was bothering him.

Once they arrived home from the failed walk, Jim coerced him up onto the dog den couch. He gently nudged Jerry to lay on one side, then rotated each paw for a closer look. "Hmm, maybe he's got something in there." As he parted the fluffy hairs between each toe and probed the recesses with his finger, the advice of Jerry's first vet echoed in his thoughts: "Run him while he's young."

It pained Jim to say it. His dog might be falling apart. "Maybe it's his hips. We should call the clinic and have him checked out."

❀ ❀ ❀

Dogs can't understand the complicated words that spill from a veterinarian's mouth, but they excel at reading human expressions. Jerry's humans were overcome with a glassy-eyed, confused look. He knew something was definitely wrong.

The tall man in the white coat sounded confident and in charge. He seemed to know what he was talking about. Those big, rough hands poked, prodded, and pulled his patient around like the livestock he'd handled in his previous life as a large animal veterinarian. Out of habit, he used unnecessarily forceful exam tactics that forced Jerry into submissive, distressing positions. While his loud, booming voice broadcast over Jerry's body and above Jim and Rene's heads, Jerry's crouched posture and trembling legs communicated a palpable fear and distrust. A vet from an earlier generation, he didn't understand that when treated with respect, all animals will cooperate when fear is banished from the exam room. Too bad neither Jim, Rene, nor the vet knew any of this back then.

The loud man returned Jerry's leash to Jim and continued, "It's arthritis. He's getting to be that age." His droning continued with an occasional recognizable phrase like "hip dysplasia" thrown in to keep Jim and Rene from becoming lost in the overly technical conversation.

Jerry ducked behind Jim's legs while the humans traded handshakes. "Okay, thanks, Doc, we'll try the medicine and let you know how it works. Sounds good!"

Jerry clearly felt great the next day. Whatever was in that liquid medication enabled him to run up and fly down the 18 stairs separating the office from home. That night they took an evening walk and he trotted with the classic shepherd gait, never once missing a beat. Jerry was like a puppy once more.

The results, however, were short-lived. Weeks went by as Jerry randomly limped on walks, then quickly resumed a normal gait if he saw Rene or Jim watching. One day he limped on the left, the next day not at all. On another day favored the right. Then one afternoon, he was no longer able to abide by his instinct to hide pain at all costs. He just couldn't disguise the hurt any longer. Back to the vet he went.

Once again, the vet seemed like he knew what he was talking about. "That medication wasn't right for him, it may take some experimenting." He threw twenty-dollar words around and pointed out the state-of-the-art equipment he had just purchased for the practice. Jim and Rene hardly had a chance to speak or ask questions, but they trusted every word.

Two more months went by. When one pain medication stopped working, the vet prescribed a different one. Each time, the limp disappeared for a few days, but the painful hobble always returned a little worse than before.

Evening walks grew shorter. Jerry could no longer walk beyond a few minutes before sitting down. They relaxed in the dog den more than usual until one night, Jim sensed something destructive was happening to Jerry's body. This was more than "just" a limp, but he had no idea about the cause. While caressing Jerry's soft fur, he quietly pleaded for help with the diagnosis. "What's wrong, buddy? Can you tell me?"

Jerry exhaled with a long, contented sigh. He always basked in human touch and at that moment, Jim's light massage overshadowed the dull pain in his body. Jerry relaxed into it while Jim gently continued observing, waiting for any sign the vet may have missed. He lightly palpated and applied pressure to different parts of Jerry's body, unsure of what he was looking for but hoping for a clue. Slowly and carefully, he walked his fingers along Jerry's spine, starting at the tailbone. When his fingertips reached the top of his shoulder, he stopped to feel the front left scapula. Instantly, and without warning, Jerry shrieked and snapped at the offending fingers.

Jim's hand jerked away, narrowly missing the gleaming fangs. "Whoa! I'm so sorry, buddy!" He paused and looked deeply into Jerry's eyes, then lightly and tenderly caressed the shoulder area to feel for anything that might reveal the problem. Jerry recovered from the insult with barely audible whimpers. Fearful but still trusting, he allowed the exam to continue.

Rene ran to the dog den when she heard the commotion. "Hey, what'd you do to him?"

Curled into a defensive ball on the couch, Jerry sighed, sensing the exam was over. Jim looked up at her with sadness in both of their eyes. "I'm not sure, but I think it's his shoulder."

* * *

The old farm vet hastily manipulated Jerry's hips and legs, but this time his only advice was, "Well, he is getting older after all. He just can't do the things he used to. Stop taking him on runs, he's too old for that now."

Eight hundred dollars, months of medications, and nothing but useless information, Jim thought to himself. Rene was thinking the same, but neither questioned the recommendation. They weren't wearing the white coat, after all. Who were they to wonder?

"Sorry, I've got an emergency surgery. You'll need to increase the anti-inflammatory dose, it should work better now." The arrogant man completely missed the bewildered look on their faces as he rushed out of the exam room.

Jerry stood at the door, ready to bolt from the exam room. Jim followed, and Rene went to pay another bill. When he walked to the tailgate to help Jerry inside, he felt a light tap on his arm. It was the vet's assistant.

"Wait, I wanna let you know something..."

Just then, Rene approached as Jim helped Jerry up into the truck. The three humans stood at the back, out of sight from the office window. In a barely audible whisper, she spoke her mind to the confused clients. "You might consider getting another opinion."

BE MORE DOG

— 6 —

Cancer Comes Calling

Jerry didn't seem to mind the five-hour drive to the University of California at Davis. For all he knew, they were headed on a camping trip when Jim helped him into the truck. But there was no tent or sleeping bag or stove to share his space. When they finally stopped, he spotted a few of his brethren waiting outside the big brick building. Jerry trotted toward them with abandon. He may have thought they were at a new version of Happy Dog, his favorite doggie daycare in Eureka. But when he caught that strong aroma of fear lingering in the air, he stopped in his tracks.

The large waiting room buzzed with attentive young vet students coming and going with clipboards in hand. A menagerie of dogs obediently waited alongside their worried pet parents while cats howled with displeasure from the safety of their locked carriers. In a quiet corner, an African Grey chattered gibberish about the confusing scene.

"Come on, Jerry, let's go sit down!" Jim tugged on his dog's leash.

With great reluctance, Jerry obeyed the command and followed. A few moments later, Jim handed the end of his leash to a fresh-faced student in scrubs. The jig was up, and he knew it.

"Hey, Jerry, this is your new friend!" Rene introduced the young vet with enthusiasm, hoping Jerry wouldn't feel the terror in her heart over what they might find. Like all smart dogs he felt her emotions, and tried to dig his paws into the ground. But on the slick clinic floors, it was useless. Gently, she tugged him along with the leash and together, they all entered the bright examination area.

❈   ❈   ❈

Two hours later, a resident vet from the orthopedic department prepared to drop his latest cancer bomb on unsuspecting clients. Only one year into his department residency, the young clinician's heart sank as he delivered the news.

"We can't be certain until we biopsy, but on the radiographs, it's showing up like bone cancer. See this white area on the shoulder here?" He pointed the laser beam at the computer monitor and circled around an oval blob on the upper left shoulder area. It was an almost daily conversation in the orthopedics department, where limping dogs get help and owners hope for anything but cancer.

Jim and Rene sat in the exam room and stared at the black-and-white picture with shell-shocked expressions. The ghostly, oval-shaped area was about the same shape and size as a mango, precisely where Jim pressed on Jerry's shoulder to make him snap.

As always, the vet attempted to deliver the diagnosis with a balance of optimism and reality. "It could possibly be a regional fungal infection, so we can test for that. But I'll be honest…it's a pretty slim chance. Most likely, this is osteosarcoma. Bone cancer." He gave the diagnosis so often that he didn't even trip over the word anymore.

But Rene and Jim had never heard it before. They didn't even know dogs got cancer. A large mass was growing inward on Jerry's scapula. How could they be so blind? For at least three months, the destructive cell grouping chipped away at his skeleton, causing excruciating pain with every movement of his leg. He must have felt it on their last hiking trip. Six miles with off-the-charts bone cancer pain? No human would have ever walked so far with something so excruciating. Only a dog.

"It's huge." Jim shook his head in shock, looking around the exam room, staring blankly at the pamphlets on the wall. "How could we miss that?"

"You couldn't have known. See how the tumor is growing inward? The pain is coming from how it presses on his spine. It is tough to notice just by looking on the outside." The vet bent over to scratch Jerry's scruff and patted him on the head. "It can really only be caught with x-rays, sometimes not even then—at first. It's too bad whoever saw him last time didn't diagnose it."

Rene's jaw clenched tight. They weren't about to open that discussion.

"Amputation is the recommended treatment for osteosarcoma. It will remove the pain, but it won't cure the cancer. This disease tends to spread quickly, so it's best to move fast." He went on to explain how the pain would only get worse if they did nothing. The bone would fracture unexpectedly, terribly.

They listened as the vet explained why more tests were needed if they wanted to get rid of Jerry's pain. And if so, they had to do it soon. Right now the cancer was only invading his scapula, and surgery could remove the painful, primary tumor.

Testing felt like a no-brainer. Jim looked at the vet and Rene nodded in agreement. "Yeah, please. Whatever tests you need to do, let's get 'em done."

❀   ❀   ❀

Less than an hour later, the vet confirmed their worst fears. Jerry didn't hear the news or see the look of shock on their faces. He was waking up from anesthesia in the recovery ward with a bald patch on his shoulder from the needle biopsy into his scapula. As he did, the vet slowly explained to Jim and Rene that dogs and cats usually return to their old selves after they recover from amputation surgery. "Animals don't have the same hang-ups we do. They don't care whether they have three legs or four. All they want is to feel good again. The amputation can help your dog live happily for the rest of his life."

Neither of them spoke, but they didn't need words to know what each was thinking. Testing was one thing, but amputation was not an option for their athletic dog. Jim remembered the vet's worst-case scenario, but needed to hear it again. "And what if we don't do anything?"

"The only other option would be palliative care. Just manage the pain with medication."

"And how long will that last?"

The vet understood their hesitation. He recognized how drastic amputation seems to most people. "Without amputation, it could be only weeks. There aren't any pain meds strong enough to control the pain once it gets beyond a certain level."

To the vet, and anyone who works in a veterinary clinic, amputation has always made sense as the best treatment for this disease. It gets rid of cancer's painful origin. It also buys anywhere from six months to a year of pain-free life for dogs who are the unfortunate victims of osteosarcoma.

"They really do get around great on three legs, I see it all the time. There's probably one or two out in the lobby right now." He put his pen down, folded his hands on his lap, and waited for the same questions he heard almost daily.

Jim and Rene would have a million of them in time, but for now, only one loomed in Jim's mind. "But how can they walk like that? How would he go to the bathroom?"

"It's easy for them!" It was one of the first questions people always ask. "They adapt, even to urinating. When they need to go, they'll go!" Then he moved his left arm toward the middle of his chest and made a fist. "Their body shifts the weight around. They compensate by moving the leg to the middle. They stay upright that way, like a three-legged stool. That's why we call them tripods."

"Tripod? Like a piece of furniture? That's harsh!" Jim didn't like the insult.

"Well, you don't need to call him that. Try to look at it this way: By not using that leg, Jerry is basically already a three-legged dog. Amputation may not eliminate the cancer, but it will get rid of his pain. He could be around for a while longer, and without pain."

Even the well-rehearsed vet couldn't convince them on the spot. Amputation sounded inhumane to most clients, including Jim and Rene. Chop off a dog's leg to save its life? That didn't make sense. But they agreed on more tests to rule out other conditions.

꙰   ꙰   ꙰

Jim desperately tried to stay calm as they returned to the busy lobby. This one could have been in any human hospital, except for the dozens of barking, meowing, cawing animals jumping out of their skin. Tufts of random fur balls floated back and forth across the slick floor as clients came and went. Meanwhile in the back office, Jerry recovered and happily posed for more x-rays with the gentle and coaxing students. He was so calm that sedation wasn't even necessary.

From the hard, plastic seats in the waiting room, Rene and Jim mourned in silent agony until a young student wearing blue scrubs walked toward them with Jerry. The good-natured patient was hobbling and tired, but not stressed by the commotion. The fur on his right wrist joint was trimmed all the way around, and the bald spot on his shaved left shoulder gave him a patchwork quilt appearance, but he didn't care. He was just happy to be back with his people. When they stood to greet him, a soft voice drifted over their shoulders. "Awwww..." An unfamiliar woman watched the happy reunion with a smile.

"Thank you." Rene had no idea why she was thanking her.

The woman got down on one knee to talk to Jerry. "What's going on with you, fella? Why are you limping?"

His long tail whooshed sideways as he nudged her cheek with his muzzle. She didn't seem to mind his wet nose kiss.

Rene could barely answer on his behalf. "Cancer. We think."

"Oh, I'm sorry. What kind?"

"Osteosarcoma." Rene hadn't even gotten to research the disease, but was trying to get comfortable with the clinical term of the cancer that was killing her dog.

"I'm so sorry. That's tough. I had a feeling. My old German shepherd had the same cancer a few years ago. We had to amputate her leg, but she lived two more years!"

She reached into her purse and pulled a photo from her wallet. A beautiful, black-and-tan shepherd stared intensely into the camera with fearless, dark eyes. "Look, this was Stella!" She appeared to be the kind of female that Jerry would roll over for if given the chance. "She had three legs, but she was so happy! She even got to go to the beach and swim."

Jerry's radar antenna ears twitched at the word "swim." Jim and Rene looked at each other, then down at their athletic dog.

"Oh, that is so good to know. Thank you." Rene couldn't manage any other words before excusing herself and running out through the double glass doors with tears in her eyes.

❈   ❈   ❈

One week later, they made the long drive back to Davis. Rene hovered close to Jerry like paparazzi, video camera recording while he hopped along outside, sniffing the lawn and greeting other dogs waiting for their turn with the vet. He wasn't using the bad leg at all anymore. Clearly, he could get along on three legs. He was in pain, but moving with a grace and strength that few humans possess when roles are reversed. With flat ears, squinting eyes, and tense facial expressions, he hopped into the lobby while his humans tried to keep their tears from flowing.

An hour later, Jerry went down the rabbit hole. Peacefully he lay on the table, perhaps dreaming of chasing rodents while a giant robotic arm slowly circled around his anesthetized body for a series of three-dimensional images. Life-altering decisions hung in the balance, but hours would pass before Jim and Rene had to decide anything. For now, Jerry's bed lay on the floor of their hotel room while daytime TV talk show banter filled the chasm of silence between the two people who loved him more than anyone else in the world.

Oprah chatted with Dr. Oz while they tapped away on their laptops. But there was no way to focus on work when Dr. Internet could be hiding something that would help them decide Jerry's future. Not surprisingly, the "osteosarcoma in dogs" query Rene typed into the search engine returned less than optimistic results. There was no disguising the brutal facts of the disease.

Amputation surgery alone results in an average survival time of about four to six months.

Amputation and chemotherapy can give a dog up to a year of additional time.

But less than 10 percent of dogs live beyond the one-year prognosis.

In her eyes, none of the options were any good. Each seemed like a pointless attempt at prolonging the inevitable. She turned to Jim. "Why bother doing anything if we only get six months?"

"Because it gets rid of the pain and buys us more time together." He sounded more hopeful than she did.

Neither liked the idea of amputation. Chemotherapy was almost as horrifying. Give their OK to turn their athletic hiking dog into a crippled, bald dog, pathetically hobbling around with one missing leg? Never!

But deep down, they also understood that he wasn't ready to die.

They had never met another dog with osteosarcoma. If they could find a few happy stories about these cancer dogs on three legs, amputation might not seem so terrible. Then, after an hour of mindlessly scrolling through search engine results, a 43-second video changed everything.

"Get the gopher, Moose, get that gopher!"

A happy male voice cheered a giant Great Dane digging in the dirt with one giant front paw.

"Get it, Moose! Gooood boooooooyyyy!"

Cartoonish, awkward, and oversized, the giant Harlequin dog could almost be mistaken for a Holstein dairy cow. Up and down and back again went his floppy ears while he burrowed deep into the gopher hole with a single front leg.

"Get it, Moose! You can do it!"

The real-life Marmaduke continued pounding the ground with one big paw, never once stopping to mourn his missing leg. This was not a disabled animal. Moose was happily doing what came naturally to any other mammal on the hunt.

"Hey, you have got to see this!" Rene got up and carried her laptop to the desk where Jim was sitting. She replayed the video again.

"Get the gopher, Moose, get that gopher!"

Jim looked up from her screen, dumbfounded but smiling. "Wow, if he can do that, then why not Jerry?"

Great Danes are nearly twice the size of an average German shepherd. Jerry only weighed about 78 pounds. This giant Moose (aptly named) was at least 125 pounds, even without that gopher in his mouth. If he could dig with one front leg—and look so happy doing it—then why not a smaller, active dog like Jerry?

The clip ended, and their eyes locked. Neither had to speak the obvious. Amputation didn't seem so cruel after all. One hour later the phone rang, jolting them from their confused haze of optimism.

"You get it, I can't." Rene knew she'd break down regardless of the news. Jim answered, his hand trembling.

"Mr. Nelson? This is Dr. Stepnik, at the hospital." He spoke quickly and was very matter of fact. "Jerry's MRI went well, and we got a good picture of the tumor. It's definitely cancerous, and bigger than we thought, but we think it's localized to the scapula. We're not sure we can get it all. If we amputate right now while he's still under anesthesia, it's the best chance for your dog to be pain-free. We can take the entire leg if you give us the go-ahead."

"So, you're saying that we have to decide right now?" This was a joint decision. Jim could not decide Jerry's fate all by himself.

"Well, yeah, that would be good, while he's still sedated." The vet took a deep breath and then added, "There is another option too. If you don't want to amputate, just tell us, and we won't wake him up."

Not wake him up? The suggestion was shocking. It hurt like hell to even consider the idea.

"Can we call you right back?" Jim pleaded. "We just need one minute. Rene's right here, we need to talk."

He hung up, sick with fear about deciding the fate of their oblivious dog. Euthanizing a young, otherwise healthy dog just didn't feel right. He needed to see his best buddy enjoy life again.

Rene's eyes filled with tears; there was no need to relay the news. She wiped her eyes with the back of her sleeve and broke the silence. "I think we should amputate."

"Are we being selfish?"

"I don't know. But I'm not ready to put him down."

Jim wasn't either. And they both knew what Jerry would do if the choice were his. He loved life; he had toughed it out through his pain to be with them. Being pain-free and enjoying life—like Moose in the video—felt like a natural choice. Jim's shaky hands reached for the phone and dialed.

❋   ❋   ❋

"I can't believe I just told him to chop off my dog's leg." Bizarre thoughts about Jerry's future as an amputee ran through their minds.

Wonder what that leg weighed?

Where does the leg go when they take it off?

Will other dogs notice he's missing one?

Time dragged on while they waited for a surgery update, hoping it was a good one. They had their laptops open, but neither was being productive. Never before had their future been more uncertain and terrifying. Rene sought solace in a desperate Internet search for more happy dogs like Moose. But web surfing wasn't doing it for Jim; he needed something more to focus on. So, he did what he does best; he began building a new website. Only this time he wasn't doing it for money, but for something much more important—to save his sanity.

Jim thought back to the vet's conversation about three-legged dogs, almost feeling guilty about referring to his own dog as a piece of furniture. That "Tripod" nickname just seemed kind of mean. And dumb, too. After all, what three-legged stool has paws on it?

That's when it hit him. "Paws, Tripod...Tripawds!" He turned to Rene. "Tripawd. Get it?" He spelled it out for her. "T-R-I-P-A-W-D. Let's empower it! I'm going to build Tripawds.com. Whatchya think?"

She smiled for the first time in days. "I love it!"

By the time Oprah's hour ended, Jim had published an online diary where he and Rene could pour out their feelings about Jerry's ordeal. Writing came easy to them, and now the skill would serve them well when they explained the amputation decision to friends and family.

※　※　※

The surgery went just as planned. The next day, on Thanksgiving morning, Jerry's surgeon met them at the unusually quiet hospital, looking much more casual in a t-shirt and sandals. Their dog was now minus one leg, but they still had plenty to be thankful for: Jerry was coming home.

The young vet felt confident Jerry would rebound in record time. He survived the three-hour surgery without any complications and all the stamina of a much younger dog. "Give him about two weeks; you'll see that he will do just fine." He studied his clients' red, swollen eyes and gently smiled, then left to retrieve his groggy but eager patient.

Minutes later, he and Jerry returned like two superheroes ready to take on the world. Less than 24 hours after his amputation surgery, Jerry was not being wheeled out on a stretcher as they expected. He wasn't attached to an IV or even wearing bandages around the large incision across his chest. Happy and confident, he hop-galloped down the empty hallway toward Jim and Rene while the vet hung on tight to his leash with one hand while carrying a plastic cone of shame in the other.

"Jer..." Rene timidly called out while averting her eyes from the eighteen-inch incision snaking around his shaved torso. Jim smiled as tears fell from his eyes. Jerry was walking! Well, sort of. It wasn't quite a trot, more of a hop. Just one day after losing his leg, he could fling his front leg forward so head and body could follow in a bucking, rocking-horse gallop. His new walk looked hard, but it didn't slow him down. With bright, alert eyes and a bouncy tongue flapping in the air, the happy amputee ran into their open arms.

"I tried to bring him out on a gurney, but he wasn't having it." The surgeon handed Jim the cone of shame, gave a stack of discharge instructions and a bag of pills to Rene, then took Jerry's leash and led them out to the parking lot where their impromptu ambulance waited. Jim had turned the back of their truck into a padded transport with a thick mattress and heavy blankets to protect Jerry on the long, bumpy ride home.

In his most vulnerable state that either could remember, Jerry seemed so physically fragile and yet so strong in spirit. Jim swore he wouldn't baby him, but he couldn't help worrying. "I'm not sure of the best way to pick him up; I don't want to hurt him."

"That's not a big deal. Just try not to put direct pressure on the incision." The vet demonstrated by reaching down to gather Jerry in his arms. "Do it like this." He scooped from the "good" side of Jerry's body where his other front leg remained, gathered his patient into his arms, and gently placed him on the truck's open tailgate. Standing tall and proud, Jerry lightly grunted, *Hrrrmphf...hrrmphf...* while circling three times to the left in search of the right position on his new, three-inch-thick foam bed.

The surgeon smiled with pride at his latest mission accomplished. "He might be a little dopey for a while, but at least he'll sleep through the ride. Have a good trip back, and call if you have any questions."

"Thank you so much. And happy Thanksgiving! Go home!" Jim shook the doctor's hand, still surprised he came by on a holiday to reunite their little family.

The green truck disappeared into the redwoods with a sleepy new Tripawd fast asleep in the back. When they arrived home five hours later, Jim scooped Jerry into his arms just like the vet showed him, then carried all 70 pounds of him up eighteen steps into their drafty, old house. Hundreds of miles away, their families were clinking wine glasses and carving up turkey. And while there were no festivities for Jerry, Jim, and Rene, their spirits overflowed with hope for more time together.

꙼   ꙼   ꙼

Dogs overcome hardship far better than people. Instead of feeling sorry for themselves, they take action, adapt, and move forward. For dogs, there is no dwelling on the past.

Jerry recovered within two weeks, which is typical for most middle-aged dogs. His textbook recuperation was uneventful, but Rene still worried. She wanted to sleep on the floor next to his bed during the first week, but Jim refused to let her.

"He doesn't want you there; that would just seem weird to him." Tough love was the best approach to a quick, complete recovery, he told her.

"But what if he wakes up and needs something?"

"He'll let us know. Think about how he would see it. Sleeping on the floor with him would be out of the ordinary. If you do that, it's for you, not him."

Reluctantly, she agreed. Over the next two weeks, Jerry healed just as his vets had hoped. It was Jim and Rene who needed more time to adjust to the new normal of a drastically different routine. She was grateful Jerry was alive, but couldn't understand how he would be happy if he couldn't go on long hikes anymore. When she watched him pant and sit down after just a few steps, she couldn't help but focus on what he couldn't do, not what he could. Inevitably, a chilling thought stabbed at her heart:

Was there any point in planning new camping trips when he might not even live long enough to see spring, much less summer?

Consumed by sadness, it didn't occur to her that neither dog nor human is guaranteed another season on the mountain or a day at the beach.

Jerry, however, wasn't consumed with thoughts about his altered life. He wasn't frustrated if he lost his footing on the slippery hardwood floors. When the sun rose, he embraced the new day with as much enthusiasm as before. And he certainly wasn't wondering about what he would do next summer. Or even tomorrow. He only wanted to know why she had sadness in her eyes. He sensed the fear and worries that ran deep in her heart.

What if he hurts that one front leg?

What happens when the cancer comes back?

How will we know he's had enough?

She fought the constant urge to carry him. She would do it if she could, but she wasn't physically strong enough. Watching him learn how to compensate and stay balanced was even more difficult, especially when he took his first tumble.

Jim's sister had sent a care package of toys that Jerry scattered around their long hallway. Rene filmed him playing with the gifts, when he picked up one of his Barney dolls and aimed it at the new squeaky football, sending it flying down the hall. He chased after the prize but fell face-forward, bumping his chin on the floor.

The face-plant almost killed Rene, who dropped the camera in shock. "Oh, Jerry! Oh no! Are you okay?"

He was oblivious, and leaped up to his feet within seconds. Unscratched and undaunted, he snatched up the ball and chomped on its delicious squeaker.

She ran to console him, but Jim grabbed her by the arm.

"Don't! He can handle it. Just let him be a dog."

"But..."

"Stop."

Jerry hopped back into the dog den, still squeaking the ball and probably wondering why the game was over so soon. Clearly not upset, he looked up at Rene with curiosity in his eyes, as if he wanted to say, "Did I do something wrong?"

She knelt down, threw her arms around him, and sobbed into his scruff. "Oh, Jerry, I'm so sorry! I'm so sorry!"

Jim looked down over her from the couch and watched Jerry's expression turn to worry. "It's okay, buddy, she's just having a hard time."

※   ※   ※

Moving out of recovery mode meant relearning their routines, and Jim was ready for the task. He tried not to treat Jerry with kid gloves, but some things needed fine-tuning, like the eighteen short, steep, slippery steps leading in and out of their hundred-year-old house. Constructed during an era without building permits or codes, the staircase had a steep pitch that was dangerous for any dog, no matter how many legs they walked on. It made Jim especially nervous to know that since dogs carry more than 60 percent of their weight in the front end of their body, the lack of a second front leg put Jerry at greater risk of falling forward. He tried carrying Jerry on the stairs, but the determined dog wanted to do it his way and squirmed with displeasure in Jim's arms.

"Okay, buddy, you do it then." One morning, he paused at the top of the staircase and put Jerry down on the floor. Then, like a proud new dad watching his infant son's first steps, Jim watched his three-legged dog lean against the staircase wall and use it for balance as he slid and hopped down to the first-floor landing.

Once safely at the bottom, Jerry paused, looked at Jim's grinning face and seemed to say, "Don't worry, Dad, I've got this."

❊   ❊   ❊

In less than a month, Jerry looked as good as the vet promised. His stitches were out, his balance was better, and he seemed antsy for his usual neighborhood walks. Nervous but grateful for the progress, Jim and Rene decided it was time. From the moment he stepped outside, their amputee dog was a head-turner. Most neighbors had positive feedback, like, "Oh wow, he does great, doesn't he?" Some couldn't help but pity the joyful shepherd with the gimpy gait and large patch of missing fur.

"Awww, poor dog!"

Sometimes the negativity was too much to bear. That's when Rene and Jim gave them something to think about.

"Poor dog? Don't feel sorry for him. He's not feeling sorry for himself!"

Jerry grew restless after a few weeks of pain medication, short walks, minimal playtime, and no socialization with others.

During the workday, he returned to his old tactics to drag Rene and Jim away from their computers by banging his paw on the back door or nudging his muzzle at their keyboards. They wondered if he was up to playing with his old friends.

"Jerry, you wanna go to Happy Dog?"

Jim could have been dangling a steak over Jerry's head. The pent-up dog jumped and danced a little twirl around the office, thrilled to hear his favorite two phrases: "You wanna...?" and "Happy Dog!"

Could he keep up with his old pals? Would they sense his new weakness? Nobody knew, but Jerry had no fears. On the morning they arrived for the carefully supervised visit, he raced into the yard and ran along the fence that divided him from the larger play area. A deafening cacophony of yapping, yipping, and deep barks filled the salty seaside air while Jerry joined the daycare party. He barked louder than usual, as if to say, "I'm back! Bet you never thought you'd see me again, huh?"

Rene held out hope that he could enjoy the one last "normal" thing he used to enjoy. Sadly, that dream didn't last long. Not long after the rowdy gathering began, Jerry stopped and slowly melted into the ground. His long tongue lazily hung out of his mouth, bouncing up and down with heavy exhales and inhales. The dog was happy, but he was done. And so were his Happy Dog days.

"Come on, buddy, let's go." Jim approached the exhausted dog and clipped a leash on his collar.

Arm in arm, leash in hand, with Jerry leading the pack, the trio walked out of Happy Dog for the last time. Sadness filled their hearts; but just around the bend, Jerry's best days were yet to come.

— 7 —

The New Normal

Jerry's best buddy, Winston, was about his height, but nearly ten pounds heavier and all muscle. His people were active folks, and they often had him wearing a harness that had loops to attach a backpack for camping trips so he could carry his own kibble. Winston sure liked food. Living room couches were one of his favorite snacks.

"It was early during Jerry's recovery when Jim went outside with him, coaching the dog to do his doody. Winston's pack walked by and, like always, threw Jerry into a tizzy. He ran to the gate, barking at Winston with a wagging tail and all smiles. But Jim was nervous for his new amputee. He'd already seen the impact on Jerry's energy during his last visit to Happy Dog. Playing together would have to wait, he explained to Win's people. They understood, so they kept Jerry's excited playmate on their side of the fence.

The dogs appeared confused at the separation. Jerry's head darted back and forth from Jim to his best friend. His eyes pleaded as if to say, "C'mon, Dad. I'm fine!" Winston appeared to want playtime just as much. Neither paid any attention to the fact that Jerry was now missing a leg. They both just wanted to run around like old times.

When those two got together, they played rough, and Jim feared Jerry would get hurt. Then he spied the handle on Winston's harness, leaned over the fence and pointed at the gear. "How does that thing work?" Jerry's gait and movements were so altered now. Maybe the contraption could make life easier for him, and Jim.

"Oh, that?" Lauren grabbed the handle in the middle of Winston's back and straightened the harness on him. "We got it from Ruffwear. It's great for going on walks!" Then she tugged at the leash attached to a ring on the harness and stepped forward. The two canine friends gave sad barking goodbyes as Winston continued on to finish his walk.

"Come on, Jer, let's go inside. Time to get to work!" They turned and headed for the back stairs. Jerry hesitated at the bottom and looked up at Jim, who was already climbing the mountain. He took a second to assess the ascent, then one hop at a time, he slowly propelled himself up the staircase on his two back legs. *Hop. Clop. Hop.* Up he went. Since dogs carry all of their propulsion power in the rear, going up was no problem. It was going down the 18 steep, uncarpeted steps that scared Rene and Jim to death each time Jerry wanted to go outside. He seemed to lack confidence going down, and helping him with the impromptu beach towel "sling" one vet tech suggested was an epic failure. Each time they went outside, Jim and Rene were forced to grit their teeth and nervously keep a close eye on him, hoping he wouldn't fall.

"Hey, did you see Winston's harness?" Jim called to Rene from the top landing.

"I did. I've seen all that Ruffwear camping gear for dogs. Pretty cool. But isn't that harness just to keep dogs from pulling on the leash, or attaching a pack?"

"I don't know about that, but I think the handle could come in handy for helping Jerry get around."

"Oh yeah, I didn't even think about that!"

One week later, the brown delivery truck arrived. "Oooh, it's here!" Rene ran to the door to sign for the package, then ripped it open to reveal the exact same harness Winston wore, but in black. Initially designed for lifting search and rescue dogs on duty, the harness also seemed ideal for helping a three-legged German shepherd go up and down stairs.

"Jerrrrrrreeeee, come check this out!"

Three sets of claws click-clacked down the hallway to her. Jerry had heard the truck pull up and was eager for a treat from Mister Brown Shorts. He couldn't see the harness she hid behind her back. He skidded into an obedient sit and looked up at her with pleading eyes.

"Good boy!" She leaned over him and gently placed the harness strap opening over his head. Begrudgingly he sat, trying to understand the game. "You are going to look so sharp, Jerry! Like a service dog!" She guided his remaining front limb through a leg loop, then adjusted the harness and straps for a good fit.

Jerry was already used to wearing a backpack from his hiking days, and the goofy sweaters Rene bought to cover his incision. Familiar with her apparel antics, he didn't flinch during the sizing session. When it was over, the harness sat perfectly across the middle of his back while sunlight bounced off the reflective trim.

"Oh, Jerry! You look so handsome! Jim, check it out!"

The officially uniformed dog brought a smile to Jim's face. "Let's go see how it works!" He gently ran a hand through the harness handle and guided Jerry over to the stairs. "Come on, Jer, let's go outside!"

Happy for a break from the workday routine, the uniformed CFO hardly missed his treat at all. He complied and cautiously started the downward hop to the bottom landing. Only this time, Jim was able to offer help by holding onto the handle while walking along Jerry's amputated limb side. With every down step Jerry took, Jim also descended one step. Finally, they arrived at the bottom without any worries. The expensive piece of gear was worth the money—and a ticket to keeping Jerry active without risk of injury from falling on stairs or stumbling up into the truck.

The harness purchase kicked off a few simple adjustments for Jerry's new normal. Rene's dad built an elevated feeding station to help Jerry eat without straining his neck or losing his balance. And when the dog slipped on their hardwood floors, Rene put down new carpet runners for better traction. Then she installed baby gates to block off their slippery, antiquated staircases. And when she saw how he tripped on his lumpy, cedar-filled dog bed she bought a firm, orthopedic mattress for him. It was nearly as nice as any human one, but Jerry avoided the bed, instead preferring to sleep on the floor. Only later did she learn that dogs often gravitate to hard, cold surfaces to help soothe their achy bodies. Just one of many lessons they learned along this new path they were taking together.

Within a few weeks after surgery, Jerry returned to his job as CFO. He got right back to work, greeting his friend in the brown truck. More friends dropped in to check out the new Tripawd in town. And while Rene researched diets that could help Jerry fight cancer, Jim grew more comfortable with the decision to amputate. Life was not nearly as sad as they thought it would be. In fact, it was much happier. Jerry was a constant source of inspiration as they watched him effortlessly move on and adapt to their new normal without any more pain.

❀　❀　❀

Shortly after the vet removed his stitches, Jerry followed Jim into the yard for his first real playtime after the surgery. Leash-free and ready to play, he quickly trotted over to favorite outside toys, like his hula hoop stash. Jim smiled at the eager dog, remembering how the first time Rene had brought a big yellow hoop home on one of their yard sale-ing days, Jerry didn't know what to do with the circular object. But when Jim rolled it, the chase was on! Jerry ran after the hoop and grabbed it—taking it down like prey and giving it the quick death shake. It only took a few times to tear the toy in two. Just like a coyote whipping a dead rabbit by the neck, he thrashed it repeatedly until it was a plastic scrap pile. The bits were now only good for playing fetch. Like with his Barney infatuation, Jim and Rene fed Jerry's hula hoop obsession by searching for replacements at every yard sale.

Since the surgery, his humans protected him from the perils of playing with the hoop—or any of his outdoor toys—whenever he did his business in the yard. Short, leashed potty walks were all he got during those first few weeks of recovery. But now Jim could see the time had come to ease up.

As soon as he spied the bent remains of that hoop, Jerry hopped over to it with a determined look and goofy grin. Jim smiled, happy to see Jerry back to his old self again.

He snatched the plastic toy with his teeth and immediately shook his head from one side to the other, giving the hoop one powerful whip. Promptly followed by a loud, *Yelp!*

He dropped that hoop like it was on fire and painfully cried out. This time, there was no second shake. The new amputee hopped away with a stumble, forgetting that his spare leg was missing. He appeared stunned and confused.

Jim gasped; his eyes grew large as he rushed to Jerry's side. He realized Jerry didn't seem to know or care that the major muscle group connecting his neck and shoulders was still on the mend. It was a good sign, in a bittersweet kinda way. In Jerry's mind, he was back to his old self again and able to romp and play like before, with no concern about the changes in his body. The old dog was back…just not quite up to full speed yet.

As he hopped back to the house, Jerry kept his eye on what was left of his hoop. Jim could tell what that dog was thinking by looking into his eyes. It's called in-seeing, a communication method he learned early on when reading a dog training book by those monks, the ones who know everything about German shepherds. At that moment, Jim looked into Jerry's eyes and knew Jerry had no limiting thoughts of what he could not do or how things had changed. No, Jerry was telling that obstinate hoop, "You just wait…"

Jim smiled. "You bet. Move on, dog." Both acknowledged the lesson. No need to dote. Jerry was back to playing and enjoying his new lease on life with just a touch of caution. One week later, the dastardly hoop finally met its doom. It then dawned on Jim that dogs are incredibly resilient creatures, and Jerry was going to be okay. Everything was going to be okay.

❋   ❋   ❋

Jerry's progress was so exciting that Jim and Rene wanted to share it with the world. They wanted others to see that he adapted better than any human would. But what they didn't yet fully understand was the importance of helping their three-legged dog avoid injury by keeping him from overdoing it.

Gradually their walks got longer, and Jerry wasn't tiring nearly as quickly as before. The short hop to the corner and back turned into a quick stroll around the block. A month after surgery, it seemed his stamina had returned. He walked at a faster clip now, and Rene and Jim discovered they were the ones who needed to keep up with Jerry. They learned it's easier for amputee dogs to hop along at a faster pace than lumber along while throwing that front leg forward.

One day while watching him move, Jim thought to himself: *It's better to hop on three legs than limp on four!* The perfect tagline for Jerry's website presented itself, and as he continued to improve, Jim and Rene made movies and took photos everywhere the trio went. The daily hops around the block gradually led back to their favorite destination—a small park down the street. They always thought of it as Jerry's park. A small, two-acre, grassy oasis, it was the nearest place where Jerry could run wild chasing a soccer ball through the field or enjoy a fun game of Frisbee after work. It was also the place they discovered Jerry's new talent.

One day, Jerry spotted a basketball somebody left behind at the park. He ran after it like he always did his soccer ball. But he couldn't pick it up, so Jim bounced it toward him. The game was on. Jerry snapped at the flying orb with his mouth and bumped it right back to his teammate. So, Jim bounced it higher. Jerry jumped, caught air, and bounced it back to Jim. Out came the camera…bounce, hop, snap.

Bounce! Hop! Snap! Snap!

Everyone laughed and cheered. Too bad nobody realized that all that hopping and bouncing on concrete was so bad for his remaining limbs. To their credit, most vets didn't even know back then. And Jerry? Well, he didn't care; all he wanted was to play. He twirled, jumped, and landed while pounding his front wrist with the majority of his body weight. Years later, a canine rehabilitation therapist enlightened them about the importance of limiting high-impact exercise for three-legged dogs. But hindsight, as they say, is often acquired through some hard lessons learned.

※　※　※

One evening, the reality of Jerry's new normal finally hit home. In their eyes he seemed strong enough to walk the eight blocks to Old Town, a distance twice as far as his post-surgery walks. On the night of the monthly "Arts Alive" downtown event that brought hundreds of locals out for free music and art exhibits, Jim and Rene set out to show off their three-legged wonder dog. They made it there just fine, and Jerry soaked up love and attention from everyone he encountered. Looking exuberant, they strolled up and down a few more blocks and along the waterfront before heading back, extending the walk even more than they'd intended.

Walking with huge smiles plastered across their faces, so proud of their amazing dog, Jim and Rene finally led Jerry home. But at the turnaround point, Jerry told them he was done—the best way he could. The exhausted dog plopped down on the sidewalk.

"Jerry? What the…? Are you OK?" Worry seeped into Rene's voice.

This time Jim didn't say, "Come on, dawg…" Something told him he'd let Jerry overdo it, and he kicked himself for being so oblivious. Dogs are excellent at hiding their pain, and they do all they can to avoid showing weakness. In the wild, their mates might kick them out of the pack if they did, or worse. Jim and Rene wouldn't, of course, but Jerry's instincts kept him going until he was incapable of hopping along any further that night. Since he was no small dog, carrying him the seven blocks home was out of the question.

"Go get the truck!" She was upset, and Jim did what she asked.

Embarrassed, sad for Jerry, and mad at himself, he ran all the way home. While Rene waited, people passed to pet Jerry, who soaked up all the affection as if nothing was wrong. He was in pain, but he didn't take it out on anyone. Soon Jim returned, and lovingly lifted Jerry into the truck. They arrived home and he carried Jerry upstairs, where the dog immediately collapsed into his new foam bed. He didn't move far from there for a couple days, obviously sore from the long walk. Jerry had overdone it. But more accurately, Jim and Rene inadvertently allowed him to overdo it.

That incident was a wake-up call. Clearly, they needed to be better proponents for Jerry's well-being. So, they started keeping tabs on his activity and making sure he didn't go too far on their walks. What was too far? They really didn't know, since most vets didn't give any kind of guidance for new amputees, at least back then. They guessed as best they could, and one month passed before they allowed him to walk more than ten minutes at a time. And it was three months before they felt confident enough about his stamina to take Jerry back to the beach, his favorite place of all.

Rene fretted about sand getting in his incision. Then Jim showed her how it had long since healed up. Jim was concerned about other dogs hurting him. But Rene reminded him that Jerry had already been playing with Winston. On his first day back at Samoa Beach, they hovered over Jerry like helicopter parents. Rene made sure he was wearing a sweater, and Jim kept a tight grip on the leash.

The moment his paws hit the sand he was so excited and raring to go, they couldn't hold him back.

"Okay, Jerry, if you insist." Jim unhooked the leash from his collar. "Just for a few minutes." But he was already off and running down to the surf line in search of some kelp.

"Jerry! Come!"

Jim brought out the Frisbee, another game they would later learn is risky for amputee dogs. Thankfully, no harm was done on this trip. Jerry played; they got some great photos and a lifetime of memories.

* * *

Over time, they learned that Jerry didn't need as much help as they thought, but it was still smart to play conservatively and avoid hard activities that used to come easy to him. A couple playdates with Winston proved that Jerry could handle himself in most situations. He needed to be a dog. It was time for more fun with his own kind.

Other, new friends and big dogs began to come around. Santo was a client's large German shepherd, with a dark-black mask and markings. That dog was 100 percent roughhousing shepherd—unlike Jerry's less aggressive play style. One morning during a client meeting with Jim, their client let Santo out of the car for a romp with Jerry. But in typical shepherd style, the younger dog wanted to play the alpha, even if he was on another dog's turf. Jerry was a timid player at heart, but when Santo started to play rough, his inner shepherd came out. He stood his ground and quickly showed Santo that even a three-legged animal is top dog in his own yard. Jerry snapped at him with a loud, aggressive bark. Santo slowly walked backward.

"Whoa…" Jim was taken by surprise and his client laughed. Both were impressed by the sweet, but territorial, amputee defending his home.

That's when Jim knew: Jerry didn't need so much protection from other dogs after all. He could stand on his own, even with one less leg. Jerry proved it again a few weeks later when a neighbor walked by with her friendly but intimidating-looking mastiff named Zeus.

"Hey, buddy? Want to play?" Her oversized puppy ran the lattice fence so he could get a closer look at Jerry. She smiled and reached over to wave at Jim and Rene, who were doing yardwork while Jerry supervised.

They smiled, and Jerry got up and let out a series of happy-sounding barks. Both dogs' tails wagged, muzzles touching through the lattice. Jim and Rene looked at each other and nodded. "OK, Jerry, ready?"

It was the right decision. Once inside, the two dogs with similar play styles burned off extra energy without incident. Zeus took particular interest in one of Jerry's tug toys and picked it up by one end.

Jerry let out a loud but friendly sounding bark to let Zeus know the toy was his. Then he snatched the other end. Zeus understood who was toy boss, but proceeded to drag Jerry around the yard anyway. This strong mastiff clearly underestimated Jerry's determination. The three-legged dog wasn't about to let go.

Tug, tug, grunt, tug. The toy stretched and grew while both dogs planted their feet and pulled harder. Tug, tug, grunt, tug. Jerry lost ground as Zeus pulled him across the yard. He then appeared to recall something Jim likes to say: Work smarter, not harder.

Zeus pulled Jerry toward the small maple tree in the corner of his yard. He hung on, positioning himself on the other side of the tree. Backing up, Jerry wrapped the rubber toy around it. Then, using the tree as leverage, he planted his one front foot in the ground. Up and down went his bobbing head while he yanked his body backwards. Again and again he repeated the maneuver.

The mastiff could no longer pull him along; it was a stalemate, but both dogs were steadfast. Slowly, each dog inched away from the tree until, *SNAP!* The rubber toy split in two, throwing both dogs backward. Zeus lost his grip and landed in a squat with a bewildered look, as if accusing Jerry of cheating. Jerry trotted off in triumph with the prize hanging from his clenched jaws.

Did he cheat? No. Was he proud of his conquest? You bet. The peaceful, three-legged pacifist watched the humans in their amusement as he trotted upstairs for a rest.

"Way to go, dawg!" One in-seeing look and Jim knew they were thinking the same thing. "Now, *that* is how you overcome."

*   *   *

Four months after his amputation, and he grew stronger every day as his one front leg bulked up like a bodybuilder preparing for competition. Jerry was ready for more of his old activities. Since the mountains weren't very far from home, when an early spring storm dumped a few feet of snow on nearby Berry Summit, they took a day off from work to have fun with their CFO. Sure, they could have stayed home working, but for the first time ever, their life was centered around Jerry, not their clients. Jim and Rene were learning to focus on the miraculous dog that brought so much joy to their days.

Slushy, wet snow was falling hard when they arrived, but there was already plenty carpeting the ground. "Get the snowball, get it!" Rene gathered up a big ball of the white stuff in her gloved hands and tossed the orb. Jim threw another, and Jerry ran off for his icy treat.

Snowballs flew through the air and landed in splats around Jerry's feet, prompting him to hop back in bewilderment as the balls disappeared with a *poof!* Too smart to chase after the vanishing prizes, he focused on catching them in the air.

He jumped high to snatch each one, only to land on that remaining front leg again. *Toss, jump, splush!* The softer landing wasn't as high impact as the basketball game, but Jerry tired faster than they expected. He plopped down in the snow and rested while Rene built a snowman. He was curious about her effort. "What's this, Jerry?" Rene patted another big gob of wet snow atop the snowman's head.

Jerry rose to his feet to inspect. Jim grabbed the camera and started filming. "Get him, Jerry!"

He attacked that snowman like it was an evil enemy. He ran over and hopped up, then with his one front leg, pawed at it fiercely. Once he succeeded at knocking it over, Rene tried to rebuild the snowman but Jerry wouldn't stand for it. In his eyes, the beastly ice man needed to be destroyed. And destroy it he did. *Bark! Pounce! Snap!* Jerry bit at the snow, shook his head, then beat at it repeatedly with his front white paw. He hit hard and he hit often, then he scraped out some snow and went back for more.

Jim recorded the whole thing, which soon appeared on YouTube as a two-part movie set to the 1970s cartoon anthem of *Hong Kong Phooey.*

"Hong Kong Jerry, number one super guy. Hong Kong Jerry, quicker than the human eye."

Jim belted out the anthem and watched snow fly into the air as the canine snowblower chomped and punched that thing to the ground.

Bark! Pounce! Snap!

"When the going gets rough, he's super tough, with a Hong Kong Jerry chop!"

They watched with pride, not quite realizing that Jerry's lesson for the day was all about determination and perseverance. When this dog put his mind to something, he got it done. The demolished evil snowman was his perfect example to show that no job should ever be left undone. When he was satisfied with his actions, nothing remained of the big, bad snowman but a hole in the drift where it once stood. To make sure his students got the point, Jerry kept barking and digging at the remains. By the time it was obliterated, everybody was tired and wet from the cold.

At home later that night, Jerry signaled that they'd allowed him to overdo things—again. They knew because when they went to bed, they heard the distinct gurgles of dog barf rising in his belly. *Hrrruupf, hrrruupf, hrrruupf…*

"Oh, no!" Rene ran to his side, rushing to get him off the carpet.

Out it flew. Apparently, Jerry ate so much snow that he couldn't hold both the water and dinner in his belly. The puking kept Jim and Rene up all night. He vomited in the hall, and he hurled in the bedroom. It spilled onto the stairs and seeped into the oak floors. The next day was even worse.

That's when the coughing started. Rene heard the first hack and froze. She immediately recalled when his surgeon explained how when cancer returns, it usually shows up in the lungs and presents as a cough. Four months after the amputation—and a projected life expectancy of six months—fear rose in Rene as she looked to Jim. The more Jerry let out one cough after another, the more they both grew frightened. The scary cough continued into the evening, so the following day, they rushed him to the vet for x-rays of his lungs.

"Are we going to jump at every single new symptom like this?" Rene hugged Jim while they waited for the x-rays to develop.

"I don't know." Jim just shook his head, hoping for the best.

After what seemed like an hour, his vet returned with good news. "Well, it's not his lungs." She held up the clear scans to the light. "He just ate too much snow. That's what caused the vomiting. Which irritated his throat."

Reality hit home one more time. Jim and Rene knew that as much as they wanted him to "be a dog" again, they couldn't keep putting Jerry in risky situations. It was a fine line: they wanted him to be a happy dog, but they needed to help him stay healthy for as long as he had left.

BE MORE DOG

— 8 —

Moving On

When Jim was young, his dad made it a point to teach the importance of keeping expectations in check. "Expect too much," he would say, "and you set yourself up for disappointment." Jim did his best to remember this whenever he thought about Jerry's cancer, but it wasn't easy. Every day he worried about the cancer returning, or Jerry having an accident on the stairs, or somehow hurting that spare leg. So did Rene; but they didn't dare speak what they both wondered each time they looked at Jerry:

How long do we have together?

Cancer was a big, dark cloud hanging over their heads, surrounding them with pointless emotions of fear, uncertainty, and doubt, or FUD, as Jim called it. He got it from his gruff old boss, who used to say, "FUD will get you nowhere!" Over time, Jim learned to accept that fears, uncertainties, and doubts are nothing more than mere thoughts. They have no power on their own. They only exist in the mind, and they definitely don't help any situation. So, each time he looked at Jerry, he tried hard to shove that FUD aside. After all, Jerry didn't fear the future or doubt his ability to love life. He lived in the now, as all dogs do. Even with one less leg, he had a "just do it" attitude that inspired Jim and Rene to try harder to do the same.

Jerry returned to chasing his favorite red ball around the yard, and even figured out how to lean against a shrub so he could lift his leg to pee. He adapted quickly, but Jim and Rene still carried the burden of agreeing to the amputation. They dealt with their feelings the way many people do: with retail therapy. Only they didn't hit stores, they cruised yard sales. They bought up all the Barney dolls they could find in Eureka. Big Barneys, small Barneys, talking Barneys. Jerry even gained a Giant Barney for his collection, a plush replica nearly as big as he was. He quickly put it to use as a support pillow for his one remaining front leg while he slept, which made him look like he was hugging his big, purple friend. Once he realized the dinosaur could serve his needs, Jerry's instinct to kill the purple beast morphed into a codependent love/hate relationship. At least once a week, a limbless Barney would be abandoned by the sofa. Or a headless Barney dropped in the kitchen. Rene always stitched the corpses back together, while Jim found twisted pleasure in producing lighthearted *KillBarney* videos that documented the destruction on YouTube.

Life was starting to feel normal again. Then Rene shook things up one Saturday afternoon.

"I have an idea!" She barely gave Jim time to finish washing their lunch dishes.

"Uhh, great." He put the last plate in the cupboard and prepared himself. "What now? More yard sales? Another bush for me to dig up in the yard?" Whenever Rene had ideas, it often resulted in home projects gone awry or some sort of extra work for him.

She suggested they go sit and talk in the backyard.

"Oh, boy!" Jim never knew what to expect, but clearly, this was a big one he thought as he watched Rene help Jerry down the steep staircase to the patio. She had a notebook and a beach towel in her hands. He appeared downstairs a few minutes later with cocktails for each of them. He assumed this big idea likely called for it. He guessed right.

"Yum. Thanks, bartender!" Jim handed her the refreshing gin and tonic, then sat down on the towel next to Jerry without saying a word. He didn't have to; his skeptical grin said it all.

He sipped his drink while she did the talking. She began by pointing out that for the last ten years, they had worked day and night to grow their business into a productive little shop. As if he didn't know. Then she reminded him how they had taken the company as far as it could go with just the two of them. "You are at capacity with your workload, I see it." She took another sip. "And I can barely keep up with all your projects."

Jim just nodded, waiting to hear what she was getting at. "We can hire help and expand, but do we really want to go that route? It would suck having employees around here!"

"I know." Jim's drink was half gone already. "If we hire sales help, I'll need some production help."

"Right! And if you had production help, we would need another salesperson to pay for them." His agreement made her so excited she spilled some of her drink while trying to sit up straight. Then she got serious by pointing out the obvious: their CFO would probably only live a few more months. "Do we really want to spend that time doing the same thing, working all day and starving him of attention until dinner?"

He looked at her but said nothing, waiting for whatever big idea it was that would change everything.

"You know we'll neglect him even more if we're training employees. That takes more time away from us." She reached over and caressed Jerry's head to emphasize her point. "Let's sell the business!"

She blurted it out in the loud, fast-talking voice she uses whenever she gets excited, then rushed on with, "And the house, too. We'll get rid of all our stuff, buy an RV, and take a year off. We'll travel with Jerry and give him a farewell tour! What do you think?"

With a blank stare, Jim groaned, "Whoooa...that is a biggie, all right." He had not expected any idea that big. Expand the operation. Cut back on business. Throw a big party. Move...plenty of ideas may not have surprised him...but this? It took a moment for her harebrained notion to sink in while rare coastal sunshine streamed through the willow tree, warming Jerry's soft fur. Jim stroked his dog's side, thinking hard about the seemingly impromptu plan. In an instant, he acknowledged how much he'd been feeling overworked. But after a long silence, and the last few sips of his drink, he spoke. "Okay. Let's do it."

He wasn't sure if he actually heard those words come out of his mouth. It all seemed so...irresponsible. A wide grin spread across Rene's face as she put down her empty glass and lunged forward to kiss him.

In reality, part of Jim thought the idea was utterly irrational, but something inside him found it intriguing. They both grew up RVing with their parents as kids, and he could certainly use a break. His heart screamed, *I love that idea!* But he was skeptical as always, and hesitated to leap at it—until he remembered one of her other "great ideas" that she presented after their first trip to Humboldt County. That one involved quitting their good-paying jobs in San Francisco and moving to that peaceful property on the outskirts of Eureka, where they first started growing their little marketing enterprise. That idea was pretty crazy at the time, but it worked out all right, he admitted to himself.

"We are both getting pretty burnt-out, I know. All right. Let's figure it out." Then, being the marketing guy he is, he brainstormed ideas with Rene and crafted a plan to make it happen.

First, she bought books about how to take a sabbatical without going broke. Then Jim researched how to sell a business, and designed a prospectus to help their home-based shop resemble the successful enterprise he knew it could become. They sought help from a consultant and crunched numbers to evaluate the business. Finally, a real estate agent listed their home office on the market. It wasn't going to be an easy sell; they already knew most locals didn't have that kind of money to buy their business and house together. But with the Internet and their marketing expertise, they could bring in more prospects with a slick website—designed by Jim, naturally. A few weeks later, as they had hoped, inquiries from all over the country started flooding their inboxes.

※　※　※

The lifestyle leap idea was getting real, but the FUD was haunting Jim. Each day he woke with a nagging feeling that they couldn't pull it off in time for—he could barely picture it—Jerry's last days. The waiting and anticipation gnawed at his mind all day long. It consumed him so severely that he couldn't see how Jerry was showing absolutely no signs of slowing down anytime soon.

One day, he noticed Jerry peacefully resting on his bed. Staring down at him lying on the deep-red carpet, a vision of Jerry's death flashed through his mind. In that instant, Jerry looked up to see a tear fall from Jim's eye as he dropped to his knees to lay his head on Jerry's chest. With each deep breath, the dog's rib cage rose and fell while Jim stroked new fur growing back where his leg used to be. He couldn't imagine life without this dog. He wasn't ready to say goodbye, so he made a vow. "Hang in there, buddy," he whispered to the sleepy dog. "You just hang in there with us, and we're going to go on a great adventure. I promise."

Jim repeated the promise to Jerry nearly every night at bedtime. Sometimes he even lay down and whispered it to him during the day, as if saying it enough times would make it real. "I'll keep my promise if you keep yours, okay?" He pleaded with Jerry to live long enough so he could enjoy their big adventure in the works. "You just gotta stay healthy and strong. It won't be long now. We'll take the road trip of your life. I swear...camping every night, meeting new people, and new dogs. Ya wanna?"

Jerry loved those last two magic words. Something fun always happened whenever Jim said them. He tilted his head to get a better sense of Jim's intention, not understanding, but never doubting something fun was ahead. And for the next several weeks, he patiently waited for their new life, never sharing Jim's fear that he might not make it to the departure date.

The doctors had said he may only have four to six months to live, but Jerry proved them wrong. He was still healthy and happy as ever when the most promising prospect came to visit a couple months later. But the day she knocked at the door holding a quivering purse dog in her arms, Jerry's personality changed from happy-go-lucky to timid and standoffish. The sudden switch had nothing to do with his cancer. It was the buyer's dog. She had a big attitude and quickly barked her way into Jerry's domain to establish her rank as the new dog in charge. Her owner, meanwhile, was a textbook case of dog and owner sharing the same personality traits. They barked and nipped at everyone, filling the air with attitude and ego. But they were also the ticket out to a new life, so Jim, Rene, and Jerry all just grinned and tolerated the behavior of the little bitch—and the big one, too.

The buyer had cash and was ready to take over. But first, Jim and Rene had to close the deal and provide her with training. She was loud, brash, and hardly ever seemed interested in the training provided with the sale. The tension between the three of them grew, and it wasn't long before the dynamic upset Jerry too. He wasn't a dog who endured strong, negative emotions spewing from the people around him. Rather than be a part of whatever pointless event his humans were arguing over, he preferred to leave the room and wait for things to cool down. And like all dogs, he didn't hold grudges, which was his first mistake around the little dog.

One morning during training, he hopped in to check on everyone. But before he could set foot into Jim's office, the angry little monster charged at him. She ran down the long hallway, screeching and barking violent threats. But rather than confront her, Jerry simply stopped and turned to hop back outside without a second thought. "Whatever," he seemed to say, as if he sensed that the adventure Jim had promised might not happen if he fought back.

❈   ❈   ❈

"She's not interested in learning QuickBooks." Rene shook her head, putting a big red X through another day of transition on their countdown calendar in the dining room upstairs.

"Tell me about it! She wasn't paying attention when I was explaining the print server. I hope she has fun with that stuff."

The deal on the house and business was going through; most of their possessions were sold off for pennies at three separate yard sales, and they were the proud new owners of a used four-wheel-drive pickup truck that would tow the fifth-wheel trailer they had on order. The bon voyage party was just weeks away, and their new life was so close, and yet so far. "We're almost there, Jerry! You're gonna make it," Jim told him every day. The sly grin his dog wore seemed to say, "You had doubts?"

Excitement replaced the fears and doubts in Jim's mind. But he was still uncertain of things to come. Silly human. He had all the confidence in the world over his computer capabilities, but his lack of RV knowledge made him uncomfortable. Could he even tow a trailer? Night after night during those final few weeks, he frantically researched everything about travel trailers and RVing. He studied towing capacities and vehicle weight ratios. He investigated solar energy, DC power, and mobile satellite Internet options. He kept reminding himself that if they were gonna live in a fiberglass box for a year, they were gonna do it right.

The closing date on the sale was just two weeks away when their shiny new 24' Arctic Fox fifth-wheel trailer arrived from the dealer a few hours north of them in Portland, Oregon. One week later, Rene and Jim drove up and the sales rep greeted his eager novice customers. Then, within minutes of their arrival, he handed Jim the keys and said, "Thanks! Here you go."

"What, no test drive?" Jim was shocked. Deep down, he was nervous. The big moment had come, and he was expected to just hitch up his expensive new trailer and pull out of the dealer's narrow driveway? How wide would he have to turn? How do you back up? What if he got stuck?

He was the man of the house, leader of the pack, the driver. He was supposed to know these things. But he didn't. So, he asked for help. "I need a test drive. Can you get someone?"

Rene was secretly proud of her husband's willingness to get assistance. She noticed the rep seemed surprised at the request, like he had never been asked to do that before. But he was willing to do anything to get these newbies off his lot. He somewhat reluctantly walked Jim through hitching up the trailer to the truck. Then he hopped in and rode shotgun while Jim learned to tow the RV around Portland. Thankfully, he didn't need long to get the hang of hauling nine thousand pounds behind him. After a few miles and a couple pointers on backing up in a nearby parking lot, they returned the salesman to the dealership.

"Happy travels!" The salesman ran inside the office before they could even say thanks or ask more questions.

After retrieving Jerry from a friend's house, where he'd stayed during the purchase, they said their goodbyes and headed to their first destination about 50 miles away—a fancy RV park with paved sites, groomed lawns, and a morning newspaper delivered to their doorstep. It was a sweet spot to spend the first night in their new home. But once they realized they could stay in other places for far less money, it was the last time they would check into a luxurious—and expensive—resort like that one.

The pristine trailer had an overpowering new RV smell, lacking the lived-in aroma of Eau de Dog they were accustomed to. They reveled in their sense of accomplishment over making the crazy plan a reality. While Rene prepped her first RV kitchen dinner that night, she wondered if Jerry would be nervous about the sudden change, but she underestimated his resiliency—again. The three-legged dog bounded up the three steep steps into his new doghouse on wheels with barely any help from Jim, who had a firm grip on his harness. He immediately made himself at home, hopping up onto the couch and looking out the window at his new surroundings—various RVs, people barbecuing, walking their little dogs—unaware the scene would soon be changing daily.

The next day, Jerry settled into the traveling life like an experienced hobo. As they drove down the highway, he rode the entire way while sitting up on the back seat and leaning his muzzle out the window, his long tongue flapping in the wind. Watching the world go by at 55 miles an hour put a new sparkle in his eyes and added energy to his spirit. After a long day on sensory overload, he quickly claimed his spot on the RV couch and fell into a deep sleep. Life seemed no different for him, only the size of his house. It was as if he had always lived like a traveling dog.

Jim, however, found his first trip less satisfying and more nerve-wracking. With their new home in tow, the drive back to Eureka was harrowing. The long stretch of narrow, two-lane highway winds through dense redwood forests, with protruding rocks on one side and a sheer drop-off to the river below on the other. By the time they got home from the white-knuckle drive, his jaw was sore from gritting his teeth the whole way. It would be years until he could cruise that same stretch of road while eating a sandwich and singing a tune. For now, he was thankful the pack made it home alive.

※　※　※

After several weeks of tension, bickering, and stress, the business deal ordeal was over. The contract was sealed with their blood, sweat, and tears. The RV was packed, and there was nothing left to do but close the door behind them, turn the key, and go. They gathered the last of their things and took one last look at the large, empty house that had consumed their money, time, and energy for several years.

"Aren't you going to miss it?" He knew the answer but asked anyway.

"No!" Rene was more than ready to walk away.

To her it was 3,700 square feet of an expensive, never-ending project that she was especially glad to leave behind. The Victorian's dusty plaster walls were still only half-painted, and all the old woodwork still remained to be refinished. The oak floors creaked underfoot as they went from room to room one last time. When they walked into the living room, Rene laughed. "We never got to painting the living room…oh well!"

At the end of the long hallway, they could see where Jerry's nails had gouged the refinished flooring. They took comfort in knowing that some part of him would remain with the old building. That house held so many ghosts, and now it had some of their energy, too. The long ordeal was over, and an unknown, exciting future was just outside the front door.

"We can check 'fix up an old Victorian' off our list now, okay?"

They were standing at Jim's office window when the new owner arrived for the house key hand-off, counting the minutes as they watched her pull up to the curb. It was a beautiful day out, with reasons for everyone to celebrate, but their buyer just looked as angry as ever. Even her walk was full of tension as she clutched her little dog tight like a handbag and approached the garage instead of coming right to the front door as they expected. Had they ever looked that stressed-out after fleeing the big city life? They hoped not. Maybe she just needed to live in the small, sleepy town for a while. Perhaps she needed a bigger dog to teach her about taking more breaks and what was really important in life. Maybe...Jim just knew he was grateful they had learned what truly mattered in their own lives, and that the door was about to close on the chapter that brought so much stress.

"Ugh, I'm so glad we never have to see *her* again!" Rene peeked through the blinds and watched her stomp up the short driveway to the garage, making herself right at home. They watched as she threw open the garage door. But the instant her hand let go, the heavy overhead door fell off its track and nearly crashed down on her head. She ducked away in time as Rene and Jim gasped at the near-miss. They didn't know what to do while watching her swear and yell at the door, then storm toward the front entrance. It was the most awkward moment yet with the woman, so instead of saying anything at all, they pretended they never saw it happen. She didn't say a word either, obviously happy to see them go. Everyone played nice; Jim handed off the keys, and Jerry's pack made a quick getaway, never once looking back.

As Jim commandeered the pack's new home away from their old house, Jerry sat upright on the back seat with his head between the two of them. Jim swore he saw Jerry smiling, then looked at Rene, who definitely had a wide grin on her face. Without speaking a word, they both burst out into laughter as they drove away, leaving their old life and all that FUD behind, for good.

BE MORE DOG

— 9 —

Hitting the Road, Back to Life

Many people wonder what it would be like to hit a reset button for their life, but few actually pull it off. Once a person leaves the freedom and spontaneity of childhood behind, they assume responsibilities that corner them into routines. Between 9 and 5 they yearn for freedom and dream about those "someday" plans to escape the daily rut they fell into. Eventually, they wake up and realize that someday is yesterday. Many fall into the trap of believing it's too late to start over.

But a few lucky dreamers out there might get a wake-up call before life appears in the rearview mirror. For them, the alarm blares: *Life is short! Do it now!* Rene and Jim were two of those fortunate people. When the siren wailed, they listened. They saw the light and drove straight into it without looking back.

"Are we really doing this? Whose truck is this?" Jim's hands clenched the steering wheel of their new-to-them four-wheel-drive Dodge Ram, amazed that the big beast was all theirs. Even more surprising was the brand-new house on wheels he was hauling behind it.

Rene joined him in disbelief. Sitting up high and feeling so safe in that big truck, she spied Jerry peacefully curled up on his comfy back seat bed. "It felt like this would never happen." A huge smile lit up her face as she watched Jim commandeering the big vehicle. She never felt more sure that leaving their old life behind was the right move.

Jerry's cancer diagnosis shattered Rene's illusions about being in control of life. For years she did her best to feed him right but apparently, cancer didn't care about what went into his bowl. "Why did he get sick?" The questions she asked herself would go unanswered, but for at least this brief moment, she felt they had seized control of their lives. Their "someday" had arrived, and from that moment on, the entire concept of "home" became a moving target. Home was no longer a place, but a state of mind. It could change according to the season or whatever impulses they followed. Home was whatever and wherever they wanted it to be. They would wander the back roads and blue highways as a pack. And instead of working all day as before, now they would camp and fish and do fun things together until…the moment Jerry was ready to move on without them.

❀ ❀ ❀

The new RV was only 24 feet long, but it was the Taj Mahal to these two hard-core tent campers. Boxy and shiny white on the outside, the Arctic Fox fifth-wheel trailer was cozy inside, with all the comforts of home. Autumn-themed wallpaper, upholstery, and dark wood accents created the look and feel of a vacation cabin. The fresh showroom floor "New RV" aroma smelled like a sweet reward each time they opened the door. It was a well-deserved payoff for the past ten years of hard work they'd put into growing their business. Their new home—and the new lifestyle they had planned—was a special reward for their CFO, who was the entire reason for their purchase. It sported the Arctic Fox logo, with its fluffy tail and pointy ears that Rene thought resembled Jerry's best features, so they knew that buying this brand was their destiny.

As RVers, they could bid farewell to sleeping on dirt and pooping in the woods. They would make meals in their tiny but fully equipped kitchen, shower in their own bathroom, and sleep on a queen-size bed that beat any blow-up mattress. It was everything they'd scorned during their tent-camping days.

Whenever car-camping on the way to some remote hiking trip, they would make fun of folks watching TV from their cozy RVs. They would shake their heads and say, "That's not really camping!" Now they had become the people they once scorned. And they couldn't have been happier.

Their new RV was spotless when Jim drove it off the dealer's lot. But by the time they pulled into their first destination, the outside was coated with an array of mud and insect guts. It wasn't long before the inside started getting that lived-in look, as Jerry's furry tumbleweeds collected in the corners quicker than they would in their big, old house. "Jerry, you are such a German shedder!" Rene joked as she swept up fur balls hiding under the table. Deep down, she knew that one day she would miss the chore.

Their first stop was a goodbye party at a campground less than twenty miles from home. The thick, salty fog hung low and blocked the sun, but they were too happy to notice. Friends stopped by throughout the day to bid them bon voyage. Rene, Jim, and Jerry were about to drive away from the place they called home for ten years, and the main thing everyone wanted to know was, "Where are ya gonna go?"

"We have a few plans, but nothing set in stone." Jim hadn't thought much about destinations. "Getting our solar put in at my brother's place down south, then we're headed to Arizona to meet up with Rene's parents."

"And after that?"

"No idea!" He looked at Rene, and they both grinned. The very thought of not having a plan was exhilarating. For the first time ever, they had no pressing responsibilities. After years of meeting daily deadlines and grueling work schedules, the new concept of true freedom left them speechless and feeling great.

The bittersweet goodbyes were met with, "We'll be back," but inwardly, Jim and Rene knew better. Humboldt County had lost its appeal. For now, they simply embraced every ounce of the love and friendship ferrying them off into the wide-open world. Their well-wishers brought RV-friendly housewarming presents, including a special plush toy puppy for Jerry. Rene assumed Jerry's voice in the Tripawds blog, and shared his gratitude with the world:

Oh, Bob and Marianne, you are so funny! And thoughtful, too. Thanks for my new buddy. I'm going to call him Hoppy. Only two creative types like you could think of me when you saw this cute four-legged Beanie Baby, then remove that front left leg, so it's just like me. I love him!

One more present awaited Jerry inside the trailer. "What's that?" Jim was looking at an extra-large padded envelope on the table.

"I don't know. What's this, Jerry?" Rene smiled, tossed it on the floor, and he immediately investigated the package. "Open it! It's from Winston." Winston and his pack had moved south to the Bay Area just a couple weeks before. Rene found this in their mail while packing and decided to keep it for the big bon voyage party.

Jerry gave her a glance to be sure, then pawed at the pouch. He must have smelled something good because once she gave him the nod, he grabbed a corner and gave it a good shake. "What is it, buddy?" Jim laughed, cut the tape on one end, and tossed it back to Jerry with a big grin.

Jerry stuck his whole head inside the bag and sniffed hard. After a pause, he clamped down on something and shook his head back and forth. The envelope flew away, unfurling pink-and-purple padded fabric. Everyone laughed as Rene held up a small child's sleeping bag with the big, fat, purple dinosaur image on the front. "Ha, ha-ha! It's Barney!"

Jerry continued smelling the envelope as she draped his new blanket over his back. He spun around chasing the end until it fell off, then sniffed it some more. From the looks of things, Winston must have slept on it a few times to break it in.

"They know you so well." She draped the gift back over his back and gave him a big hug. What was soon named The Barney Blanket became Jerry's new security blanket. It found a new home on the back seat of the truck, where Jerry would sit on Barney's face for the thousands of miles to follow.

✵   ✵   ✵

After driving south for just a few hours of their first day on the road, they arrived at Jim's brother's house. He still lived in the small farm town where they both grew up. Two rough-and-tumble farm dogs met them at the gate of the spacious property. Rene didn't see them and opened her door to let Jerry out of the truck. But then she saw the dogs, and froze. Jim saw the panicked look in her eyes.

"Why are you standing there? Let him go."

"What if those dogs come after him?"

"He can hold his own." Jim reached around Rene to help Jerry out of the back seat. "You saw how he handled Santo. Remember?" Deep down, he was eager to know if his amputee mutt could run with these rough dogs. He assisted Jerry down by his harness handle. The moment his paws hit the ground, the two stocky black Labradors rushed over to investigate. The dogs circled around Jerry, who barked with excitement at his hosts.

"Back off, dogs!" Rene yelled as she stepped in between them like a protective mother, but Jim ran interference.

"We agreed to let him be a dog, remember?" He wrapped his arms around her in a hug and guided her backwards. "So, let him go. They'll work it out."

Jerry stood tall and stiff with his broad, white chest puffed out and big ears pointed straight up. The farm dogs barked and spun circles between him and the humans, but his three paws stayed cemented to the ground. The two energetic Labs were as heavy as concrete sacks and could easily overcome Jerry, but he kept his head high and stayed alert.

If the stocky, brash dogs intended to do harm, it was their perfect opportunity to try. But instead of beating up their cornered guest, they pranced around. Then, one dove into the universal sign of doggy friendship: a play bow. Jerry responded with a fast pivot and play bow of his own.

Within seconds, all three muzzles made contact and the dogs were off and racing around the open, grassy field. From a distance, it was almost impossible to notice the "handicapped" dog who was keeping up with the fast, four-legged farm dogs.

"See? We don't need to worry about that." Jim let go of Rene, and she turned to him with a big smile.

"Yeah, I guess he can hold his own!"

Rene watched as Jim backed up the trailer right next to his brother's large workshop. It was the perfect place to install a solar power system. Off-grid power could feed their craving for "boondocking" away from utilities and RV parks. They bought everything needed for a system to keep them comfortable without always needing to be plugged in. The upfront cost was hefty, but Rene justified the expense, knowing they would save on rent by camping in free and low-cost public lands campgrounds.

Two days later, they were fully equipped with an off-grid home. Jim piloted their truck and fifth-wheel trailer toward the tall, snowy peaks of the Sierra Nevada mountains, eager to use the new solar power system. Rolling foothills and anxiety disappeared in the rearview mirror while relief, hope, and joy settled in for the ride. The most significant moment in their lives was happening, and Jerry was alive to enjoy it.

Just ahead on the horizon loomed a big alpine lake nestled deep in the granite mountains. "Hey, pull over when you can." Sudden stops for roadside photos required a bit of pre-planning when towing a ten-thousand-pound trailer, but Jim was able to find an adequate selfie spot. The landscape was exactly the scene he'd envisioned the first time Rene sprang the plan on him.

Jim grabbed their camera and crossed the highway to capture the moment. He stood proud, looking at his impressive truck and new trailer modified with satellite Internet and solar panels on the roof. With the spectacular mountain scenery behind it, the spot looked like a Camping World ad. He snapped the picture just as Rene ran into view yelling in glee, "Woo hoo!" In a freeze-frame instant, she jumped up to celebrate their once-in-a-lifetime gift of more time with Jerry and an all-new life ahead.

Finding adequate space to pull over for photos with the truck and trailer was just one thing they had to get used to. New RVers often underestimate the size of their big house on wheels. When Jim and Rene pulled into their first mountain campground, it looked like the perfect spot to kick off their new adventure. It was the kind of place where they would have eagerly pitched a tent in their backpacking days. But within a minute of driving that 24-foot trailer down into the campground, Jim knew they'd made a dumb mistake. Giant pine trees lined both sides of the narrow road.

Scraaatch… A tree limb scraped along their rolled-up awning.

"Oh, crap!" Rene shut her eyes tightly, hoping they hadn't just done what she thought they did.

Jim stopped the truck and got out to inspect the trailer's first battle scar. "Well, it was going to happen eventually. Now that we got it over with, the next scratch won't seem so bad." Rene was still upset, but she pulled herself together and guided Jim out of the campground to a more RV-friendly spot.

Many dents and dings would occur over the years, and they both learned to take these tough situations in stride. One look at Jerry was all it took. He had no idea what the big deal was all about; he was only eager to get out and sniff around the woods.

❖   ❖   ❖

RVing required a whole new way of thinking about what made for the perfect camping spot. That first scratch made them realize that certain concessions were necessary when hauling a big trailer instead of pitching a tent. Many of the more remote, wilderness-type camping sites where they once enjoyed solitude simply wouldn't accommodate a big truck and trailer. Often, the only option was to suck it up and camp among other RVers like them. At first they didn't approve, but soon realized that the constant socialization played an essential role in helping Jerry thrive. Unlike Jim and Rene, who had always preferred to keep their own company, Jerry could love anyone. And now that he had three legs, everyone loved him.

Walk anywhere in public with a Tripawd, and you soon discover two groups of dog lovers in this world. The first one takes pity on the animal. But the second is more curious. When they see a dog like Jerry, these friendly folks don't say, "Awww, poor dog!" Instead, they want to know more. The most common question was usually, "What happened to his leg?" Jerry attracted many curious onlookers whenever walking around a campground or RV park. Before long, Jim and Rene came up with a long list of creative comebacks.

"What missing leg? Oh my, look at that!"

"If he had four legs, we could never catch him!"

And Jim's favorite, "Ssshhh...don't tell him, he doesn't know!"

When children asked the same question, their comebacks changed. Jim, Rene, and Jerry would stop, and while the parent usually looked on in pity, they would try to educate the child.

"His leg was sick, and hurting him really bad, so the doctors took it off. Now he feels better, and he's so happy he can run and play again. See?"

Then, as if on cue, Jerry would do something cute to show off. He might chase a ball, fetch a stick, or sit for a treat. Kids loved these antics and treated Jerry like a celebrity. They followed him on walks while chit-chatting about his three-legged hop. Jerry had his own paparazzi around every bend and he loved all the attention.

At Lake Francis, kids were everywhere and the campground buzzed with youthful energy. One morning while out for a walk, Jerry encountered two little girls playing basketball. They saw him from afar and couldn't take their eyes off the three-legged dog. Slowly and cautiously, they approached as each took turns hiding behind the other. Jerry lunged forward on his leash when he saw their ball.

"Oh, you want to play?" The smaller girl held out the large, orange ball.

"Sure he does, check it out!" Rene took the ball and showed it to

Jerry, saying those favorite two words. "Ya wanna…" She bounced the ball in front of him. "…play ball!"

Jerry lunged hard to give that basketball his best head-butt. He pushed it to the girl, who caught it, then bounced it right back. He quickly snapped a return pass and waited for it again.

"Wow! He can still play?" Both of the girls laughed as they ran after the ball.

Each time he bounced the ball back, the girls squealed with excitement, which only drove Jerry into a frenzy. Jerry nabbed almost every shot with that long, pointy muzzle of his. They continued playing as the sun went down until the girls were called home for dinner by a woman smiling in the doorway of a nearby travel trailer.

The game was now over, but not the fun. Both girls had giant smiles plastered across their faces when they walked back to their campsite. And Jerry was just as happy as he went home to his. It wasn't the last they heard from those little girls though. The following week, Jerry received his first fan letter on his blog, with this comment:

Hi Jerry, Remember us? We camped across from you at Lake Francis this weekend. It was a pleasure playing ball with you, and we had a blast! You're such a beautiful dog, and we will never forget you. Keep up the good work and stay strong. You're the best, Jerry! Love, Ashley & Kylie

Stay strong. The words stuck with Jim and Rene. They never really knew what to expect from a canine amputee, until Jerry actually did something new. They feared his old acrobatics might hurt a remaining limb, but all their rationale got tossed aside each time his eyes begged for playtime. After his surgery, some vets implied that worrying about injuries and long-term health was pointless for a cancer dog like Jerry, since he may not even survive another six months. So, they decided to just let him be a dog, all the while still paying attention to keep him from overdoing it in any single session, after learning that lesson a couple times already.

Since the campground was at a lake, Rene had also worried about Jerry trying to go in the water. He only recently had grown to love swimming, but that was before the amputation. Now, Jim and Rene assumed his swimming days were over. Would he sink? Or just swim in circles?

Winston would bring those questions to light the next day when his people drove several hours to get the dogs together for a final, bittersweet reunion. "Win, hang on!" his mom hollered as he tried jumping out the car window. The minute his lanky legs leaped out of the car, Winston broke into a happy dance when he saw Jerry and that shimmering mountain lake.

Forget group hugs and hellos; the bird dog gave a quick sniff, then bounded toward the water, Jerry following closely behind. "Jerry, wait!" Rene's worried-mother attitude quickly came back. She turned to Winston's mom, Lauren. "I'm really not sure he can do this."

"Well, let's just see how it goes," she suggested. "If he can't, no big deal. The lake looks shallow here. We can always wade in and get him." She was more confident than Rene about Jerry's next milestone.

They walked to the lake and found sticks for the two dogs to retrieve. "Go git it, Win!" Lauren let the stick fly far out into the lake as Rene's eyes widened. The lean hunting dog glided into the water while Jerry studied his path, ready to follow.

"Here ya go, Jerry. Get it!" Jim flung a large stick just far enough to test Jerry's ability to swim, but close enough to retrieve him if he got in trouble.

As Jerry galloped past Rene, she bent over to grab him but caught herself and closed her eyes. "Let him be a dog. Let him be a dog." She repeated the mantra several times, then opened her eyes. "He's swimming! Look, he's swimming!" Jerry dog-paddled through the murky water toward his reward. The only thing that was different about his paddling was a more exaggerated head bob on the surface. Otherwise, he looked just like any other dog swimming for a prize.

Jerry snapped up the trophy stick and returned to shore, gracefully gliding through the water. "Right on, Jerry! Come on back!" Everyone cheered as Jerry bobbed his way to the sandy beach.

"Whoo hoo!" Rene ran to give her soaking-wet dog a big hug.

"All right, Jerry!" Jim was just as proud.

"You're awesome, dog!" Lauren patted his wet head and turned to Rene. "See…"

BE MORE DOG

— 10 —

Making Friends Everywhere

Dogs lean on the pack for survival and comfort. Intuitively, they understand how maintaining strong relationships creates a stable, harmonious life for all pack mates. But humans are buried underneath piles of work and family stress. Their over-complicated lives leave them too tired to build strong relationships outside their inner circle. Even relationships within their circle can suffer. With too small of a circle, when a tragedy happens, they are often left out in the cold, alone in their ordeal, their decisions, their pain.

Giving the okay to amputate a dog's leg is one of those tragedies that can leave a person feeling isolated after the decision. That's when well-intentioned friends and family unexpectedly reveal their true feelings about "handicapped" animals.

"What kind of quality of life is that?"

"Dogs aren't meant to live that way."

"It's kinder to put him down."

Even some veterinarians are cynical. A few crusty, old-school practitioners still think euthanasia is the best alternative.

Rene and Jim wanted to share Jerry's story. Maybe they needed to share it as a way to cope with his cancer, with their decisions, and with the reality of their new lives together. They knew they might face more people who would disagree and not understand. But, like reaching out to the human pack for help, they needed to express what had happened to them to a broader circle.

With each new blog post they published, they discovered they weren't alone in their journey. Jerry's little website was getting attention from others in search of answers about their own dog's recovery and care. Some just wrote to cheer Jerry on, while others wanted to know why their own dog wasn't doing as well as he was. Each time Jerry shared his latest bucket list accomplishment, he ignited genuine emotional connections between total strangers. Now, nobody had to feel alone after an amputation recommendation. Somewhere between California and Maine, Jerry's growing community had blossomed into a haven for passionate pet parents who don't listen to naysayers.

Clearly, kindred spirits understand the acquired wisdom that blossoms when living with a three-legged dog. They are the pet parents who have watched their animal heroically bounce back from losing a leg, the ones who understand that pets have no qualms about being different. At tripawds.com, amputation is accepted, and life on three legs is a reason to celebrate a renewed chance for a pain-free life, not wallow in grief. Jerry's story was showing that cancer wasn't something to be depressed about, but embraced as a catalyst for life-changing lessons that animals teach us about living in the now.

The website grew quickly, and while it may have appeared that Jerry was always busy blogging, he was usually offline having real-time fun. Still full of stamina, he seemed to love his new routine of not having any routine at all. Every day was different, as he shared with friends in one of the first blog posts he wrote from the road:

> *Used to be that my daily walks we re the same old same old. We'd walk up past the beauty college, where I'd try to sniff the latest muck on the street. Then I'd hop a little more, say hi to my neighborhood pals, turn around the corner and come back. Same thing, every day. But not anymore. Now there are so many new things to discover every day! From kids, to bear scat to rivers and lakes, my tail can't even keep up with the trail of crazy scents and activities on my walks.*

> *Yesterday I met some fun kids near my camp spot who wore me out playing before I could even go on a walk. Today, I went for a hike on the river that goes to Silver Lake, in the El Dorado National Forest. I ate pine cones and swam in the shallow spots. Now, this is different!*

🐾   🐾   🐾

Of course, Jim and Rene were the thoughts behind Jerry's voice in all those blog posts. They shared such a strong bond with their bright-eyed shepherd mix, they could almost read his mind. From his broad smile to his rocking-horse head bobs and cartoonish spins, no words were needed to communicate his fondness for their new lifestyle. His joyful demeanor, no matter the weather or location, alleviated the guilt they felt all those years Jerry sat in the office day in and day out—just waiting for the few, carefree minutes they played each night after closing up shop. Jerry finally had the life he deserved, with the added bonus of helping others facing amputation and cancer. Life was good for the pack.

As they began meandering across the country, they made more friends on the road than they ever did while living back in Eureka. Socializing with new people was much easier once they eliminated the daily burdens of chasing after clients and contracts. Once on the road, strangers became friends, with Jerry as their greeter and tour guide for all the adventures that lay around the bend.

With every mile traveled and new adventures shared in Jerry's blog, more letters from other amputee families arrived in their email inbox each morning. Be they good or sad, silly or serious, Jim and Rene knew they needed to get them out into the world. Each was a learning experience in its own right, like the story about Bill, a big, black dog from Illinois. He did great after surgery, but his people worried whenever he used the stairs or played too hard. They now lived in a constant state of panic, which made Bill edgy and nervous. Jim and Rene understood the self-defeating nature of such feelings, so to help them relax, Jerry shared some wisdom with Bill in the blog:

> *Silly humans. They think we are as slow to adapt to change as they are!*

Tripawds blog stories were usually on the lighter side, but like the yin and yang of the universe, amputation also has a dark side that Rene and Jim eventually discovered. A Doberman named Rumpelstiltskin drove it home when he gave them the hardest lesson they needed to learn if they wanted Jerry's community to help others. After being diagnosed with the same cancer as Jerry, veterinarians were convinced the Doberman would do well on three legs. With nothing but encouragement from Jerry and his growing band of amputee friends, Rumpelstiltskin's parents proceeded with the amputation. But the next day, Jim and Rene learned that he did not even survive the surgery.

It was the first time Jim and Rene clearly faced the risks of amputation surgery for any dog, even healthy ones. From that moment on, they always made sure Tripawds members understood that with the amputation decision comes a considerable leap of faith—faith in the veterinarian doing the surgery, in the dog's ability to get up the next day, in cancer playing nice long enough so the animal could recover and enjoy a good quality of life. To honor Rumpelstiltskin, Tripawds published a touching sentiment expressed by his broken-hearted humans, which included the phrase:

If love could have cured you, you would have lived forever!

The Doberman's death was also a big reality check for Jim. It was the first time he accepted that Jerry remained sick with terminal cancer and could start that downward slide anytime. Yet, it also reinforced just how fortunate they were for having this extra time together.

      ❄   ❄   ❄

Jerry's blog was thriving. But Jim and Rene tried to stay away from their computers and gadgets as much as they could. They weren't about to squander their gift of more time by being sucked into technology. Instead, they focused on enjoying Jerry's life, just as they had planned. Once or twice a week, they wrote blog posts in Jerry's voice to explain how amputation did and didn't affect him, and how strangers reacted when they encountered the galloping three-legged dog. Jerry told it best:

I love this full-time RVing road trip I'm on with my people! I enjoy traveling and meeting all the new folks and dogs everywhere we stop. I just wish strangers wouldn't feel so sorry for me when they see me. I get along just fine on three legs, thank you. I have one more than most people, after all.

Neither Jim, nor Rene, and especially not Jerry, cared what disapproving strangers thought while he joyfully wagged his fluffy tail and chased after his latest adventure.

A few months and hundreds of Tripawds readers later, Rene and Jim realized the potential impact—and the possibilities—of Jerry's little blog. One morning, they received an email from a woman named Sasha. An ocean apart, she was from Israel, and her beautiful female black Lab had just lost a rear leg to bone cancer. Against the expectations of those around her, the dog was doing quite well. Sasha wrote to the Tripawds community in Lalla's voice to explain the rarity of treating pets with cancer in Israel. Feeling alone in her search to give the dog a good, pain-free life, she reached out to Jerry's community for an authentic connection with others going through the same thing.

The global connection further validated the need for Jerry's community. In honor of his courageous approach to life on three legs, Jim and Rene had created a safe place where anyone, anywhere in the world, could share their tales and treatment tips. At Tripawds, their pet's stories would be documented forever, and provide hope for newcomers to the journey.

Jerry and Lalla's parallel experiences highlighted the common connection among all animals: determination and a strong will to survive. Like Jerry, Lalla didn't have any chemotherapy. "It would have really disrupted my normal happy routine," Sasha wrote on her dog's behalf. The Israeli canine happily shared the keys to a happy life after cancer and said, "I honestly think that the reason for my well-being is the beach." Later she disclosed that, "Love, canine survival instincts, and joy of life are also crucial to recovery." Her feelings accurately reflected the right attitude that could help any animal enjoy life on three legs with their people.

Lalla beat the cancer odds for nearly two years after her amputation. Her accomplishment was more remarkable considering she lived in a place where, "the public is not very well educated in terms of animal health," as Sasha put it. Meanwhile, Lalla and Jerry's love affair blossomed over the Internet as they published fun doggy dialogues, details about long-distance gift exchanges, and an original series of comic strips describing a dog's deeper understanding about the important things in life.

"The Tri-Stix Chronicles" were comical adventures Sasha created about life on three legs with two stick-figure Tripawds. In each episode, Jerry and Lalla shared wise words for pet parents new to the amputation journey. Later, when Jerry was reunited with Lalla in doggie heaven, Sasha created her final episode. Simply titled *The Wisdom Tree*, the graceful silhouette figures of Jerry and Lalla sat on a limb against a bright-blue sky. Lalla asks Jerry if he has any words of wisdom for Jim and Rene. His answer?

Look at life through the windshield, not the rearview mirror.

❀   ❀   ❀

To many people, a three-legged dog is a sad, handicapped animal. But each time Jim and Rene looked at Jerry, they never saw a sick or debilitated dog. Underneath those satellite-dish ears and the soft, black-and-tan fur was the burning spirit of a timeless soul with something to teach humanity. His leg was gone, and invisible cancer cells were floating through his body, but that didn't stop him from helping other people faced with the same difficult decisions. Rene and Jim were duty-bound to make his legacy last.

No longer striving to grow a business solely for the sake of making money, their new mission got them excited about building the Tripawds community. Within a few months after kicking off their sabbatical on the open road, Jim, Rene, and Jerry were already back to work. Only this time, their "job" felt so different. Jim was no longer slaving away to meet some client's urgent deadline for another electronic gizmo. Rene wasn't having nightmares about business debt. What they lacked in material things they made up for by committing to a less complicated, more affordable life. If growing Tripawds meant ranking in a lower bracket, they were happy to do it. Because gone were the demanding clients who required constant babysitting, the frustrating conference calls, and the endless late nights in the shop. Jim and Rene finally found something they were passionate about, or rather, it found them—and in the most unexpected way.

— 11 —

Cool It

Jerry's behavior turned lazy and lethargic after leaving the Sierras. His reluctance to get outside and play became even more apparent when the pack met up with Rene's parents at a campground in Flagstaff, Arizona. It was the first week of July, and the hottest weather they'd encountered so far. Rene's parents were also miserable, and there was no better time to test the RV's air conditioner. Jim flipped the switch to cool everyone down, but before long, one of the campground's workers knocked on their door and announced, "You can't run that here."

"What do you mean? We paid for this spot, and it's running just fine."

"No, you're not allowed. It's in the rules. Take it up with the office." This guy was nothing like the happy workers pictured in the campground advertisements.

"But...?" Tilting his head as Jerry often did when confused, Jim was at a loss for words.

The grumpy-looking worker waited at the door until Jim complied, then squeezed into his tiny golf cart and rolled away. Disgusted and angered by the restriction, Jim did take it up with the office, only to discover that the woman behind the counter didn't appear to like her job either. She only shook her head, explaining that they were parked in a 30-amp site. "You can only run the A/C in a 50-amp site. You can't do that on 30 amps." It was apparent she had argued this point before.

"But I can run it, it's working fine! I have a sick dog and old people in the RV, they need to stay cool!" He tried playing the cancer card, but she would not budge, citing rules and pointing to some tiny print on the back of a colorful park brochure. "Fine! Then move me to a 50-amp site."

"Can't. We don't have any open."

The RVing newbies learned hard lessons that day: Avoid Arizona camping in the summer, stay away from busy RV parks, and don't bother arguing with underpaid campground staff. She looked around Jim to the next customer who walked in the door. "Can I help you?" This lady was done with their conversation.

Jim walked out, bewildered. They were stuck in this heat for at least another week, but were already making plans to head north once Rene's parents returned to Los Angeles. Meanwhile, Jerry constantly panted no matter how many cold, damp towels Rene draped over him. Everyone was hot, so instead of sitting around complaining, they made the most of it by spending their days taking road trips in the cool comfort of their air-conditioned truck.

Their first stop was the mountain mining town of Jerome. They set off on their two-hour trip with the windows rolled up and cool air blasting. Within minutes, Jerry was comfortable and up for exploring. So was Rene's dad. He lived there as a kid when his father worked the nearby copper mines. The small town is nestled into a hillside, with steep stairways connecting residential areas, narrow, winding streets, and three switchback turns to direct drivers along Main Street. The air was dry and dusty as the bright sun beat down on the truck while Rene's dad took a trip down memory lane.

A little higher in elevation, it wasn't too hot to get out and walk along the steep and narrow sidewalks, with Jerry hopping alongside. One gift shop after another, Rene went in to look at knick-knacks while her mom shopped for souvenirs. Her dad tagged along to take advantage of the air-conditioned stores while Jerry waited outside gulping water from the portable dog bowl Jim always carried on his belt.

Eventually, they ran out of bric-a-brac to browse, and Jerry was the first to show that he was done with this new adventure. As they walked back toward the truck, they crossed paths with a construction crew working on a retaining wall. Jim noticed a hose and picked it up, getting the attention of the workers over the noise of their portable concrete mixer.

"Hey, can I get some water for my dog?" he yelled, and held up the hose while pointing at Jerry. All he got was a nod from the foreman. After filling the water bottle, he doused Jerry with the hose.

Surprised and chilled, Jerry shook vigorously. But when he felt the cooling water flow through his thick fur, the blast of cold water seemed to make sense to him. He stood in place to let Jim hose him down while the workers laughed at the skinny, soaking-wet, three-legged dog. Jim and Jerry then rested in the shade while Rene's parents ducked into the air-conditioned mining museum.

Walking back down the steep hill to the truck was easier on Jerry, but as his cooling wet coat dried, he eventually called it quits in front of a bar. "Paul and Jerry's Saloon. How'd you know, Jer?" Jim laughed at the appropriately named pit stop. Wearing the most pathetic look on his face, Jerry plopped down in the open entry to the old-timey bar. Just behind him, a set of creaky wooden swinging saloon doors allowed some of the cool air to escape and help Jerry feel better.

The bartender felt sorry for the panting dog out front. She emptied the dollar bills from a pitcher on the bar, filled it with water, and placed it in front of Jerry. Without standing up, he lapped at the water, then laid his head down next to the plastic pitcher with the "Tips" sign taped to it.

"Too funny, I gotta get a picture of this!" Jim and Rene laughed and snapped photos of the adorably pitiful three-legged dog begging for change. Neither of them could imagine that someday they would use that photo for years to come when soliciting donations to keep Jerry's growing website online.

Everyone looked forward to cooling off in the truck again, so they headed to their next stop in Sedona. The lazy river in shady Oak Creek Canyon was a perfect place to pull over and have a picnic. Rene's parents sat at a table while Jerry ran straight for the water. The irresistible temptation to retrieve a partially submerged tree from the shallow river breathed new life into him. Without hesitating, he plunged his head underwater to retrieve the large limb.

"Jerry, get the stick!" Jim and Rene smiled as they watched his energy return. Jerry came up for air, shook his head, and dove under again and again. Jim caught his excavation on camera for a video that included the final scene of a damp Jerry napping on his pink-and-purple Barney blanket in the truck.

The short movie captured another fan for Jerry. Within minutes of Jim posting it, the first comment appeared on YouTube: "What an awesome dog. Kind of ironic, my name is Jerry, too."

❊ ❊ ❊

They bid farewell to Rene's parents and made immediate plans to head for the colder climate of northern states. For the first time since they'd left Eureka, they felt totally free and on their own to travel anywhere they pleased. Meet-ups with friends and family were done, and they had no other obligations other than touring the country with Jerry. Today their only goal was to cool off at a campground in Moab, Utah.

"And we can run our A/C, right?" Rene called the RV park office to make sure Jerry would stay comfortable.

"Uhh, yes, of course. It's a 30-amp site; do you need 50-amp to run it? What do you have?" The woman on the other end assumed she had another RV rental novice on the line. After the call, Jim steered them to the park to avoid the afternoon heat. They blissfully ran the A/C all day, but eventually decided to explore the town as the sun sank lower on the horizon. Several neat shops offered their wares, and the Moab Barkery greeted Jerry with fresh-baked dog treats. Jerry seemed fine, but about halfway home, he coughed. Then he hacked. And then he coughed again.

Jerry needed several breaks during the short walk back to the RV park. They offered him water from a portable container Jim wore on his hip, but the tired dog refused to drink. Instead, he sat under a shady tree and panted. When a slight wheeze came from deep in his chest, Rene heard it and panicked. She knew Jerry's cancer would eventually spread to his lungs. Was it already happening? she wondered. The next day, Jerry continued to cough after the slightest exertion. Then Jim heard the wheeze. Without saying a word, they both feared the worst.

"Already...?" The thought of cancer returning so soon was devastating.

Rene needed to know what to do. She called their vet back in Eureka, but Jim didn't want to hear the news he suspected was coming. He went outside and climbed up on the roof to measure the height of their RV—something he'd been meaning to do since they'd sideswiped those pine trees at the small campground back in the Sierras.

He sat cross-legged next to the humming air conditioner, lost in contemplation. They had kept their promise to Jerry, and Jerry kept his promise to hang in there until they hit the road. "We did it," he spoke into the mountain air. "But why so soon?" He squinted to fight the tears welling up in his eyes, then straddled the ladder to get down off the roof. As he opened the RV door, he heard Rene talking on speakerphone.

"Allergies? You think?" she asked the vet.

"Quite possibly, yes." The vet sounded hopeful. "The heat can have something to do with the coughing, too." Then it made more sense to Rene and Jim. Two days prior, Jerry had gulped tons of water to retrieve that tree from Oak Creek. He was coughing now, just like he did last winter after the Kung Fu match with that snowman up on the mountain. What a relief!

They had just endured another learning-to-live-with-cancer experience and were now clear on what to look and listen for when the nasty metastasizing cancer cells finally appeared. Eventually, they would, and Jim felt better about being prepared. This current cough was shallow, like one that accompanies a dry, scratchy throat from lack of humidity. "Duh! We are in the desert, after all!" When lung tumors did make their debut, the vet explained the cough would sound deeper, more moist, and guttural.

For now, everyone could breathe. "Panic equals death," had been Jim's mantra back in their scuba diving days. Now he thought it could help them through Jerry's cancer journey. He knew it made no sense to panic. They'd learned to rely on experts instead of jumping to any conclusion, and now felt determined to share reliable information about pet cancer in Jerry's blog.

The coughing mystery was solved, but one more thing still didn't make sense, and that was staying in that godforsaken heat. It was time to cool off in the north.

In the wilds of the Southern Rockies, they put their RV investment to good use. With a four-wheel-drive truck, solar power, and satellite Internet, they could camp anywhere they wanted. Minutes after the rustic wooden billboard announced, "Welcome to Colorful Colorado," they picked up a better map to scout out remote locations. Rene had rough plans to get to the Northeast in time for the fall colors a couple months away, and they wanted to see the Great Lakes too, so it made sense to set their sights on Colorado for now.

The small town of Carbondale was their first stop. It was one of the early contenders to make it on their shortlist of livable communities where they might someday consider living. It was as intriguing a place as they'd imagined, with all the features they wanted in a new place to call home—stunning forest scenery with rivers and lakes, plenty of sports and activity choices, bike lanes and paths everywhere, and year-round tourism. That last part was important because they were crazy enough to consider buying or starting a tourist-based business once they settled down. Carbondale ranked high on their possibilities list, but they still had many more states to explore.

For now, Rene wanted to explore the town, and Jim was anxious to get parked. He had fishing to do after a long day of driving.

Always budget-minded, Rene chose an inexpensive campground just outside of town. When they arrived, she understood why it cost less than the others. The park had steep roads, tight switchbacks, and small RV sites carved into a hillside. As Jim backed the trailer into their off-kilter campsite, he had to angle the truck more than usual just to fit inside on the parking apron. The action caused the front of the fifth wheel to scrape along the side rails of the truck bed. He didn't hear it happen, but as soon as he got out to check his work, he saw that the truck's shiny, diamond-plate rail protector was now crunched up at the end.

"Dammit!" He was pissed. Frustrated, he rushed to disconnect the trailer and started pulling away before putting the tailgate down. Wham! One more ding on their new Dodge.

The dents were small, but the damage hurt like hell. Jim forgot all about his calm reaction to that first scratch he'd put on the trailer and sought solace from his master of comfort, who stood proudly on his cockpit perch. He looked at Jim's frustrated face, cocked his head, and gave him a questioning stare. Jim looked back into those deep-brown eyes and answered, "You're right...what's my hurry? I need to slow down, take my time. I hear ya."

That week, they fell in love with Colorado. The giant brown trout Jim caught on his hand-tied flies also helped. Most importantly, Jerry seemed to like the climate. His ears perked up, the cough was gone, and his energy returned. But they didn't dare stay too long and get too comfortable, or they might not see the rest of the country. The next day, they set out to put their solar power system to use in the Routt National Forest near Steamboat Springs, where a small, primitive campground sat at the end of a long, washboarded road.

"What kind of hellhole are you taking us to?" Jim joked about Rene's choice of destination as they bounced along the dusty trail. They laughed while unbeknownst to them the slow, bumpy ride was jolting dishes out of the RV's cabinets and filling the living area with a fine grit. One hour later, when they arrived at the deserted, remote campground with a slightly battered rig, they felt deflated and wondered if the ordeal was worth beating up their home.

In the heat of the moment, they found it hard to remember how they believe that there are no coincidences, everything happens for a reason. From the people you meet, to the places you go and the events you experience, everything is part of a coordinated life journey. Once they cleaned up the kitchen mess, they understood why the universe directed them to the remote spot.

Jim was unhitching the trailer and Rene setting up camp when a middle-aged couple wearing official-looking forest service t-shirts walked over to say hello. The only others in the campground, Jim and Mary explained they were college professors taking the summer off to work as campground hosts.

"Hey, that sounds like fun. What do you have to do?" Jim struck up a conversation, smiling at the coincidence that his own parents shared the same names as this couple.

In no rush to get back to their work, the Missouri couple introduced Jim and Rene to the concept of workamping. It's an arrangement where RVers can get a free campsite, and sometimes a paycheck, in exchange for working limited hours at a campground or other scenic spot. In a slight drawl, they explained how the job was a pretty sweet summer gig. They were set up deep in the woods, with no work to do if no campers arrived. The ranger came by every few days to collect any cash inside the self-pay station, so all they had to do was answer questions and clean up messy campsites.

The four of them became fast friends, and Jim and Rene took mental notes on the arrangement. "Free Rent" stuck out in her mind, while he liked the idea of working outdoors for a few hours a week. Workamping would come in very handy down the road.

Later that day, the towering trees and solitude reminded Jim and Rene about their promise to spend more quality time with Jerry. Stormy weather prevented them from getting online with their satellite dish and with no cell phone service, they were forced to explore their new surroundings. Jerry had fresh air, new forest smells to sniff, and flittering birds to chase. Jim and Rene were finally living their dream, spending time fishing, mountain bike riding, and just having fun with their resilient canine. At night, they made Hobo Pies over a small campfire.

Jerry had his own take on their first off-grid adventure. The next week in his blog, Rene shared a picture of him sitting on a piece of fake grass her father gave them when they met back in Arizona.

I'm cool, and I'm loving it! Finally, we found some real forest and got out of that hot sandy desert scene...I played, I hiked, I swam. And when I was done, I got to relax on this lovely piece of 'lawn' that my Grandma and Grandpa gave to us. My Mom and Dad used to make fun of people who had AstroTurf in their campgrounds, but now they're finding that it helps keep dirt out of my fur, and they aren't making jokes anymore!

I had a great time at this campground, but there was a lot of thunder and lightning in the afternoons, and I didn't like that one bit. I'm glad to be moving on!

Move on they did. It was time to keep meandering toward the East Coast. Jerry had his first major road trip milestone. He crossed the Continental Divide for the first of many times in his travels. They snapped a photo at the summit to commemorate the crossing. High in the Rockies, the weather was cool and pleasant, but as soon as they descended the pass, the temperature rose. Jim drove with purpose, and made the 300-plus-mile drive to Devil's Tower in one afternoon. By evening, he realized that driving an RV that far was much more exhausting than piloting a passenger car. Road-weary and beat-up, he sipped a cool beer with dinner and vowed to keep their travel days shorter.

Growing up in the eighties, all that Jim and Rene knew about Devil's Tower was what they saw in the *Close Encounters* movie. Neither of them had ever been to the landmark, but now the landmark ominously lurked high over the campground, the perfect landing pad for an otherworldly visitor. One night, as a joke, Rene made mashed potatoes for dinner, just so Jim could entertain them by recreating the scene where Roy makes a spuds mountain on his plate. They kidded about aliens, never once realizing the deep, spiritual meaning this destination would eventually hold for them.

Not many people know that the Native American Cheyenne refer to Devil's Tower as Tso' Ai', meaning Bears' Lodge. The name refers to the Native American legend of the Kiowa people. The Kiowa were a nomadic tribe, too. One day in their travels, seven young girls were out gathering berries when they caught the attention of some hungry bear warriors. The girls ran across the open prairie as the bears chased down their lunch. When they came upon a large, gray rock, the girls climbed to safety, or so they thought. The bears quickly scrambled up behind them. Thinking they were doomed, the girls began to sing and pray to the rock. The Kiowa say it was a lonely rock, who had laid quiet for centuries. Nobody had ever respected it in such a manner before, so it decided to help the girls. The stone foundation stood tall and started rising. It grew taller, lifting the girls high into the sky as boulders fell all around it.

This angered the warriors, who sang to the Bear gods. They, too, began to grow in size. The bears grew taller as the rock rose up. The large rock became steeper and higher as the bears clawed at its sides. The bears tried and tried to climb the rock as it continued to rise up into the sky. But their huge claws only split the rock face into strips as the butte grew up out of their reach. The rock was cut and scarred all around as the bears fought to climb it. Finally, the bear warriors tired and gave up, turning back toward their own houses, leaving the girls safe atop the tower. Walking away in defeat, the giant bears shrank as they plodded across the plains, slowly returning to their original size.

Noticing the approach of the giants, the Kiowa people broke camp, leaving the girls behind, fearing they had been eaten by the bears. They fled in fear and looked back at the towering mountain of rock. They guessed that it must be the lodge of these bear beasts. The girls? They were left on their own atop that tower, alone and afraid. Again, they began to sing, this time to the stars. Happy to hear their song, the stars came down and took the seven girls into the sky. Today, each night, the Seven Sisters still pass over Bears' Lodge and smile in gratitude to the rock spirit.

A Lakota forest ranger giving a talk near the tower enlightened Jim and Rene about this legend. It wasn't until later that its deeper meaning settled in. For now, the reasonable weather and intriguing monolith inspired them to take Jerry for a closer look at the Kiowa's sacred place. Dogs weren't allowed at the viewing station, but Jim convinced the ranger to let Jerry walk up a short portion of the trail.

"Okay, but make it quick, and don't go past the paved section." The ranger looked around and smiled at the happy dog while trying to sound stern and official. Having only three legs worked wonders when playing the pity card.

The boulder field begins at a tree filled with flags, photographs, pieces of yarn, poems, and other Native American prayer offerings. Touched by the spirituality of the place, Jim gently pulled some fur from Jerry's thick coat. Jerry darted his head back with a quick glance, then relaxed. He had plenty of hair to spare.

Later that week on Jerry's blog, Rene shared the experience in his voice.

We only walked up to the boulder field at the base of the tower, but that was far enough for me. Jim pulled a bunch of my hair and wove it into a strand he tied around a tree with all the other Native American prayer offerings. Hopefully that will bring me good health and well-being for years to come. Later we ran and played a lot...

Jim quietly wrapped Jerry's furry offering around a string that held small prayer flags flapping in the wind. He made his wish with tear-filled eyes and prayed for the dog beside him to live a long, happy life. Then he asked the rock to keep the cancer away. They turned and walked back down the path, quiet and respectful of the sacred site. After thanking the ranger, the pack proceeded back to camp, with a quick stop to admire the playful prairie dog residents of Dog Town.

Jerry never got excited by rodents, and quickly grew bored watching the little creatures at play. He made it clear that it was his turn for fun. Bear's Lodge is warm in July, but nothing like the scorching heat of the Southwest. Grass and shade blanketed the campground, making it a perfect setting for some low-flung Frisbee tossing. Jerry's eyes lit up when he saw Jim toss his favorite floppy flying disc to him. Back and forth, again and again, he went after the flying saucer prize. Rene ran alongside Jerry with the camera to capture his mid-air retrievals. It didn't take long to make Jerry happy, and within minutes, they plopped down under a tree to rest. Jerry eagerly slopped up all the water from the portable water dish on Jim's belt. Most of it spilled out his jowls and onto the grass, but he was satisfied and sat happily panting as his thick, long tongue flopped out one side of his mouth.

They chuckled at the bobbing organ so long it practically swept the grass under Jerry's paws. While he rested, Rene zoomed the camera lens in on the bouncing tongue. Jerry's afternoon finale became the setting for another epic video showing a dog loving life on three legs. In those days, Jim would spend hours making videos, but not this one. He made a quick clip showing just a few seconds of a close-up shot of Jerry's long tongue. Little did he know that the silly snippet would be their first video to receive more than one million views. Why? Because at first glance, the movie's thumbnail of Jerry's thick, pink tongue resembles a certain private part of the male anatomy.

That night as Jim drifted off to sleep, the legends of this sacred place floated into his dreams. He envisioned the Bears' Lodge lifting the three of them up to the sky as Jerry sang. Dreadful thoughts had nagged at him as they'd started this journey, but the vision put his worries well out of reach as he and Rene rose on the rock. It was Jerry's spirit lifting them up, encouraging them to seek solace on the foundation they had laid for the road they now traveled. The dream was vivid, and it wouldn't be the last.

In the morning he awoke, slowly recalling the vision, then realizing the road trip was more than one last hoorah for the dog he loved so much. This had become a spiritual voyage and Jerry was their guide. The amputee dog was their spirit animal who clearly had many lessons to teach them on the road called life.

At Bear's Lodge and beyond, the lesson was: Go and Do. Every morning, Jerry would hop up the three steps to their small RV bedroom and squeeze into the tight spot next to Jim. His polite whimpers said, "Get up!" Go out and do things, seek adventures, create memories, and love every moment. Don't waste your time watching the world go by. Get out there and live the life that makes your heart happy. Jim and Rene got the point; his messages were sinking in with every new adventure.

✿   ✿   ✿

With Bear's Lodge in the rearview mirror, they headed to Roy Lake, a favorite spot for the speedboat and Jet Ski crowd. The shady, grassy campground lacked much of any accessible shoreline for Jerry to go swimming, and the RV sites were hidden under big trees. Jim maneuvered the trailer through the canopy and crept slowly along the road, looking for a site with good southern sky access to get online, while carefully assessing the height of all the low branches.

"Look out!" Rene's shout startled Jim so he tapped the brakes, causing Jerry to bump into the back of their seat.

"What?" Jim was frantically looking for low limbs or trees that might hit the RV's air conditioner. Clearance looked good, and there was no one else around. Jerry even looked at Rene and sniffed her ear, wondering what the big deal was. He could always sense her stress, and she was clearly worried. Jim started to creep the truck and trailer forward again.

"Stop! There's another one." Jim stopped. It was frogs. There were frogs everywhere, and Rene didn't want to run over any of them.

"Aw geez," Jim droned with his best Midwestern impression. Happy it was nothing serious, he convinced Rene they needed to pick a site, since it was getting late. The darker it got, the harder it was to find a suitable spot while watching out for all the amphibians. Jerry noticed them as soon as they let him out of the truck. He may have met a toad or two in his time, but he had never seen so many actively leaping around in one location. The campground was so saturated with little frogs they had to be careful where they walked. Jim made a comment about some biblical plague, and out came the camera.

Jerry hopped after them on that one front leg, but as soon as he got close to one, it would leap away. When another caught his attention, he trailed behind to investigate. Sneaking up on them was impossible, they were far too fast. Others stood their ground when they saw him trotting through the grass. He stuck his nose right up to the brave toads while Rene zoomed in for an extreme close-up of the big, black nose versus the little green critter. Never once did gentle Jerry bark, bite, or try to eat a single frog, he just shook his head if one startled him by hopping away when his giant proboscis made contact. It was a real-life Frogger game that went on into the evening while fireflies lit up the darkness around them. They were exhausted by the long drive and playtime, and the chorus of croaking frogs and clicks of crickets lulled the trio to sleep at night.

The episode reaffirmed Jim's belief that their furry Zen master had another message in store, this one about loving-kindness— the tenderness and consideration toward others taught in various religious traditions.

Maybe he was simply being the calm dog he was by nature, but Jerry's act of kindness sank in. Somewhere along their journey, Jim or Rene clipped out this quote and added it to the other meaningful mantras they have taped inside their bathroom cabinet.

> *Presume innocence of each piece of life, at least until you know better, and the joy of a loving community will be yours.*

They believed this is what Jerry was telling them at Roy Lake. It is why he didn't eat any of his new frog friends. He was merely happy to be going about his business of enjoying life's new surprises, and making friends along the way.

— 12 —

Crossing the Mississippi

The Midwest was kind to the wandering pack. From Fargo to Duluth and beyond, the temperate weather lifted their spirits as they settled into their new nomadic lifestyle. The meandering had a loose itinerary, but people always wanted to know where they were headed. "We're just following Jerry's lead," was Jim's comeback, often calling him their co-pilot. It was mostly correct, but there was one destination he and Rene both wanted to reach more than anything: the Atlantic Ocean.

"He needs to splash in the Atlantic. Can you see it? Coast to coast! From the Pacific to the Atlantic. That will be awesome!" Jim was determined to see Jerry play at the beach again. It would be his victory lap, the most authentic way to show people that a cancer diagnosis isn't the end of the road.

Once over the Continental Divide, they knew they had to let Jerry hike on the AT—the Appalachian Trail—so he could score his own Triple Crown badge. He'd already conquered bits of the Pacific Crest Trail and Continental Divide Trail. The AT would be the culmination of his trail dog glory days.

So many milestones came to mind as they dreamed up their eastward journey. The more they thought of new places to visit, the longer their bucket list for Jerry grew. They had to see him splash in the Atlantic, and a visit to the Ben & Jerry's factory in Vermont was a must since that was on the way. Florida and swimming in the Gulf were the next significant milestones, and Jim was already looking forward to seeing Jerry back in the Rocky Mountains to complete the circle. Burdened by the human obsession over time and goals, Jim and Rene found it hard to focus on the here and now. Packing so many milestones into whatever time Jerry had left seemed like exactly what needed to be done at this point in their lives, and in his. It also kept their minds on a more positive note than dwelling on the inescapable inevitable.

Meanwhile, Jerry wasn't paying too much attention to the circled names and dots on the big road atlas. He was too busy trying to show them how to appreciate each day instead of fretting over his future. Every new day held another new adventure, and while enlightened humans call it "Living in the moment," Jerry didn't need to call it anything. Living in the now was just in his nature.

He lay sprawled across the cool dirt while Rene leaned over the atlas, plotting their route on the picnic table. He studied her expression as if wondering why she was in such a hurry. If he could talk, he may have told her to stop, sniff, and look around. Nature wasn't in any hurry; why was she? Birds don't let a GPS tell them where to go. They go where their instinct takes them. The beauty of life is in the here and now. Could she even see that?

Most days, they made time for a little blogging and a lot of fun. One day, while exploring the college town of Bemidji, Minnesota, they stopped for a picnic at the feet of the massive Paul Bunyan statue that towers over the town's visitor center alongside Lake Bemidji. Jim helped Jerry out of the truck while Rene reached into her backpack for some sandwiches. She looked across the lake at the scenic countryside and smiled. "I think I could live here; I really do!"

"Yeah, just like you said you could live in Hoven, South Dakota, because you thought it was so cute. Just wait for winter!" Jim's logic kicked in again, much to her annoyance. She loved the charm of old Midwest towns, but he knew that his California girl would flee at the first sign of snow.

They ate their lunch at a picnic table near the lake while Jerry patiently sat beside them, monitoring for falling scraps. Rene browsed the town brochure she'd picked up inside the center and pointed out all the good qualities of the community. As she read the material aloud, Jim looked up to see a weathered old man with long, black hair and leathery skin coming toward their table. He wore a tattered dress shirt, torn jeans, and carried a large, dirty tote bag. The stranger made eye contact just as Jim took a bite out of his sandwich.

"Don't look," he whispered to Rene. Living in cities had made him skittish about strangers approaching without reason. Memories of the junkie at their door in downtown Eureka were etched deep into his mind.

"Don't look at wha...oh." She looked up and right into the man's dark-brown eyes.

The man appeared to be Native American, and he had their attention. In a deep, slow voice, he spoke first. "Hey, can I tell you a story?"

Jaded from dodging city panhandlers in their previous life, they assumed that if they said yes, it would cost them something. During the split second it took to size him up and decide if the answer should be no, Rene looked down at Jerry. He was already standing up to greet the stranger without any judgment whatsoever.

The old man looked down and grinned at the relaxed dog, then reached out his weathered old hand to pat Jerry's head. Without a moment of hesitation, Jerry fully accepted the man's introduction.

"Your dog reminds me of these two old Indians. I'll tell you a story about them." He began his tale without waiting for their approval. Jerry looked up at the big man, soaking up the gravelly voice, and leaning against his strong legs.

"This Ojibwe and Choctaw were sitting at a bar..."

Maybe it was the beginning of a corny joke that would lead to a handout request, but Jim's gut feeling was to take a hint from Jerry. "Want to sit down?"

"No, this won't take long. Listen. The Ojibwe, he's got a dog with him. The dog only has three legs, like him." He stooped down to give Jerry a firm rub and continued. "Then the Choctaw, he asks, 'Hey, what happened to your dog?' The Ojibwe looks down at his dog's missing leg and says, 'Oh that?'"

Jim and Rene hung onto his words with a reserved curiosity. Then the man flawlessly delivered his punchline with a well-rehearsed poker face.

"A dog this good, you can't eat all at once!"

Jim gasped with a bit of disgust, then looked up at the tall man and chuckled, grinning out of kindness. He wouldn't understand the cultural significance of this tribal wisecrack until researching it after they got home, finding it a joke that laughs in the face of racial bias inflicted on this man's people. But for the moment, he turned to see Rene's reaction as she responded, "Uhh...okay."

They each wondered when the man would hit them up for money. But as the big stranger let out a deep bellow at his own joke, they joined him in genuine laughter—more at his deadpan delivery than the appalling punchline. When the laughter paused, they could see that Jerry and the old man had made a connection. The funny story wasn't meant for them, it was the old man's gift to Jerry, a way of laughing at adversity, be it from prejudice or physical affliction. Here he had found a kindred spirit, someone with whom the old Ojibwe man shared much in common. Like Jerry, he was also set apart from the mainstream and wearing an outward appearance that compelled most others to judge.

"That's funny! We'll have to borrow it for a comeback when people ask how he lost his leg." Jim offered his hand, and the man accepted with a gentle grip from long, calloused fingers that dwarfed his own. The man then grinned down at Jerry, turned, and walked away without saying another word.

Like many dogs, Jerry believed that people are mostly good. Even after he was abandoned in the drop box at the animal shelter, he made his way in the world holding out for the good in others, instead of becoming jaded and making unfounded judgments of all people. It took his cancer diagnosis and life on the road for Jim and Rene to see this wisdom he shared.

🐾   🐾   🐾

The great river dividing the wide-open west and the dense eastern states was more than the halfway point of their journey from California to Maine. Eight months after vets predicted cancer would kill him within a year, Jerry was ready to prance in the cool shade of the towering pines that grow along the shallow waters near Lake Itasca, at the headwaters of the Mississippi River. There was no telling how long or how far he would travel, but for now, they didn't care.

"We're going to cross the Mississippi River, Jerry, on foot!" Rene was more excited than any of them. She treasured the idea of her little tribe walking through the water, then going for a swim, but it didn't quite work out that way. From the parking lot, they could see that the Mississippi River doesn't begin in a deep, blue lake, but rather in a shallow stream with pure, clear, gurgling water spilling out onto the grassy land. You don't swim in the headwaters at Lake Itasca State Park, you wade. Jerry was okay with either though. He reveled in the excitement of his human's voice and galloped ahead at the end of his leash, looking like a younger, healthy dog. He just happened to be missing a limb.

"Come on, Jerry, let's go to the water!" Jim led him past the visitor center. A family of foreign tourists watched in awe as they passed. Wildflowers carpeted the bumpy terrain while songbirds celebrated another gorgeous summer day. The wide, shallow creek was dotted with flat rocks that created a natural path for visitors to tiptoe across the narrowest point of the headwaters. Jerry led Jim and Rene straight toward the gentle water. Behind them, Jim heard a tiny voice declare, "Hey, that dog only has one leg!"

"Wait, Jerry!" Rene and Jim kicked off their shoes and stepped in behind him. Carefully they waded on the wet rocks as Rene snapped dozens of photos of the kids swarming the bouncy three-legged dog in search of a swimming hole.

"How come he only has one leg?" The boy from the parking lot followed Jerry into the water, amazed at how he hopped along on his one front leg.

"What do you mean, one leg?" Jim stopped to turn Jerry around with his leash. "He's got three—that's one more than you!"

The child looked puzzled, but eventually, he understood. "Ohhh... yeah, I guess so!"

More onlookers walked up to Jerry. "What happened to him?"

Jim was considering a reply with the new Ojibwe joke, but Rene was ready with her usual five-second version of Jerry's story. "Oh, he has cancer. But he's doing great now."

With his bad leg gone and standing strong on his remaining forelimb, Jerry's proud stance showed the public that this was a dog living with cancer, not dying from it. As he splashed his way across the gurgling stream, Rene and Jim never felt better about agreeing to the amputation surgery.

❄   ❄   ❄

Like all friendly dogs, Jerry had a way of luring his people into conversations with strangers. Each time they slipped the leash on, they knew it might be an opportunity to meet someone new who found him irresistible. Over time, their skepticism at meeting others faded. Thousands of miles later, socializing with strangers felt natural instead of inducing paranoia.

Michigan had enough pretty scenery to keep them happy for a while. One evening while they enjoyed the peace and quiet of a remote forest campground, a man driving an unusual truck showed up. The truck bed had a dozen square steel boxes that resembled small jail cells. When he turned the engine off, a loud chorus of barking dogs pierced the air.

"What the...? He's got dogs back there!" Rene had never seen such a thing, but Jim grew up in the country and knew right away the guy had a truck full of hunting dogs. They watched through the tinted RV window as one by one the man opened each little box, led a white-and-brown dog out to the forest to pee, then tethered the dog to a ground stake.

She stared in amazement at the whole process. The tethered dogs were strategically placed in rows, and weren't allowed much room to roam. They looked a little too skinny, she thought.

At least a half-dozen similar trucks arrived over the next hour. Each driver freed his own captives until the entire campground was filled with dozens of barking German Shorthaired Pointers. Jerry jumped up on the couch and peered out the window as the excited howls from all the dogs grew louder.

"What the heck is going on? Are they breeders?"

"They're all hunting dogs, silly. They must be here for some competition," Jim explained.

"Well, that's just mean!" She didn't understand why people would use dogs in any sport, and the whole scene seemed cruel as the dogs' ear-splitting baying and barking interrupted their solitude.

"Whatever. I'd rather hear barking dogs than a bunch of screaming kids." Jim grinned, and she agreed, but still questioned the curious sight. He then grabbed Jerry's leash to get outside and check out all the dogs. The excitement escalated Jerry into a frenzy. All the hunting dogs lunged to the ends of their tethers when their new neighbor approached. Jerry was equally curious.

"What's going on here?" Jim shouted over all the barking as the three of them approached the man who first arrived with his dozen dogs. Rene trailed behind, wondering if the dogs were happy.

"Oh, we're here for a trial." The hunter pointed to the "Hi-Five Kennels & Gamebirds" sign on his truck. The teams were there for a weekend competition to test the dogs' birding skills.

"How long have you done this?" Rene became immediately interested in the man's business since it was all about dogs.

"Ten years so far!" The trainer explained that he used to be a drafting and design engineer, but when his job got outsourced in 2002, he decided to do what he loved most: train hunting dogs. "Now I get paid to hunt!"

"So, you get to play with dogs all day? Cool!" Rene became more curious about his story, and her whole opinion of hunting with dogs changed in that instant. This man's canines were not as skinny as she first thought. He explained how the breed is muscular and lean when they get to do what they love. These dogs were bright-eyed, and clearly well-bred and cared for. The idea that this man worked with them every day sounded like a dream—to her, and for the lucky dogs. Operating a kennel seemed like a fun way to make a living, maybe even something they should add to their list of potential next business ideas. Maybe.

"Well, it's not all play or fun." The trainer willingly participated in the impromptu interview. "I mean it mostly is, but there's a lot of maintenance and cleanup most people don't think about. I have lots of dirty work. Horse and cow poop are fine and dandy, but there's just no glamorizing dog crap!" The three of them laughed over that reality and then talked more about how their lives were all about the dogs.

The work was hard and his hours were long, he explained, but he was happier than ever for the chance to do what he loved. It was just what Jim and Rene needed to hear. Neither of them had any idea what they might do for a living when their road trip was over, but they knew two things: one, they wanted to remain self-employed, and two, animals would always be a big part of their lives, in one way or another. Being their own bosses made them happy. As they continued to meet other like-minded people following their passions, they hoped that in time, the universe would provide them with precisely what they needed.

— 13 —

Tripawds Coast to Coast

The pack's new daily routines had little resemblance to their old life. The scenery changed outside their dining room window almost every other day, and they never quite knew where the road was taking them next. But even while their home frequently changed locations, a few old habits remained. Each morning, Jim and Rene woke up, walked Jerry, ate breakfast, and got on their computers. Even with this new life of theirs, they couldn't break free from the Internet. But without the drudgery of demanding project deadlines, they found great joy each time they went online to share Jerry's latest adventures.

Just a year after starting Tripawds, Jerry's blog was a resource for others facing the same struggles they were. But it wasn't the dogs who needed the support. It was the people. Amputation is harder on the pet parent than on the dog having the procedure. Jim and Rene could relate. They had not truly believed Jerry could do well on three legs until they saw another dog doing it. Humans are like that: they want proof. Now that these two had it, they wanted to show the world. Every few days they made new videos of Jerry loving life, shared photos of him having fun, and composed short blog posts in his voice. Their goal was to show that life didn't end after amputation, and more importantly, that he wasn't dying of cancer. He was living with it.

To prove Jerry wasn't an anomaly, they shared stories about other amazing dogs. One of the first was Finnegan, a three-legged Irish Wolfhound in Pennsylvania. As large and lovable as a small pony, Finnegan proved that canine osteosarcoma doesn't always play by the rules. At six years old, and twenty-four months after being told he wouldn't last more than six, the giant Tripawd showed the world that all dogs—of any size—can enjoy life as an amputee. His mom, Andrea, believed in this long before most people. Back then, even most vets automatically dismissed giant breed dogs as candidates for amputation surgery. But Andrea was a trailblazer. She ignored the doubters and found a vet who held just as much optimism as she did.

Nearly two years later, her miracle dog was still going strong against all the odds, and Jim and Rene wanted some of Finnegan's good luck to rub off on Jerry. On a rainy August afternoon in Erie, Pennsylvania, they got their chance.

They turned into the playground parking lot and Jerry sensed something was up. Feeding off his humans' energy, Jerry was ready to dive onto asphalt when Rene opened his door. But a split second before his leap, she caught him by his harness handle. "Wait, Jerry! Hang on," she gently scolded him. In the throes of excitement, this mellow dog often forgot his obedience.

A tall, grey creature walked his human toward them and all bets were off. Jerry was ecstatic. The giant dog ambled closer with an awkward walk that was a cross between a hop and a step. With each step forward, his head bucked up and back while his one long front limb strode ahead and the back legs bunny-hopped him forward. Andrea took extra-long strides just to keep up. Watching the pair's movements felt very familiar to Rene and Jim.

Jerry lunged ahead while Rene hung on tight to his leash with a big grin on her face. Nobody cared about the steadily falling rain. After all, it wasn't every day they got to have a three-legged dog party. "Hi, Andrea! I'm Rene, this is Jerry, and that's Jim."

"Nice to finally meet you!" She smiled, extending her hand to introduce the miracle dog. "Here he is; this is who you've been waiting for."

"Oh, Finnegan, let me touch you!" Rene didn't need to bend down to plant a kiss on the tall dog's forehead. Finnegan's wooly fur was softer than it looked, and he stayed calm and patient while she smothered him with affection. The gentle giant didn't care about her, though, his eyes were fixed on Jerry. Finnegan pulled Andrea to the grass as he and Jerry walked in sync to get there. Finnegan dwarfed Jerry by at least ten inches. For the first time ever, Jerry switched roles and played the little dog. Being the short guy gave him the advantage of easily sniffing around Finnegan's undercarriage.

Dog encounters can go either way, but Finnegan and Jerry were a good match. No growling, no barking, no drama. They simply sniffed each other up and down to decode one another with their powerful noses. The humans watched closely, lost in their own interpretation of the encounter. Andrea peeked out from underneath the hood of her jacket and asked what they all had been wondering. "Do you think they know they're both different?"

"Seems like they would know that there's supposed to be a leg there." Rene is good at overthinking such things. "But maybe they forgot?"

Humans instantly size each other up to draw conclusions. They look at clothing, hairstyles, skin color, and language, then make huge assumptions about others. Dogs, however, are beyond this superficial thinking. They don't allow missing or damaged body parts to define an individual dog. What they look for is presence. Calmly allowing another dog to approach sets the tone for everything that follows. Finnegan and Jerry were both blessed with this sense. They had serene, confident personalities that immediately gelled. Was it because they were different? Doubtful. Their temperaments simply blended well, and as they got to know each other on the muddy playing field, the grateful humans could see that there was no fear, worry, or doubt showing on their dogs' expressions. Forget amputation, chemotherapy, and supplements. These dogs just did what dogs do best: live life to the fullest and send happy energy into an uncertain world.

🐾　🐾　🐾

Just three months after leaving their old life behind, Jerry's new white doghouse on wheels had cruised almost the entire way across North America. Jim and Rene weren't in a rush to follow any itinerary, but they added more destinations on their growing bucket list. From the Badlands of South Dakota to the cold waters of the Atlantic Ocean in Maine, arriving at each new mark on the map would become a victory celebration of Jerry's fight against cancer.

"I can't wait to see Jerry playing in the Atlantic." Jim had high hopes for this major milestone.

"Me, too! He's gonna love it!" Rene's route planning had them just a few more weeks away.

Neither of them spoke about the what-ifs of how to cope with Jerry's inevitable cancer metastasis. Statistics indicated the disease had probably already spread in Jerry's body and was growing every day. Soon they would be forced into discussing how they would handle that situation, but not now. Today, Jerry was the energetic, happy dog he always had been, and that was all that mattered.

The more they just sat back and enjoyed the ride as Jerry did, the better off they all felt. Sometimes Rene wondered if they were burying their heads in the sand, but as the miles rolled on, it only seemed right to enjoy each moment as it unfolded. She knew that if cancer became the focus of whatever time they had left with Jerry, that damn disease would win. By putting their worry on the back burner and following his lead, the two of them came to understand how focusing on the gifts right in front of you is the best path to happiness. There's no point in worrying about things that may or may not happen, she reminded herself. Nobody can control the future, so why try?

An osteosarcoma diagnosis always comes with a recommendation for routine follow-up chest x-rays every few months after amputation. The tell-tale results would show if or how the cancer has progressed. When the vet recommended x-rays to Rene and Jim, they struggled with the decision. Of course, if Jerry showed any signs of discomfort, they would immediately seek out a vet. But if he seemed pain-free and happy, couldn't they just enjoy their time with him?

"I don't think that's a good idea." Jim made his feelings clear. He did not want any remaining time with his beloved dog spent with frequent vet visits and worry about each result.

"It would change everything." Rene looked at him with a sad expression.

They agreed. Skip the x-rays until trouble appears on the horizon. The adventure would continue. With so many miles ahead of them and no guarantees about tomorrow, for now, the best medicine for Jerry was a peaceful, blissful life with his people. Inwardly, however, both wondered: if that cancer came back in his lungs, the way it usually does, and they did nothing to save him, could they live with their decision?

Months passed before they were forced to see a vet. Jerry wasn't showing any signs of sickness, but when it came time to travel through Canada, they discovered he needed the canine equivalent of a US passport. If they were going to visit the small town north of the border where Jim's parents were married, Jerry needed a Certificate of Good Health. And that required a health exam. All this time they had done their best to avoid stepping inside any veterinary clinic, but now the time had come to hope for the best while preparing for the worst.

The bare-bones animal clinic they found in upstate New York was unimpressive, but would serve its purpose. They sat and waited for their appointment time on hard benches in a sterile lobby with dark, wood-grain walls and a harsh Pine-Sol scent that made the place even less comfortable for the animals.

"Hi, we're here for Jerry's health exam." Rene rushed up to the desk, hoping to be done with this visit in a few minutes.

"This must be the guy! Hi, Jerry." The tech bent over and gently scratched the top of his head. "You can come on back now."

They waited under bright florescent lights that bathed the room in an eerie green hue. Then came a soft knock at the door, and a tall man in a white doctor coat walked inside. "What a good-lookin' fella!" The vet bent down to scratch Jerry's soft ears. "What seems to be the issue?"

He was the classic country vet. Older, with white hair and lacking certain bedside manners, he reminded them of Jerry's first vet who'd botched his diagnosis. But he would have to do for what they needed now.

"We just need a pet health certificate so we can go to Canada." Jim was also hoping for a quick and simple exam. Neither the tech nor vet had asked about the missing limb. Car accidents claimed a leg from many animals, so Jim hoped they simply wrote Jerry's three-legged situation off to just another run-in with a car.

"Oh, we can do that, it's easy!" The vet explained his simple checkup. "I'll just need to go over his health history and check for any unusual lumps or skin conditions. I'll also listen to his lungs to make sure they're healthy." His last words hung in the air, shadowing the couple like a dreadful shroud.

This was the moment of truth. For the first time since Jerry's amputation surgery, a vet would put a stethoscope up to their sick dog's lungs. They needed to explain Jerry's condition, but Rene couldn't bring herself to say, "My dog has cancer."

Jim found the strength to do it for her. "Jerry's got bone cancer. We amputated his leg nine months ago. His lungs might sound kinda weird." He really had no idea what they might sound like, and he truly didn't want to know.

"Ohhh…" The vet reached for the stethoscope hanging around his neck. "Well, there's only one way to find out."

He bent down on one knee to face Jerry, then gently placed the stethoscope diaphragm on his chest. Jerry stood softly panting while the vet concentrated on his breathing. Rene and Jim tried hard to interpret his reactions, but the man's face remained indifferent to whatever sounds came through the device. Time seemed to stop, then he turned to them both and grinned.

"Well, he sounds like any other perfectly healthy dog his age! His lungs sound fine to me."

"Whew!" Jim made an exaggerated motion to wipe his brow with the back of his hand, and Rene's face lit up with a broad, happy smile.

"Yay! Did you hear that?" Jerry had no idea why Rene was so giddy and patting his head so hard, but the feeling was contagious. His tail started wagging in double-time. Ten months after his diagnosis, Jerry was happy and healthy. Life was looking good, and they were going to Canada.

The vet inspected Jerry's current vaccination records, then reached into a filing cabinet to retrieve a form. He bent over the official-looking paper, scribbled his signature in triplicate, then handed copies to Rene. "Have fun up north!"

❖   ❖   ❖

They made the brief side trip to Toronto in their truck and after a quick stop at Niagara Falls for another epic photo-op with Jerry and Barney, the Atlantic coast beckoned. But neither had ever driven East Coast roads before, and the native West Coasters quickly surmised that eastern drivers make their own rules. Shocked by the Amish horse-drawn buggies and speedball truckers jockeying for pole position on impossibly narrow country roads, Rene constantly shrieked at the gruesome animal casualties left in their wake. Her reactions put Jim on edge, and hauling the trailer became a chore. She tried to teach herself knitting to keep calm, but her new hobby often left Jim without a navigator.

"Is that my exit!?"

"Huh?" Startled by his question, Rene looked up from her knitting. "Wait! Slow down. Yes!"

Sudden stops and swerves put them on the wrong roads and tollways more than once. Jim couldn't wait for their next milestone, where they could park the RV, relax, and play the tourist for a few days.

❖   ❖   ❖

In between the crazy drivers and frantic turns, there was still plenty for them to love about this new region. Ticking off their dream destinations was easy with eastern states being so close together. Places and activities that seemed impossible for Jerry to reach just a few months ago were now within their grasp, each stop only a few highway exits away from the next. Their entire cross-country route was planned so that many of Jerry's bucket list stops were near towns with potential as a place to put down roots. Burlington, Vermont, was one such community. They loved everything about its laid-back, hippie vibe. Not since they had been in Carbondale, Colorado, had they visited a town that even came close to their aspirations. As a bonus, Burlington was a short drive from the Ben & Jerry's ice cream factory, a must-see stop along their New England tour. The famous ice cream duo was partially the reason behind Jerry's name, and Jim always said that if Rene ever insisted on adding another dog to the pack, he would call him Ben.

The quirky Ben & Jerry's factory in Waterbury has dog-friendly picnic grounds, so Jerry felt right at home on that unusually cool afternoon. Rene and Jim joined a tour to get the scoop on how their favorite ice cream is made while Jerry waited patiently in the RV. An hour later, they fetched him for a picnic on the grassy lawn. Jerry strutted his stuff for tourists, sharing the happy energy of everyone around. Rene held onto his leash while Jim walked to the ice cream stand. On the way, he spotted a giant, round replica of a Ben & Jerry's ice cream pint container lid. The graphic designer geek in him stopped to inspect how the piece was crafted. It had two holes cut out where Ben and Jerry's faces should be, making it a perfect picture spot for visitors.

Jim smiled a wide grin and looked over at Rene. He didn't have to say a word. She immediately reached inside her backpack for Barney and waved it in the air. Jerry looked up at the two smiling fools with a tilted head that once again told them, "Really? What are you gonna make me do now?"

Jim returned with the two cups and placed them on the picnic table. Then, with the little purple dinosaur in his right hand and the end of Jerry's leash in the other, Jim walked around behind the giant lid and stepped up onto a platform with Jerry. He told Rene to take the picture as he squished the Barney doll into one of the cutouts—the one for Ben, of course. Then he bent over and scooped Jerry into his arms. Jerry wiggled around but when he saw Rene through the hole he stuck his head through, as if on cue. "Okay, now! Ready? Shoot!"

Rene snapped a dozen pictures of the unlikely pair of faces on the big lid while Jim muscled Jerry's 75-pound torso at shoulder height. The tolerant dog cooperated and helped create another legendary photo for the blog. "Perfect! Let's go eat our samples, they're melting." Rene stuffed the camera back into her bag.

They sat and savored their tasty treats in the bright August sunlight. "Here you go, Jerry, all yours." Jim let his photobombing dog lick the bottom of the cups while Rene captured Jerry's delight on video. After putting up with another one of their crazy tourist stunts, he had earned every lick.

❈   ❈   ❈

Burlington made it onto their short list of livable communities, but they couldn't linger long. Jerry had an important date with his Internet pen pal, Heidi the German shepherd. Long before he left Eureka, YouTube algorithms paired the two pointy-eared dogs' videos on the same page.

"Jerry reminds me so much of my dog, especially when he tosses his head to shake his opponent loose," Heidi's dad, John, wrote in a comment on their Jerry vs. Zeus tug-of-war video.

Jerry responded with equal praise for beautiful, four-legged Heidi. It was the beginning of an Internet romance between two rising stars on opposite ends of the country. Now that Jerry had made it to Vermont, the star-crossed lovers would meet in real life.

Rene brushed Jerry's fine, flyaway coat before they drove to Heidi's place. "Come on, Jerry, you gotta look nice for your lady!" He put up with the brushing, but only for a few minutes. The dog didn't care what he looked like when they got there. He immediately knew something fun was about to happen when they arrived.

"Look, Jerry, it's Heidi. Your girlfriend!" Jim helped him out of the truck, and Jerry hopped over to meet the lady of the hour.

Heidi's dad, John, walked out of the old wooden farmhouse. "He's just as good-looking in person! Hey, Jerry, nice to meet you." John greeted Jerry before looking up at Jim and Rene. "Oh, and you two, of course!"

The tall, tan German shepherd beauty strolled up and sniffed Jerry. Calm and confident, Jerry let her take all the time she needed to check his credentials. When he passed the test, she stood still and allowed him to do the same. Then, before the chit-chat even commenced between the humans, Jerry and Heidi were off and running through the tall, grassy field as golden sunlight dappled their shiny coats.

Jim reached into Rene's bag for the camera. "Hey, John, I think we need to do a video smackdown, don't you?"

"Oh, man, you're on!" Heidi's dad was already filming.

Jerry was energetic and happy to be off leash. He was in a playful mood and ready to wrestle and run around with Heidi, but she was being calm and coy. Once he realized the elegant canine wanted to slow things down a bit, Jerry settled down to show her some respect.

Rene watched the encounter unfold. "She's a real lady, isn't she?"

The date lasted an entire afternoon. Jerry and Heidi never saw each other again, and nobody had to state the obvious: Jerry probably wouldn't live long enough for a second date. But there was no sadness when these two friends parted ways. Dogs don't indulge in worries over the future with dramatic goodbyes, nor in promises to meet again someday. The humans followed their lead because, after all, if a dog doesn't look back, why look too far ahead? There was no need to spoil a perfect day with worry about the future.

※　※　※

Finally, Jerry's East Coast celebration was just a few days away. But first, Jim and Rene had to check an item off their own list: see a real, live Maine moose. "There's gotta be moose up here, don't you think?" After six long hours driving narrow northeastern parkways and harrowing lumber truck roads, they arrived in the far north at Moosewood Lake. This pretty spot deep in the woods sat on a lake near Mount Katahdin, the terminus of the Appalachian Trail. They were relieved to see a Vacancy sign on the rusty, old campground marquee. With school back in session, they had the entire place to themselves.

All the moose were in hiding, probably because of people walking their dogs along the lakeshore. Jim and Rene did the same, when a sweet older couple tried to approach Jerry. Their two dogs, however, didn't care for the interruption. The man made eye contact with Jim and tried to speak over the barking chorus.

"Wow, he gets…"

BARK! BARK! BARK!

"…around great!"

"Yeah, Jerry doesn't care…"

BARK! BARK! BARK!

"…that he's missing a leg."

"Hang on a sec." The gentleman walked his two dogs back to his RV and put them inside. He returned with his wife to meet Jerry. Like most people, they wanted to know what happened to him. Once Rene explained Jerry's story, they fawned over him even more. Jerry soaked up the love and attention as the couple scratched his ears and gently patted his sides.

"Wow, what a great dog. He's an inspiration."

"Thank you, he certainly inspires us." Jim enjoyed another proud moment with their three-legged hero. He handed the man one of the first Tripawds business cards he ever made, with a picture of Jerry and his website address.

The two couples only chatted for a few minutes, but the universe saw to it that they would meet again. A few months later, an email addressed to Jerry arrived in Rene's inbox. It was from this same couple. Their dog Holly—one of those vocal, galloping dogs on the beach that day—had been diagnosed with a limb cancer that required amputation. When her humans searched online for "dog amputation help," the Tripawds community appeared on the first page of results. Now, their own dog was going to lose a leg, but after meeting Jerry and reading his blog, Holly's humans already knew this wasn't the end of the road for their girl. She had just become another traveling Tripawds ambassador, exactly like Jerry.

❀　❀　❀

Maine was as beautiful as they imagined, but the narrow roads were maddening to them, especially the drive to Jerry's biggest milestone yet, dipping his paws in the Atlantic. Late-summer crowds jammed Bar Harbor's main drag as Jim did his best to remain calm while maneuvering the truck and trailer through the tiny town midway to Acadia National Park. He wondered why Rene was frantically looking for the map and asked, "Are you sure this is the way?"

Nowhere else in their travels had they encountered such a tight road leading to a national park. She reassured him they weren't on another wild goose chase, and he continued down the skinny road toward the park entrance. By sunset, they were neatly tucked away in their campsite. Tall trees obscured the view overhead, but a small patch of open sky allowed their satellite dish to get them online. Now that Jerry's community was growing, being online was becoming more critical than ever, but they still tried hard to live in real-time. Jerry was always their number one priority, so early the next day, they headed to the beach for their long-awaited celebration. Upon pulling into the parking lot, it was clear that the distance to the shoreline was going to be a stretch for him. Inwardly, both fretted about whether or not he could make it.

"Hey, Jerry, look where we are...we're at the beach!" His nose was already out the window smelling the ocean breeze, and Rene's high-pitched voice sent him into a frenzy. Long walks were tough on Jerry but his spirits were high, and on that sunny day he gave every indication he could handle the walk to shore. That's the way dogs are. They'll try anything, without thinking about whether or not it might hurt.

"Come on, buddy, let's go find some kelp!" Jim was eager to see Jerry get his feet wet. They could see that the rocky terrain at Sand Beach looked bad for swimming, but it had the familiar feel of the Northern California beaches where Jerry grew up. It was the perfect setting for his greatest accomplishment yet.

With a backpack full of fresh drinking water for Jerry, the smiling trio set off on the long walk to the waves. Jerry hopped along and with each step, it felt as if every onlooker was celebrating with him. "Whoa, look at that dog go!" they heard a young voice say. "Mom, look! That dog only has three legs!" said another. They took their time getting to the water and gave Jerry plenty of opportunities to rest and greet his fans.

The salty sea breeze and crashing waves lured Jerry down to the hard-packed sand. The moment Rene unclipped his leash from his collar, her revved-up dog was off and running. "Go, Jerry, go!"

He barreled into the shallow water where he danced, hopped, and leaped in the small waves lapping up on shore. The tide rolled in and rolled out, gradually exposing the top of a submerged rock that sent Jerry into a barking furor. For whatever reason, he was going to attack it. Down came his mighty front paw, and deep into the wet sand it went. Over and over again he dug, determined to expose this buried treasure, barking at it every time the waves retreated. But the water relentlessly rolled back in, covering up his hard work. And the ruckus started all over.

Jerry pranced around the rocks, hopping through breaking waves and barking with joy. The sun danced on the water as elated Rene and Jim watched him enjoy the sandy playground so far from home. Could this be the same dog with a death sentence hanging over his head? The idea made them laugh hysterically. All their worry about his disease was pointless! Jerry had just proven that nine out of ten statistics are wrong. He was still feeling great and enjoying the things that brought him so much joy during his four-legged days. Only this time, he was doing it on the opposite side of the country on a sunny afternoon. Jerry's lesson for the day was clear: we can all die at any time. Why worry about it? Make the most of what you have in front of you, and every day is a celebration.

❄ ❄ ❄

By now, it was clear that New England wasn't going to be the new home of "Jerry's Acres." So they didn't waste any time making their way to Jerry's next milestone. When they arrived at the Appalachian Trail near Bennington, Jim and Rene itched for a short hike together on this important landmark.

"Don't expect him to hike like he used to," the UC Davis vet had warned them when Jerry went in for surgery. That day, Rene and Jim secretly mourned the loss of weekend trips with their steadfast trail dog. They were grateful that Jerry was still around, but cutting trail hikes out of their life was almost as hard as amputating his leg to save his life. Still, they were determined to see him walk the Appalachian, even if only a short section.

"Come on, Jerry, ya wanna go for a hike?" Jerry knew anything with "ya wanna" was going to be exciting. As soon as Jim grabbed his harness handle and guided him out of the truck, Jerry was ready to go. His front paw touched the leafy ground as gentle dew from a nearby river misted the tips of his velvet ears. The earthy scent of a mountain trail wafted into his powerful nostrils with all the promise of a joyful afternoon. The humans couldn't move fast enough. Jerry bounced around so much that Jim could hardly connect his leash. Rene grabbed her daypack, and off they went hiking the Appalachian Trail.

A minute later, at the trailhead sign, Jim unclipped Jerry from his leash. "There you go, dude, run!" Joyfully, he bolted free and hopped ahead on the leafy trail. His nose worked overtime all across the ground as his body propelled him forward at full speed. Jerry zoomed up the short hill ahead of them then back down, as if telling them to catch up. Then he headed back up the path, filled with joy to be playing in the woods again. If anybody is ever in doubt that a three-legged dog couldn't have fun on the trail, all they need to do is watch that moment captured on video. They would see a determined dog with all the graceful balance and strength needed to maneuver through woodsy terrain.

"Did he grow another leg!?" Jim smiled as he watched his dog come alive. The new smells, crisp air, and gentle stream welcomed Jerry back to his old self, if only for a few minutes. They knew, however, that such explosive activity all at once is not ideal for any amputee dog, so out came the leash again. They hated asking him to slow down because he was having so much fun, but Jim and Rene had both learned the hard way that regulating his activity was the best way to avoid injuries.

The trail was slightly downhill as they returned to the parking lot, making it easier on Jerry's tired body. Once they reached the trailhead marker, it was only appropriate to pose for a selfie at Jerry's biggest backcountry adventure yet—complete with Barney at his side, of course.

᛭   ᛭   ᛭

Locals warned them the New England summer was already winding down. It was time to roll south for winter, but not before the West Coasters experienced their first real fall season. They had never enjoyed the sensory pleasure of watching seasons change in dramatic East Coast fashion, so despite chilly temperatures, they camped out for a couple more weeks to watch the leaves change. Plenty of campsites were waiting at a nearly empty RV resort nestled along the Battenkill River, where giant maple and elm trees were showing off blazing red, yellow, and orange foliage. Each afternoon a gentle breeze scattered large, colorful leaves into the sky, spreading brilliant hues that served to remind Jim and Rene that time was moving on. Jerry, however, wasn't bothered. After all, dogs don't keep calendars. If they did, every day would simply say: "Now."

The rustic riverside campground had a funky flair with mismatched lawn furniture, uneven campsites, and leaves left to decompose where they fell. This suited Jim and Rene just fine since they despised the leaf blower racket playing daily in fancier RV parks. The generations of campers who faithfully returned each summer clearly loved this campground, leaving their own handmade trail markers and welcome signs around the property. Something about the scene made them feel right at home, as if they had landed right where they were supposed to be. When they met the campground manager, they knew why.

※　　※　　※

Lesley was the daughter of the campground's founders, who'd built the place from scratch fifty years earlier. The New England native was a calm woman with a confident demeanor who also enjoyed another life that drew her to the animal kingdom. After observing Jerry for a few days, one evening she dropped by their campsite to say hi. But she wasn't there to meet her paying customers. She wanted to meet Jerry.

"I'm a shaman," she explained after introducing herself. "I work with pets and people to take them on spiritual journeys. I try to heal souls and make people happier by helping them understand their animal companions better. Do you mind if I do a reading on Jerry? He's such a beautiful creature." She spoke in a soft, pleasing voice as she gently stroked Jerry's ear, somehow knowing that was his favorite greeting. "I usually do this long-distance, using a photo, through my shamanic trance. But in this case, he is right here for me to make a connection. Am I lucky or what, Jerry?" She put both hands on his neck, gently massaging his one shoulder.

Anyone else might have wondered where she was hiding her tinfoil hat, but not Jim and Rene. Something about Jerry's spirit had compelled this stranger to communicate with him on another plane of existence. Jim was quick to agree, thinking it would make for great content on the blog. Rene was intrigued and wanted to learn more. This was their first foray into the spirit world of animal communication, which would become quite popular in the Tripawds community over the years, so they weren't exactly sure what to ask. They did know one thing for sure: They did not want to know about the condition of his health. They were solely interested in knowing if Jerry was happy and content with their decision not to pursue further treatment or diagnostics. They did not divulge this, nor did they give Lesley any further direction other than to proceed and share the findings from her trance.

A few days later, the communicator returned to share what she had learned during her special trance time. It occurred to Rene that this kind of thing might be helpful for people coping with health challenges in their own pets.

"Do you mind if we share it on video? People need to know about you."

"Yes, that's fine, I don't mind."

Jim adjusted the camera's video settings and began recording. Rene started by inquiring about how Lesley takes these journeys. After explaining the trance process, she described her time spent with Jerry in what she called the non-ordinary reality. "I used my hands, and energetically scanned his aura. I didn't feel I needed to go into anything else in his body at this time."

Deep down, Jim wondered if maybe she had seen something ugly there and didn't want to alarm them. With his curiosity piqued, he asked Lesley if she could see beyond any photo she sent to discover any underlying issues or emotions about the animal. "So even if the picture shows the dog playing, you'd be able to read through the..." As if on cue, Jerry hopped right past the camera to her side.

"Right, because I'm tuning into the energy of what's now, not tuning into the energy of what was captured on that film." Lesley was clearly in tune with what Jim was getting at.

Content with her living-in-the-now analogy, Jim pressed her, saying, "And your initial impression of Jerry was...?"

"Oh, happy. Jerry is a very happy dog...very much into his job, and his being, as to what he's here for. And he really is here to be a healing animal." Leslie looked at Jerry and continued. "He feels really happy with life. This has given him a chance to explore life that he wouldn't have done before. And he's very pleased about his opportunity to do that."

Jim and Rene looked at each other and smiled. They liked what they were hearing. This shaman woman, a complete stranger with nothing to gain, had just confirmed the one thing that was most important to them.

"You know, it's the combination of all three of you that really matters...it's part of your path. And Jerry is a big part of that." Rene giggled as she panned the camera to catch him tossing his rubber chicken toy in the air and chasing it around on his own.

Part of their path...Jim and Rene both knew that somehow, Jerry's cancer diagnosis and amputation had some sort of higher purpose for them. But they never quite understood exactly what that was. They only knew it was Jerry's job to teach them. As he already had.

He taught them to make time to play when they struggled with their business.

He taught them to be aware of problems and pursue an answer.

He taught them to accept changes in the present without fear of the future.

He was constantly teaching them to enjoy life.

He'd taught them to accept others and the gifts they give, without judgment.

He continued to teach them lessons at every turn of the road.

And, now, somehow, it all fit into the path for the three of them with Jerry as a healing instrument.

❋ ❋ ❋

While the prediction felt odd at the time, eventually, all the pieces fit. Lesley's shamanic journey with Jerry was spot-on. Nearly ten years later, Jerry's little Tripawds blog would evolve into a worldwide community of support for animal amputees and their people, which would surprise Jim and Rene as much as anyone. They may not have known where they were headed, but their unexpected encounter with this animal communicator showed them they were clearly on the right path. Jerry's spirit world visit with the shaman was meant to be. She had a knack for knowing an exceptional soul when she saw it: one healer recognizing another.

— 14 —

Celebrations

Time is such a human thing. Humans are obsessed with cramming their lives into neat little boxes of 24-hour increments, marking off failures, wins, and sentimental milestones along the way. So when any doctor breaks the bad news about a terminal illness, humans immediately focus on the calendar. They need to know precisely how much time is left. "Give me the prognosis, Doc. How long does he have?"

As if anyone knows how long any of us have. Doctors are smart, and some are pure genius, but they are not fortune-tellers. That's why none of them could have told Jim and Rene that Jerry would thrive far beyond the typical prognosis for dogs who don't get chemotherapy after an osteosarcoma diagnosis. They could never have predicted that with every new mile rolling under their wheels, it seemed extra days magically got added onto Jerry's life.

Dogs will tell you in their own way that ignorance is bliss. Jerry didn't know whether each new day was his last or the first of many still to come, and unlike the people who loved him, he just didn't care. He sailed into each new city or remote campground as best he knew how, even with cancer trailing them from behind.

Now that Jim and Rene were free from the daily burdens of the working world, they could study how Jerry made the most of 24 hours. For the first time, they saw how Jerry and his brethren can make every day the Best Day Ever, no matter the circumstances. Jerry saluted each sunrise with a downward dog stretch, then patiently awaited the adventure in his path.

"Can we go back outside? Can we? Now?" His nose nudges and full-body, side-to-side wags interpreted his heart's greatest wish every day during their morning routine, after his brief potty time and breakfast.

"Okay, Jerry, okay...just give us a minute." He had heard that one before, many times, in their previous life. Now he had learned if he patiently waited for them to finish their morning cup of coffee and computer check-in, he would get his reward. When Rene finally put the mugs in the sink, the day was theirs to do as they wished. Or rather, as Jerry wanted. Sometimes he led them onto a muddy riverbank where frantic frogs went airborne, trying to stay one leap ahead of his thundering paws. In the afternoon, he might show off his dog paddle prowess for kids gathered at a local swimming hole. Later, if he was lucky enough to get a cow bone for an evening snack, he flexed his powerful front leg muscle by pinning down the prize with one paw and sinking into a blissful gnawing session that lasted until bedtime.

Wherever the day led, Jerry never hesitated to give something a try. Not once did he pause to consider that dog-paddling was harder with only three legs. Nor did he fret that his walks were shorter because his strength was waning. With a happy heart, Jerry simply made the most of each day by enjoying what life put in front of him.

Jim and Rene observed their wise Zen dog and diligently tried following his lead. Now that they had the mental space to focus on the moment in front of them, they found it easier to set aside fears that lurked in their hearts, at least temporarily. Each day they worked hard to remember that Jerry wasn't dying from cancer; he was living with it! Nearly a year later, that three-legged hero appeared as healthy as ever, and nothing like the cancer patient they'd envisioned when the diagnosis broke their hearts. This led people in his Tripawds community to ask, "What's his secret? Is it his diet? What kind of super-supplements is he taking?"

❀   ❀   ❀

A food upgrade is one of the easiest ways for a pet parent to feel like they're making a difference in the fight against cancer. Rene was no exception. She scoured the Internet for new "anti-cancer" nutrition plans that would keep the disease in check, and shared Jerry's new diet with his online fans. She wanted to incorporate all sorts of fresh herbs and tinctures touted on the web, but Jim made her promise not to go overboard with changes. "Do you think you would enjoy eating ten different supplements each day? I know I sure wouldn't. And I doubt Jerry would."

She stared at him for a minute, trying to accept what she knew in her heart: he was right. Their picky eater would probably hate all that stuff. "Okay, fine. I'll just pick three supplements. Would you agree to that?"

Even after extensive research, they had no idea if the natural supplements Rene was considering would help, but they did know they wouldn't hurt. The raw meat, powdered kelp, flaxseed oil, and alfalfa powder might have helped Jerry battle the cancer inside him. But even if these new herbs and supplements didn't help Jerry, they did help Rene by knowing she was doing her best.

"Try it and see what happens. You can always stop if he won't eat them." Jim wanted to play an active role in Jerry's nutrition planning, but Rene was doing all the homework. He only had one request. "Just pick a plan and stick to it. If we keep changing up his diet, we'll never know what's working or not."

It made sense. Plus, they wouldn't be financially stressed about paying for any of the expensive "miracle cures" out there with no hard scientific proof to back them up. In keeping her word to Jim, each week the dedicated vegetarian cruised the carnivore aisles in the grocery store to make sure Jerry ate healthier, fresh meats. She squeamishly portioned out cuts, then pureed a daily selection of vegetables to hide the three supplements. For now, Jerry didn't seem to mind and ravenously devoured the rotating fresh meats in his meals.

Other than the diet change, there was no magic potion keeping him going. There was only one thing that could possibly account for his longevity, and it didn't cost a dime. It didn't come in a bottle and couldn't be found on the Internet, either. Every sentient being is born with this potential, but dogs are masters at harnessing its power. Jerry simply had the right attitude.

He didn't waste precious energy trying to predict his future. Every day he just focused on doing things that delivered joy instead of pain…

Exploring his surroundings and seeking out new friends.

Digging in the dirt, chasing sticks, and chomping on logs.

Sitting in the sun. Walking in the woods.

As Jerry did these things he enjoyed with abandon, Jim and Rene watched and learned. They embraced the unexpected gift of a joyful dog thriving against all predictions, just like Moose the Great Dane. A year after Jim and Rene found the YouTube video of Moose digging for gophers with one front paw, the giant galoot was thriving. Until one day, he wasn't.

"The vets think he has Wobblers disease." Moose's human dad delivered the sad news in an email. "It's a condition That's really affecting his balance, and it could get worse, we just don't know. Vets just don't see too many three-legged dogs with this disease."

Neurological disease is tough on dogs, but exceptionally hard on a tall, three-legged one who already has balance challenges. And while all the humans in Moose's life fretted over what the future may hold for him, that big dog simply could not care. Like Jerry, he continued to embrace each day with all he had, physically and mentally. In between his daily physical therapy sessions and doting affection from his parents, the oversized lap dog kept up his regular rodent patrols and afternoon sunbathing snoozefests in the warm California sunshine.

Moose's tenacity with the extra challenge in his path was a real eye-opener for Jim and Rene. He helped them realize that no matter what curve balls might linger around the bend for Jerry, they knew that nothing would change in his eyes. He would still be Jerry. As obedient students and guardians of his happiness, they felt it was only right that they should approach the future in the exact same way.

🐾　🐾　🐾

Crisp fall air drifted into the northeast, but Jerry paid no attention to the weather shift. On October 1, 2007, that once goofy little puppy turned nine, and Jim and Rene were elated at the thought of more adventures. They had just accepted their first "workamping" job at a North Carolina animal shelter—an arrangement to exchange volunteer hours in return for free rent. Rene submitted an application to explore their latest goal of starting an old dog animal sanctuary. It was a no-risk way they could put that crazy idea to the test—or lay it to rest.

"We'll settle down on some property somewhere and pull all the oldest dogs from the local shelter! We can contract with a local vet to help us with hospice care." She had clearly thought this through.

"Uh, okay...sounds kinda depressing." Jim wasn't so sure about her latest scheme.

"We can create a nonprofit and get donations to pay for it. Who doesn't want to help old dogs?" She was starting to get excited, just as she had about all those other crazy ideas over the years.

"Right, and we can call the place Jerry's Kids!" Jim couldn't help it.

His marketing mind was already hard at work, even though he wasn't so sure about the venture. "But first, let's see how this workamping deal at the animal rescue works out. Okay?"

❦ ❦ ❦

A big-hearted veterinarian ran the rescue. Single and in her late 40s, she was like many vets and had a better way with animals than people. She allowed Jerry to roam anywhere he wanted on the spacious rescue grounds, which gave him the unofficial role of job site supervisor while Jim and Rene pitched in for whatever needed doing. The old farmhouse and its surrounding acres were still being developed, so they were put to work right away. From painting fences and pulling weeds, to poop-scooping and feeding the residents, they worked through the autumn afternoons as a one-eyed pug, a lanky Doberman, and a pack of all-American mutts looked on. Tending to the cat house took up the rest of their day to manage and medicate more than twenty less than appreciative felines—including one particularly ornery hairless Abyssinian.

The vet had a soft spot for Jerry when she learned he had cancer. One morning as she observed him hopping around, she approached Rene and offered to give him a checkup. "What do you say I listen to his lungs? Let's just make sure they sound good. It's been a while since he's seen a vet, right?"

Rene was caught off guard. She thought Jerry seemed to be moving around a bit slower lately, which caused fears about cancer to creep back into her thoughts. She'd tried to convince herself it was due to them spending more time outside, which was more tiring for him than traveling. But burying her head in the sand was so much easier than confronting the truth about what was happening inside his body. Later, after another long day of clearing brush and cleaning cat boxes, Jim and Rene were relaxing on the tailgate of their truck when the vet dropped by.

"How you guys doing?" She wore the grimy evidence of a long, hard day tending to the animals, along with a stethoscope around her neck. Despite the long hours, she wanted to check up on Jerry. "Want me to do that exam?"

"Sure, I think we'll take you up on that," Jim answered. Rene wasn't sure she had the guts to find out the truth, but Jim felt confident Jerry was still happy and healthy. He lifted Jerry up onto the tailgate for her.

The vet ran her hands over Jerry's body and gently palpated his lymph nodes. Always the cooperative patient, he didn't mind the attention and relished in the unexpected massage. She lightly pressed on his abdomen, aimed her flashlight in his eyes and ears, and pressed an index finger on his gums to check his blood flow. Then she put the bell of her scope up to his chest.

Jerry obediently kept still while Rene and Jim held their breath. If he did have lung mets, it could change everything and put an early end to their road trip. They just didn't know what they would do if they found out the cancer was back. Their lives revolved around traveling with Jerry—nothing else.

The vet removed her stethoscope from her ears, looked at Jerry, and smiled. "His lungs sound great!"

Celebrating the joyful expressions on Jim and Rene's faces, Jerry shook his body from side to side and wagged his long, bushy tail across the vet's cheek.

"For a nine-year-old dog with cancer, he's pretty healthy." She explained how Jerry's lungs sounded clear, and she could tell he had good circulation by how the color returned to his gums right away. "Whatever you're doing to keep him healthy, keep it up."

It was Jerry's best birthday present ever. At least for them. Clearly, something they were doing was working, and for now, their never-ending road trip together would continue. The vet kissed Jerry lightly on his head, rubbed his ears, then left the three of them alone to enjoy the good news. Jim and Rene sat, stared into the setting sun, and smiled. Their miracle dog just might live to see another birthday.

The next day, Jerry revealed the good news to his blog readers:

> A year ago the U.C. Davis vet said I might be good for 3 or 4 months. Now look at me! Must be all that great food my Mom feeds me. That, and all of the exciting travel adventures we've been having lately.

Shortly after sharing a potluck Thanksgiving dinner with fellow volunteers, a brisk autumn chill settled onto the region, making Jim and Rene antsy. They were ready to move on in search of the warmer climate where their next workamping assignment was waiting. The night before heading to their job on a small organic farm in Vero Beach, Florida, Rene announced her latest big idea.

"Hey."

"Yeah?" Jim was engrossed in something on his computer, but he looked up to find out what she had to say.

"I'm not cut out for this. The rescue thing. It was tougher than I thought." She admitted her final heartbreaking truth about the month they had just put behind them, assuming it would come as a surprise to Jim. It did not. Instead he just nodded knowingly, always figuring she had to find out for herself. During their month of cleaning up cat boxes and pulling poison ivy from dog runs, his gut constantly screamed out that starting their own rescue was too much of a stretch in so many ways. But he wasn't going to be the one to break it to her, assuming she would reach the same conclusion eventually. Plus, there was another aspect harder to swallow than the physical work.

"You have to be bulletproof to do animal rescue work." Rene came to her final conclusion after seeing what they'd both been through. "That's not me. I just don't have it." She looked disappointed with herself.

"Oh, thank dog. Neither do I! I don't care to ever clean another cat box." Jim was relieved that Rene agreed. "Can we check that off our list now?" She frowned, but he wouldn't let her wallow in their decision. "Hey, remember; we're already helping animals. The three-legged kind! That's how we can help them. It's already here." He pointed to his computer screen.

He was right. Jerry's community was growing, and needed their guidance to continue. Every day more worried pet parents desperately wanted to know why life wasn't so bad for three-legged cats and dogs. Even when they didn't have all the answers, just being able to support someone going through a hard time was good medicine for everyone. Their new work felt right, especially because it didn't feel like work at all. As they drifted off to sleep with grateful hearts, they knew that for the first time in their working lives, they were making a real difference in the world.

❀　❀　❀

On a chilly, 50-degree morning, they jumped on Interstate I-95, also known as the snowbird express. Each fall, the north-south route is driven by thousands of eastern RVers heading to warmer climates for the season. The fast-moving traffic on the crowded highway was terrifying. As Jim focused on his driving in silence, Rene considered all the ways to give Jerry a happier life. She would do anything to help him stay healthy and well. Since they were headed down the Florida coast anyway, it seemed appropriate that they visit the mystical Fountain of Youth.

Many places in the world lay claim to a magical spring with pure water that restores youth to anyone who drinks it. Saint Augustine was probably the one that attracted more tourists than any of them. The quaint, Spanish-style seaside resort town was built around the legend of the Spanish explorer Juan Ponce de León and his watery discovery of eternal youth. A festive atmosphere drifts in and around the maze of stone and brick plaza shops as barkers vie for dollars from white-haired snowbirds ready for a miraculous rejuvenation.

Whether the magic water existed or not, Rene could not disregard the mere possibility of giving eternal youth to her three-legged cancer dog. She imagined splashing the sacred water over his head in a Baptist-style tent revival ceremony that would magically turn back time and obliterate cancer cells from his body. Impossible dream or not, they would at least go to the fountain and find out.

Underneath the gold and bronze rays of late afternoon, she directed Jim into a tight parking spot at a beachfront campground. They would not waste time on their quest—who wants to wait a moment more for youthfulness? In record time, the trio had the trailer set up and were back in the truck headed toward town. A salty breeze blew in Jerry's face as he leaned out the window to sniff out their latest adventure.

Upon arrival, they could clearly see the Fountain of Youth attraction was their cheesiest milestone yet, but Rene and Jim happily paid the admission fee to the dog-friendly gardens. They strolled underneath the cool, jungle-like canopy populated with conquistador statues while Jerry willingly hopped along, sniffing every edifice and resisting the urge to bark back at the squawking peacocks parading around in front of them.

Rene spotted the grotto that housed the famed fountain. They stepped inside the dark, cave-like monument, out of the stifling heat and humidity, and stopped in front of a low fence gating off a man-made spring filled with burbling water. A life-size diorama surrounding them depicted dusty, darkly painted Seminole Indian statues with outstretched arms, enthusiastically greeting Ponce and his crew. Rene reached for her camera to capture the fictitious scene and teased Jerry over.

"Hey, Jerrrrry, do you want some waaater?"

He stared into the shallow pool, ready to jump in, but the picket fence prevented him from getting any closer. He looked confused with no way to access the water, but Jim would make sure Jerry got to enjoy it. He grabbed their portable dog bowl from Rene's bag, then he reached over and filled it with water from the bubbling spring. "Look, Jerry! Drink this; it will make you feel like a puppy again."

Jerry leaned down and eagerly lapped up the refreshing water. Jim smiled at his enthusiasm and watched him drink every drop while Rene took pictures of the miracle unfolding before them. This was the dog that wasn't supposed to be alive right now.

"What the heck, right?" She locked eyes with Jim, and they smiled.

"Sure, who knows? It can't hurt!"

Perhaps Ponce was right; but even if he wasn't, as long as they had faith in the lore, that's all that mattered. Sometimes just believing is the best medicine there is.

— 15 —

Life and Death on the Farm

The week-long party lit up the shores of the Atlantic Ocean at Jetty RV Park in Port Canaveral, Florida. It was the first week of December, and the revelers weren't there for NASCAR or Daytona Bike Week. Everyone at the park came to celebrate NASA's latest victory, the launch of the Space Shuttle *Atlantis* from the Kennedy Space Center.

All afternoon older, retired RVers lounged the day away at tailgate parties leading up to the big blastoff. Rene and Jim weren't old or retired, but they happily joined the fun before starting their new workamping job on an organic farm in Vero Beach, just a bit farther down the coast. Meanwhile, Jerry didn't care about the celebration or the big, upright rocket on the horizon. To him, it was just another packed RV park filled with interesting new people excited to meet him.

Jim and Rene chatted with neighbors setting out holiday decorations. It didn't feel like the holidays to these native West Coasters, until one morning when Santa Claus paraded into the campground on the back of a Port Canaveral fire truck. Decked out in a Hawaiian shirt and shorts, the jolly visitor was the epitome of Kris Kringle straight out of Margaritaville.

"Now it feels like Christmas!" Rene looked at Jim and smiled while watching the parade. A neighbor set out a fake fir tree complete with lights and ornaments. "Can we get one, too?"

"No!" Their small rig hardly had room for extra socks, much less holiday clutter.

The Space Shuttle *Atlantis* was scheduled for liftoff on December 6, 2007, but technical delays scrubbed the mission day after day. Campers stayed upbeat as they shared daily updates about the launch schedule, but the excitement faded with every new delay. "Let's just stay one more day," Jim pleaded with Rene after every new postponement. One day turned into five until he agreed they couldn't keep the farmers waiting any longer. Good thing they didn't stick around. Space Shuttle *Atlantis* mission STS-122 didn't take off until February the following year.

❀   ❀   ❀

Their goal with these first few workamping jobs was to try their hand at businesses they considered starting after the road trip ended. Rene loved gardening and dreamed of owning a farm. Jim grew up in a Northern California agricultural town and liked working outside. Their next job at White Rabbit Acres would give them an up-close look at the dirty work of organic farming.

"Get settled in and just let us know what you want to do whenever you're ready to get started." The farmer eyed the sandals on Rene's feet when she got out of the truck and chuckled, "You might want to put on some real shoes, too."

"Ouch!" Within a few seconds of exiting the truck, she knew what he meant. Florida fire ants were everywhere. She noticed Jerry licking at his paws as she felt the first sting. Red ants swarmed at her bare feet while Rene danced around, paying more attention to her dog than herself.

She never walked outside without shoes and socks after that. And Jerry quickly learned to steer clear of the infested mounds. After a quick Google search, she found various ways to keep fire ant armies from marching on the new spot they'd call home for the next couple of months.

Between gritty farm chores and keeping Tripawds online, Rene and Jim's afternoons were booked the rest of that December, but Jerry didn't seem to mind. He found his own tasks that needed doing. A particular plastic tub required his attention.

The cracked, gray Rubbermaid tote sat in the weeds near the trailer, waiting for recycling. Maybe he was trying to help, or perhaps he had a flashback to those early days in the shelter when he destroyed that laundry basket in his kennel, but one thing was certain: the tub would not survive to see another week on his watch. Every time Jerry hopped out of the RV, he sprinted toward the basket with gusto. Never mind that it was nearly his size. Laser-focused and ready for action, destruction filled his eyes every time.

Rain or shine, Jerry made sure he gave that tub a scolding each time he went out, even if just to pee. Day by day, the tub slowly disintegrated as Jerry thrashed it around, whipping his neck with a grunt as plastic bits dropped around his paws. The mayhem continued as the pieces grew smaller.

Then one day, nothing more than tiny shards of shredded plastic dotted the grass where the tub once lay. Jerry sat down next to his pile of plastic and appeared satisfied with a job well done. The project was complete. He puffed his broad, furry chest out like a bullfrog and sat with pride. Mission accomplished. He showed his people that persistence really does pay off.

※　※　※

Jerry still appeared healthy, with no signs of cancer progressing inside him. Each time they spied on their beautiful dog so alive and happy, Jim and Rene struggled with the daily task of balancing optimism and reality. Christmas was coming, and they were joyful for having another with Jerry, but deep down they knew it could be his last. Bittersweet emotions flooded their hearts, but they remained upbeat and showered the unsuspecting dog with treats and presents. Rene even wrapped a few favorite toys he already owned, just to give him more time shredding wrapping paper on Christmas morning.

Old toys or not, it didn't really matter what was inside a box. Opening it was all that mattered to Jerry. Using his one front paw to hold the gift down, he peeled the wrapping paper with his teeth. When one of his presents started singing before he'd ripped off the rest of it, his eyes lit up and his ears quivered at the familiar voice. It was his special occasion toy, the Singing Barney. Rene always hid that one because it never failed to throw Jerry into fits of excitement at the annoying "I Love You" Barney song chanting from the toy's heart:

I love you. You love me. We're a great, big, family...

On that Christmas morning, Barney sang from beneath his Sunday comics wrapping paper. Jerry growled and bit at the soft, lumpy package until the paper was almost gone, then flung his nemesis across the room and right into his water bowl. Score! He retrieved the soggy doll for another round, then shook it hard, splashing water onto walls, windows, and his people. Laughter filled the RV as the trio celebrated a real Christmas miracle.

— 155 —

❀   ❀   ❀

Over those couple of months, they had fun learning the ins and outs of organic farming. Their new morning and evening routines didn't feel like "real" work, especially when it came to tending to the chickens. Jerry accompanied them to help out, since the coop was just the right distance for the two daily walks his body could still handle. The shepherd lived for tending to that flock, and although he was a loving soul, he couldn't resist the temptation of catching a squawking hen. Jim didn't believe the gentle dog could actually capture a running chicken, but Jerry apparently had other ideas that Rene shared in a blog post during their first weeks on the farm.

My Mom and Dad and I are living on a farm right now, and there are so many things for me to do here, I don't know where to begin.

Wait, I know. I could begin by chasing chickens around the yard and eating them up for dinner. After all, my Mom feeds me raw chicken and eggs all the time. Bet a really fresh chicken would taste so good! I see them, all plump and tender, flocking about. I want one so bad, but every time I get too close, Mom freaks out, and I have to sit back down like a good dog.

And what a good boy he was. They didn't even have to shout at him or grab him by his harness. Jerry was well-versed in the art of resisting temptation. Somehow, he had learned that rewards always follow good behavior. One day, a big bonus came to him from an unexpected source: the death of a farm animal.

It was just another morning when the trio started their shift at the farm's open-air produce store. There was a small kitchen in back where they washed and packaged produce they picked, or portioned out other organic goods the farmer's wife purchased from a local distributor. While Jim and Rene managed the inventory and customers, Jerry made friends with everyone. It was a welcome change from the days when he sat around their quiet office all afternoon, waiting for a friendly visitor.

From the freshly laid eggs to the wrapped cuts of organic beef piled high in the walk-in cooler, every day on the farm featured a different experience about life—and death. Most days, they didn't know which lesson would happen first. The day before, Rene had been holding a newborn baby lamb just days old, but today, as she washed and cleaned lettuce greens, she listened in horror while the farmer relayed some bad news.

"Oh, man. The neighbor's cow fell into a ditch. Broke its leg. You guys wanna come help take care of it?"

Jim understood the request. Rene did not. The cow would be put out of her misery and sent to the slaughterhouse. Nothing gets wasted on a farm. He turned to Rene with a questioning look, and only then did Rene recall that horses with broken legs don't get sent to surgery. Neither would this cow. The passionate animal advocate realized what was happening. "I think we'll pass."

She cranked hard on the oversized salad spinner, then shocked everyone with her request. "Hey, wait, don't throw the heart away, we'll take that. Oh, and yeah, the liver would be great, too!" She had no interest in helping the animal die, but she had no problem feeding the cow's valuable parts to her dog. Rich in vitamins, minerals, and fatty acids, organ meat wasn't just a treat for Jerry, it was included in the anti-cancer diet strategy she fed him each day. Jerry loved organ meat but never had the pleasure of eating it straight from the cow.

"Okeydokey! You got it." The farmer turned around in his big, black rubber boots and clomped off out of the farm stand and into his truck.

Jim stood looking from the open door at Rene and wasn't so sure about her great idea. "Do you have any idea how big a cow heart is?"

"Oh, come on, I'm sure we can deal with it."

They went back to spinning and bagging up all the fresh greens. Jim drained water from the big sink again after rinsing the final batch of delicate leaves. Rene munched on another handful as she finished packaging the day's harvest. Before they were finished cleaning up, the farmer's wife appeared with a big, black trash bag.

"Here ya go, we saved Jerry the best parts!"

The squishy sack was warm to the touch as Jim took it from her. He hesitated for a second, then looked down with wide eyes as he carefully opened the package over the sink. He knew it was going to be big, but he wasn't prepared for the massive, slithery liver. Then the large heart rolled out into the deep steel basin with a loud thud.

"Whoa...uh, thanks!"

Rene jumped back in horror at the warm heart and liver laying on the shiny steel surface. She was grateful, but surprised at the sheer size of the organs. She knew a human heart was about the size of a clenched fist, but this cow had a heart as big as a boy's head! The shiny and floppy liver flowed over the edges of the large cutting board and weighed in at over ten pounds.

"What are we going to do with all this?" Rene waited for Jim to say, "I told you..."

"Uh, start our own dog food company?" Jim sized up the body parts and wondered how long it would take for his 75-pound dog to consume it all. Meanwhile, Rene forced herself to get up close and personal with the steaming pile of fresh meat.

Jim wiped sweat from his brow as he prepared to play the part of the butcher. "We have to cut this all up and freeze it now." In the humid, 80-degree heat of the day, they needed to process the counter full of fresh meat before more flies caught on to the scent. They were already swarming in on the gruesome mess. And with his nose darting back and forth, Jerry had also taken notice.

"Uh, you go ahead. I'll film you." Rene didn't know what to capture first: the butcher's bloodbath or Jerry's wild antics over the rusty aroma coming from the counter. Long strings of drool dripped from his jowls and smeared across the stainless steel sink as he paced back and forth, snout pointed into the air. The peace-loving canine was going mad over the fresh cow heart! He barked and salivated at the aroma of the hidden treasure until Jim finally pulled the melon-sized heart from the sink and held the whole thing out toward his frenzied dog.

Jerry stopped and sat stock-still for a moment, startled by the massive hunk of meat. The dog had never seen anything like it. He sniffed, licked, then lunged toward the prize just as Jim snatched it away.

"Just a minute; not all at once." Jim reached for the sharpest knife on the counter and vigorously sawed into the marbled, rugged flesh. A few minutes into the massacre, he handed Jerry a large chunk. Jerry gulped it down before Rene even had a chance to capture it on camera.

"That's enough for now, big fella. Or we'll all regret it!"

After Jim finished slicing up the heart and portioning the huge liver, Rene divided the nasty bits into freezer bags. Flies buzzed around while waves of nausea hit Jim as he made the last few cuts. Blood coated his bare arms, and in the heat of the day, it didn't take long for it to dry and cake on his skin. He reached for the faucet and turned the handle, but nothing happened.

"Ugh. No water. Great timing!"

The farm's well water pressure had not yet recovered from the morning lettuce wash. It needed at least an hour to build back up, and until then, Jim stood over the sink in a bloody mess with no way to rinse off. Jerry appeared willing to help, so Jim held out his hands. Wild-eyed and crazed, Jerry licked the sticky residue, but not even his giant tongue did any good. The only thing Jim could do was walk far out into the field where high water pressure direct from the irrigation wellhead could clean him off.

Flies followed him as he walked along rows of lettuce seedlings holding his bloody hands up in the air like a villainous ax murderer. When he arrived at the wellhead, he reached down to turn the valve and open the four-inch pipe of untreated irrigation water. With no way to regulate pressure, the unfiltered water splashed into his face, reeking of rotten eggs and iron from its high mineral content. He felt even more nauseated as the warm liquid blasted the dried blood off his hands.

"The things I do for that dog!"

❄   ❄   ❄

Each Saturday morning, Jim and Rene rose before daybreak to pack coolers with newly harvested lettuce greens, organic produce, and fresh bean sprouts to sell at a nearby farmer's market. On their final day of the season, Jim took a break from unpacking to admire the breaking dawn. Brilliant shades of dark purple, pink, and orange streaked across the horizon, while dark palm tree silhouettes gently swayed in the morning breeze. He was happy for their time on the farm but relieved the gig was over. He'd witnessed the investment of time, effort, and money it would take to buy and maintain a farm and determined it was too much to consider. Weeks earlier, he and Rene didn't need any convincing to check farming off their list.

Later in the day, after shoppers had depleted their inventory, a beautiful German shepherd nudged through the crowd, anxious to meet Jerry. He was on the darker side of the breed, with stunning angular features and large, pointed ears. The dog walked under the table and with one bark and swift paw punch to Jerry's shoulder, he quickly established his rank.

Jerry's right ear sat low as he looked up at Jim without barking. He seemed uncertain about how to greet the big, bold dog Rene was fawning over.

"See, this is what you're supposed to look like!" Rene called from the other side of the table as she leaned over to caress the shepherd's coarse, black fur. Like most purebred shepherds, he was aloof and wary, but claimed his territory by sitting at her feet.

"Jerry, look up! Over here!" Rene quickly snapped a photo of the two dogs, never knowing that someday the snapshot would ultimately reveal their future as a pack.

*　*　*

Just before the sticky heat of a tropical Florida spring arrived, Rene and Jim put farm life behind them. It felt good to be mobile again, pointed west toward Texas for their friend Luke's send-off party to kick off his own cross-country adventure.

He was another one of those crazy pet parents who would do anything for his dog. The previous year, Luke and Jim met online through each other's YouTube videos and quickly discovered they shared parallel lives. Both once worked in the tech industry, and both turned their lives upside down for the love of a three-legged dog who'd lost a leg to cancer. Now, they were each embarking on life-changing, cross-country journeys ignited by a deep desire to prove cancer can't keep a good dog—or his people—down. But that's where the similarities ended.

Jim and Rene were traveling in their comfortable home on wheels. But Luke would make his journey with two dogs, on foot. He had just lost his beautiful, big Great Pyrenees Malcolm to the same cancer that took Jerry's leg. Now, he was about to start walking with his two new dogs, Hudson and Murphy. They would travel from Austin to Boston, raising awareness and money for canine cancer research along the way. In a few weeks, Jerry, Jim, and Rene would be at Luke's starting line in Texas, excited and ready to help kick things off.

*　*　*

The long east-west drive along Interstate 10 is as generic as highway travel gets, with not much more than injury lawyer billboards to break the monotony. Texas was days away, and they were making decent enough time to add one more bucket list item to Jerry's list of post-cancer accomplishments: swimming in the Gulf Coast. Rene spied the perfect spot as they drove along the Florida Panhandle where the long, sweeping shoreline along a calm, blue bay called out for disruption.

Jim parked the truck as close to the shore as he could, and they waded into the warm Gulf waters with Jerry treading alongside. The tennis ball in Jim's hand lured him further into the water until it reached just up to Jerry's withers, a perfect depth for a proper resistance workout—and better yet, spectacular pictures of the watery milestone.

He pitched the ball far out into the knee-deep water. Before the green orb even left his hand, Jerry launched himself airborne out of the bay. Resembling a great white shark in flight, hungry for prey with wide, gaping jaws, an invisible set of wings propelled him toward the prize. One throw, two throws, three…they could have spent all afternoon watching exuberant Jerry go for the ball. But now, Jim and Rene knew better. Before he grew too tired to swim ashore, Rene called Jerry to the beach, then swaddled him like a burrito in a big, colorful towel to dry him off. Smiling from ear to ear and feeling more pleased than ever about their choice to take their "dying dog" on the road, Rene and Jim stood over Jerry, hearts overflowing with gratitude at their Chief Fun Officer's continued longevity.

— 16 —

Following Their Passion

The party with Luke in Austin was just what they hoped it would be: a celebration with dozens of dog-crazy people like themselves. On a warm, sunny day, dogs and people kicked off Luke's human and paw-powered public relations journey to raise awareness of canine cancer. After the hoopla, he went eastbound on his own cross-country trek, and Jim pointed the rig in the opposite direction. They had been on the road fourteen months, exploring potential occupations and enjoying beautiful places they might eventually call home. Each job and new town was interesting or fun in its own way, but none had enough appeal to hold them for more than a few weeks. Finally, it occurred to them that they may never decide on the perfect place to lay roots. "Why couldn't we just keep going?" Rene said aloud one day. The idea of living full-time in their RV with no end date in sight began looking like an option.

❊   ❊   ❊

I could get used to this… Jim thought quietly to himself and smiled, gazing out upon the long, empty road ahead of him as they headed west on Interstate 10. He adjusted the rearview mirror as he always did so he could look Rene in the eyes without turning his head. She was nodding off again, which always made him chuckle. Like a fussy baby being taken for a car ride to settle down, road motion was an instant sleeping pill for her. Her head lolled over to one side, then the other, then back again until she settled into a gentle snore as they rolled on down the highway. She reminded him of Homer Simpson falling asleep on the job at the nuclear reactor plant. At least her dozing posed no threat to her career or national security. But the thought of his career and their own financial security made Jim wonder…just where were they headed?

Living on the road was an intriguing idea, but the FUD nagged at him. He was a responsible guy, after all. Jim needed to know that if they were to become permanent nomads, they could still cover costs. Making an income this way felt overwhelming. Living expenses, retirement savings, insurance—these were the usual things hardworking adults do to make sure they don't end up living in a cardboard box. Normal people wait for retirement to do something as crazy as living in a RV by choice. He never considered himself "normal," but a deep fear of growing old without enough money nagged at him around every bend in the road.

"How are we going to make a living?" His brow tensed with the very idea. When he glanced up in the rearview mirror hoping for some feedback, he saw Rene was out cold. He looked to the back seat, but his other copilot was sound asleep too. "Am I the only one who's worried?" The vast expanse of West Texas flatlands was just ahead, a perfect opportunity to focus on their future.

Sure, he gave up the presumed security of his Silicon Valley career path to become an entrepreneur, but ten years after doing that, things were different. Way different. Now he and Rene were totally on their own, burning through their savings. They were flying blind with no business plan or bank loan to launch them into success. If a constant wandering lifestyle was to be their new normal, they had to find a way to make their savings last until whatever "next big thing" revealed itself. Whatever they ended up doing next, they would be starting over from scratch. Ten years earlier, they took a similar leap of faith when they left the big city, bought a house, and started up their graphics business. The building, overhead, supplies, and fulfillment drained their time and their bank account, but they had a plan to follow and made it work. This time around, their home office had wheels, with little overhead but no storage for supplies, either. Yet their skills remained. All they needed was a niche market to apply those skills and generate an income from anywhere they pleased.

He thought long and hard about their next business. And somewhere between Odessa and El Paso, it hit him: the growing fanbase for their website was their biggest asset. But could sharing pet amputation recovery and care advice help them pay some bills? Sure, it's as narrow as any niche gets, he thought, but Jerry had a big following, with new fans arriving almost daily. The Internet could help them share their passion for educating people about the great quality of life three-legged pets can enjoy. But unlike last time, when they sold printed posters and displays to corporations, this time they couldn't—no, wouldn't—do any sort of hard sell or aggressive marketing to people in emotional and financial distress. By the time they crossed the New Mexico border, growing Tripawds.com seemed like a logical move.

A year earlier, Jim had inserted subtle affiliate ads on the website for pet-centric products. Each time someone clicked, Tripawds got a few pennies. Literally. Fifty cents here and a buck there was better than nothing, but monthly earnings never covered all the costs of keeping the site online. They both had their hearts in Tripawds, but how could it become a business and stay true to their goal of not selling out for the sake of a dollar? Their best-selling "product" was a warm, fuzzy feeling of comfort and support from others who had also faced amputation for their beloved dog. "Hmm, pretty slim profit margin," he said to nobody in particular. "There's got to be products that people would find useful. Maybe we could resell them and make money that way?" It was a gamble, but as Jim kept driving toward the West Coast with his sleeping passengers, more ideas appeared on the horizon.

*   *   *

Every day for many months, Jerry received messages from people with lots of questions. "What's your diet like?" "How long did it take your fur to grow back?" "Can three-legged dogs swim?" Jim and Rene did their best to answer every email, but it didn't take long for them to admit they could only do so much. After all, they only had experience dealing with osteosarcoma of the front limb in a large-breed dog. Neither one had any idea how a pug missing a rear leg might cope with mast cell tumors. Or how a blind Great Dane could handle life on three legs. Jim realized that the best way to help all these people was to create a way for them to communicate directly with each other.

In late February 2008, Jim spent long hours making their website ideas happen. He researched ways to help a website's members talk to one another, and within days, the Tripawds Forums were born. Jerry shared the exciting news in his blog, but the new discussion forums remained quiet for a few days. Jim—who posted as "Admin"—created a couple test user accounts to post replies and make sure everything was working correctly. He and Rene—who became the voice of "Jerry"—added helpful information in the empty forums, which gave them a place to point people with questions about amputation and recovery. Then, they waited.

Six days later, a reply appeared from their very first registered member with the user name singlepaw. The pet parent introduced Eisen, a 110-pound German shepherd, and gave details about his recovery and treatment. Jim was relieved. The new forums worked, and members were doing what they were supposed to do—sharing stories and encouragement with each other for all to see.

Singlepaw, Admin, and Jerry became fast online friends. Eventually, they all met in person when Jerry's road trip returned to Colorado months later. Eisen was the first to embody the hopeful spirit that Jim and Rene wanted to convey with Tripawds. Despite the six-month prognosis he got, the confident shepherd loved life on three legs for more than four years—beating all the odds against him. Later, Jim and Rene would share numerous stories about dogs of all different breeds and sizes. These heroes eventually inspired thousands of pet parents just like them to seek encouragement and hope from the community.

❋   ❋   ❋

As Jerry's survival story unfolded along the highway, more Tripawds members registered and participated in the forums to share details about their own dogs' treatment plans and results. Each time Jim and Rene checked in, they could see a pattern developing with all the new forum topics. First, a new member posts in a panic, distraught by the news of their dog needing an amputation. Next, existing users would calm their fears, answer common questions and then provide reassurance about how pets handle amputation. Eventually, that same frightened member often returned to welcome and help other newcomers.

The plan was working. Tripawds was helping people. Jim and Rene were passionate about what they were doing, but they still had a problem. They weren't making any money. A business expert might have blamed their lack of income on the absence of a business plan. But they didn't care. Tripawds was less of a business and more of a calling. Shoving their life's work into a business plan seemed like it would rob the joy from their new "job." Tripawds had no market analysis and no forecast, but winging it just felt right at the time. Besides, workamping jobs were plentiful and an easy to way to cut rent expenses. Their next gig was starting soon, so at least they had the luxury of time to think about where Tripawds was headed without worrying about rent.

In their old life they sold products to people, but in this one they were on their own, with no clients to pitch. Or so he thought. One evening, Jim noticed Jerry was still wearing his Web Master harness as he slept quietly on the bed, his vanilla-colored chest gently rising and falling with each breath. That harness was so helpful for getting Jerry into and out of the truck, going up and down stairs, and in other situations too. Then it hit him. Maybe the harness manufacturer, Ruffwear, would work with them so they could sell the harness they loved so much. With no way to stock different sizes and colors in the RV, Jim worked up the courage to call the company anyway.

The friendly sales rep explained that becoming a dealer was easy. But before he could ask about shipping services the company might provide, the sale rep beat him to it. "We can ship them for you from our warehouse—for a small fee, of course. You'll just need to sell at least a dozen a year to maintain your distributor status."

Nervous about having even asked, he stammered, "Oh. Well, uhh…we serve a pretty small market niche, but we will certainly give it a try!"

Jim felt enthusiastic enough to get on board as a distributor, but deep down, the FUD factor knotted his stomach. They would only make a few dollars off each harness. Most Ruffwear retail dealers made up for that in volume, the rep explained. Then, despite the minimal profit from each sale, Jim eagerly agreed to sign up. "Even a buck or two is better than the few cents we're getting from affiliate sales," he explained to Rene at the dinner table. She was onboard, and the very next day after Jerry announced that his favorite harness was for sale on his blog, Tripawds received its first sale. Others soon followed.

They could see that Tripawds had the makings of a so-called real business, but Rene and Jim never saw it that way. "Forget a business plan!" Rene half-joked, knowing that any smart entrepreneur would have one by now. Their lack of one didn't matter. Offering compassion and support was more important than profiting off people in distress. Doing otherwise felt like betraying their mission to make amputation and cancer a little less scary. With the first few harness sales behind them, Jim and Rene agreed to let any commercial aspect of the site just happen naturally. If they followed their passion and stayed true to their goal, they knew the money would appear.

Whenever Jim had doubts about this crazy niche market's ability to support them, he reflected upon a favorite Deepak Chopra quote: "Always go with your passions. Never ask yourself if it's realistic or not."

❖   ❖   ❖

Like Chopra, animals never ask if it's realistic to live happily on three legs. They just do. When Jerry lost his leg, he never wondered if he would swim again, he just did. He let passion drive his activity, and now Jim and Rene were doing the same.

Two years later, their passion would lead them to Blog Paws, a pet industry blogging conference, where they hoped to learn more ways to help Jerry's growing website pay for itself. Whether they realized it or not, Jim and Rene were now in the blogging business. This pet blogging and social media conference had educational seminars and networking with pet industry brand representatives they looked forward to meeting. The first time they attended the event, both realized Tripawds could become a "real" business, even when considering the sensitive nature of their niche and their desire to not make the site too commercial.

At a social mixer being held one evening, they noticed a well-dressed woman sitting by herself. They made eye contact, and the woman invited them to her table. "Hi, I'm Lena."

Jim and Rene introduced themselves. She had questions about their three-legged dog blog and held herself the way powerful women do, with a calm yet strong presence and a warm, engaging smile that made them feel comfortable discussing their unique blogging niche and how it all began.

"So, what's your business model?" She was direct and straightforward.

A blank stare fell upon Rene's face as she turned to Jim. Every other blogger they had met only wanted to talk about dogs and cats. Or ferrets. This woman was strictly business.

Thinking fast, Jim replied, "We operate on the Freemium business model." He had learned about the term long before, but it was that very moment when he was put on the spot to answer such a fundamental business question that the term came to mind. "Freemium" was precisely what they were doing.

"We offer a bunch of free content and services and charge a premium for extra features and benefits." He went on to describe their Tripawds Supporter Blogs platform. This allowed members to create their own free blogs, which he explained have ads that are automatically removed if a user upgrades their site for a nominal fee. He then discussed how they turned much of their free blog content into a couple e-books they sold for those who would rather not spend the time searching for answers in the blogs and forums. Without realizing it at the time, their business plan was taking shape, right as Jim described it.

"Smart!" Lena nodded with a look of acceptance. The three of them returned to small talk as they enjoyed the complimentary happy hour fare.

It wasn't until the next day during the big luncheon that Jim and Rene realized this was The Lena West—a social media and marketing guru, business growth expert, and keynote speaker for the conference. They hadn't just made a new friend; they had met their new mentor. This straight-talking, self-made entrepreneur who knew all the right questions to ask would prove instrumental to Rene and Jim over the years for helping them grow Tripawds as a business while staying true to their philanthropic aspirations.

        ❖   ❖   ❖

Between the methods they learned at Blog Paws and coaching from Lena, the Tripawds community slowly started to generate income. It wasn't much, but it was money they could feel good about, and it allowed them to stay on the road instead of searching for a traditional business. Every day, Jim tinkered with the website and watched it grow with pride. Tripawds was reaching more people than ever, and other pet parents were helping one another get through the same traumatic situation they had faced with Jerry.

Jim was clearly on to something. But after a couple more years of barely making ends meet by publishing sponsored content campaigns and pitching new engagement partners, he came to another realization: Tripawds could never become their only business. Not if they kept paying the ever-increasing hosting costs necessary as the site grew, out of their own pockets. But every time he approached the subject of charging a membership fee to use the site, Rene fought back. "It has to be free! We aren't money-grubbers!" she protested every time. Eventually, he realized he felt the same way.

They were doing good things, but maintaining more than 1,000 member blogs and producing more free resources was taking its toll on both their time and their bank account. Hosting and management costs were steadily increasing right along with the growing Tripawds network. It was time to get serious or give in and start another real organization. Instead, they did both.

With the help of a generous lawyer who had her own three-legged dog, the 501(c)(3) Tripawds Foundation came together in 2014. It had one simple mission: to help amputee pets and their people everywhere. Now they could host real fundraising drives, not just beg for donations during sporadic campaigns with more effort than actual revenue. The nonprofit structure not only gave them the ability to keep the website free, but also to help members directly with services like a toll-free helpline, financial help for amputation surgery, and paying for a Tripawd's first rehab therapy visit. And it all started with one cancer diagnosis that felt like the end of the world.

If you had asked Jim if he ever thought Tripawds would be what he'd be doing for a living on the day he headed west along that Texas highway, he would have laughed out loud. He'd have laughed even harder if you'd told him he and Rene would be running a nonprofit foundation for amputee pets, or that they would be chosen to give the keynote speech at a canine cancer conference. The title of their talk? *Be More Dog.*

❧   ❧   ❧

Blazing orange and yellow bands spread far and wide across the horizon while Jim piloted the RV west, his hopes and dreams for Tripawds growing clearer by the mile. He glanced in the cockeyed mirror, then let out a loud, exaggerated gasp and tapped the brakes just hard enough to jolt Rene awake. The stunned expression she wore made him break into hysterics.

Rene's eyes snapped open as she abruptly sat upright. "Whoa! What?" A second later, she realized the brake tap was another one of Jim's pranks. "Don't do that! You scared me!"

Jerry clued in, jumped up, and poked his head over the seats to investigate.

"Some navigator you are." Jim pointed at the map on the floor at her feet. "It's getting late. Care to find us a place to stay?" Darkness was minutes away as the setting sun shone brightly through the windshield.

"Yeah, yeah, I'll find a park. Just don't do that again!" She grabbed the map and thwacked him softly. "Where exactly are we?"

Jim paused a moment, his voice turning soft as he answered, "You know, I'm not sure. But I have the feeling we are on the right path."

Rene squinted at him with a quizzical look. "Uhh, okay...somehow I don't think you're talking about this place." Lost in thought, he didn't respond, so she suggested, "How about we just start with where we are, here, right now?"

He nodded. "One road at a time, baby. One road at a time."

BE MORE DOG

— 17 —

Now What?

Jerry's pack usually preferred meandering along rural back roads to get to their destination, but this time Rene was anxious to surprise her family with a quick visit before their New Mexico workamping job started in a few weeks. Driving the west's wide-open roads came easy to Jim, and he didn't mind making the long-distance haul to get them to Los Angeles in time for a quick visit.

Rene put down her knitting and turned to Jim. "Oh! I just remembered that Jerry's out of heartworm medication. I'm sure my sister's vet will squeeze us in when we get to LA. We gotta do that, okay? Remind me!"

"Don't forget to call your sister's vet about the heartworm stuff."

She smirked and shook her head, returning to look at her latest yarn project.

"Hey, you can't say I didn't remind you!" He grinned in return, knowing he would never remember to remind her.

Managing Jerry's veterinary needs on the road was less complicated than they expected, once they decided against the frequent follow-up x-rays that come standard with every osteosarcoma diagnosis. Seventeen months after surgery and ten thousand miles later, Jerry's good fortune had been on their side. He still looked great, and all he needed now was some vet-prescribed parasite prevention. His cancer might have been growing, but it was laying low. Every day the so-called dying dog woke up just as energetic and happy as always, ready for another adventure. When they looked in his glowing eyes, denial came easy. How could Jerry have one of the fastest-growing bone cancers lurking around inside him? He sure didn't appear to be sick.

❖　❖　❖

More than a year before, the UC Davis vet warned, "There's a good chance cancer has already spread." He wasn't trying to scare them, but was just giving the standard information to educate his clients. "Usually, by the time we see the tumor in a limb, microscopic masses have already appeared in the lungs. It's called micrometastases, or lung mets. We know they are usually present, just too small to see on an x-ray."

"So, how do we know if he has them?" Rene had already been worrying about the next stage of the disease.

"Well, you can do a CAT scan, which will pick up the smallest mets." The vet described how the expensive procedure would cost a couple thousand dollars and require another sedation. "Or, you can choose to get more routine x-rays to monitor their growth. Mets tend to appear in the lungs first, but won't become a real concern until they grow large enough to impact his breathing and energy.

"And then what?" Jim wondered where this discussion was heading.

"Well, chemotherapy is always an option to help slow the spread of metastatic disease. But when that does occur, we can also try to remove any large masses with another surgery, called a lobectomy." The vet noticed their dual frowns, which clearly showed they weren't interested in any further surgeries for Jerry. "Or, you can skip the operation and do nothing."

"I'm all for doing nothing." Jim made it clear that chemotherapy was off the table. He and Rene were in total agreement there, without even really discussing it.

"I am too." She reached down to rub Jerry's ears. "If we really only do have a few months left with him, driving down here for all those treatments seems unfair to him. Remember, we live six hours away."

Jim nodded and thought of their remaining time with Jerry. "Frequent checkups, huh? I think that we'd rather not know."

And now here they were, seventeen months later, still confident that doing nothing had been the best decision. Life on the road seemed so good for Jerry's health, and there was no denying that constant change was the best medicine to help him thrive. They were both pretty certain Jerry would agree. All he ever wanted was for everyone around him to be happy, and not even cancer could take that away.

Gridlock greeted them at the Los Angeles county line. Nothing had changed. For the first time since he got behind the wheel of their RV, Jim gripped the steering wheel tightly through the stop-and-go traffic. Over one stressful hour later, he navigated the RV through the narrow side streets of Rene's hometown, then slowly pulled their rig under the big tree in front of her parents' house. Once he shut off the engine, he swore he would never drive the trailer into LA again.

"Rene!?" Her mom opened the front door and squealed in her high voice, shaking her head in disbelief. "Jim! What are you doing here!?" She reached up to hug her youngest daughter and favorite son-in-law. "Oh, Jerry, you too!" Jerry was already squeezing between their legs for his hug, too.

Her plan to surprise Mom and Dad had paid off. "We just made a little detour before we go to New Mexico."

"Hah! We thought you ran away with the gypsies." Rene's dad appeared in the entry. "I can't believe you're here!"

Rene and Jim couldn't believe it either. They had just circled the entire country and traveled as far away from California as possible, and now they were back to the state where they'd started more than a year before. She missed her family, but the frenetic pace that made her leave LA in the first place seemed worse than ever. Jim loved her parents as well, but found Southern California so exhausting. "There's just too many people!" After ten years in the "Lost Coast" up north, and more than a year roaming the back roads of small-town America, he felt like a foreigner in California.

It was nice to see the folks, but it wouldn't be long before they were back on the open road. Their job in New Mexico was an excellent excuse for a short but sweet visit with the family. That, and the heartworm medication they needed for Jerry. Before they unpacked their overnight bag, Rene was on the phone scheduling Jerry for a wellness appointment. Three days later, she and Jim sat in the vet's exam room with Jerry and waited. Minutes later a tall, thin man in a white lab coat entered. "Hi, I'm Dr. Mazzy. This must be the famous three-legged dog I keep hearing about!"

"Yep, that's him!" Rene knew he had already received the backstory from her sister, whose daughter was best friends with the ET's own kids. It felt nice to meet a doctor familiar with their gypsy lifestyle and Jerry's cancer.

"How's he doing with all that traveling?" The vet got down on the floor and placed his hands on Jerry's body to check for mystery lumps. Jerry responded gleefully, as if getting a massage.

"He's great! So far no signs of cancer, and he's as happy as ever." Jim was eager to get on with the exam. "We're just here for some heartworm medication before we go east again."

"Ah, sure, we can help with that!" The vet pointed a flashlight into Jerry's pointy ears and soft eyes, then asked the usual health questions. "How's his appetite? What about his energy level?" When Rene reached into her bag and handed him a short stack of Jerry's medical records, he grinned. "I like that you're prepared; that's great."

"Well, we never know when we'll need to see a vet. I'm just glad this is for something simple." She was looking forward to another stellar checkup.

The vet then took the bell of his stethoscope and placed it on Jerry's lungs. He listened intently to Jerry's breathing. "So, when was the last time he had radiographs of his lungs?"

His inquiry caught them off guard. They had just come for the heartworm medication; why was he asking this? Would they look like bad parents if they told him the truth? Rene inwardly searched for the best words to explain their decision to skip x-rays.

Jim was ready though, and didn't flinch. "We haven't had any done since his amputation. That was over a year ago; seventeen months, to be exact."

The vet could see they loved their dog but was curious as to why they would skip such a vital step in standard cancer care. "You know that routine chest scans are a good idea for a dog with this kind of cancer, right?"

Yes, Rene and Jim were aware of the recommendation. She did her best to justify their decision. "But since we aren't doing any chemotherapy, we decided to skip it."

Jim backed her up with a firm voice full of conviction. "It's not like we're living in denial or anything. We do know what signs to look for when it returns. We wouldn't do anything differently if we did find out he had mets, so we prefer not to know."

The curious vet sat cross-legged and quiet as he stroked Jerry's back. His shiny coat, pearly white teeth, and bright eyes gave no clues that cancer could be spreading somewhere in his body. But when he listened to Jerry's lungs, he didn't like what he heard. He knew he had to choose his words carefully. At the time, it was unusual for a canine cancer patient to survive more than a year with this disease, especially one who didn't get chemotherapy. Without a doubt, the miracle dog sitting next to him was living on borrowed time. He had seen this kind of cancer before. Based on the rasp he heard in Jerry's lungs, odds were pretty good that the disease had progressed. He hoped he was wrong, but ethically, he had to encourage the diagnostic options.

"So, here's one way to look at it. No, you're not going to do chemo. But if you knew what was happening, you would feel more in charge of the cancer instead of letting the disease take charge of you."

Rene and Jim stared into each other's eyes. It almost made sense.

"Knowledge is powerful stuff. For a disease like cancer, it can help you prepare for what may be next, instead of being surprised by it. This is just me, but I really do think it's better to know than not know."

Jim and Rene sat quietly looking at each other, then watched Jerry happily return the vet's affections by leaning into his gentle scratches. He seemed so enamored of the kind man, as if they had known each other for years.

"It's better to know than not know..." The vet's words echoed in their heads.

Part of Jim couldn't believe this nasty disease could be killing his healthy-looking dog. Jerry seemed in such good shape. He had good stamina, went on walks, did things like any regular dog. This was no sick dog. He was confident they weren't going to find anything, but the vet kinda made sense.

Rene, too, struggled with the recommendation. Cancer had knocked them down once, but they got back up and went on with life. And what a life it was! Jerry showed them how to be happy even in the worst-case scenario, and that was how Rene wanted to live too. Sure, she and Jim carried the burden of knowing all about his diagnosis, but after seventeen months, she'd gotten pretty good at forgetting he had cancer. Now, this vet was about to pull her out of the very denial they pretended not to have.

Dr. Mazzy said nothing, and played with Jerry while his suggestion sank in. Jim looked into Rene's eyes. "What do you think?"

"Well...yeah, I guess that all makes sense. If we want to be smart about this, we should probably do it." She sighed as Jerry stepped over and licked her face.

Jim turned to Dr. Mazzy, and with all the confidence he had in him, gave the go-ahead. "Sure. Let's do it. As you said, it's better to know… right?" He was questioning himself more than asking the vet.

❄   ❄   ❄

The look and feel of vet exam rooms seldom changes. Sterile and cold, with uncomfortable chairs, bright, florescent lights, and the faint aroma of rubbing alcohol make it hard to tell one practice from another. While Jim and Rene sat in silence waiting for Jerry to return, it felt as if a time machine had transported them back to the time and place of his amputation day. Jim rubbed his cold, sweaty palms on his lap and stared at the floor. Rene gnawed on the edge of her pinky fingernail. Neither spoke, and when they finally heard footsteps coming closer, they half-expected to see Jerry's surgeon from just over a year before open the door. But this time, it was their moment of truth with the family vet.

Jerry nudged his muzzle through the door and hopped to Jim as the vet let go of his leash. "What a good boy! He didn't even need sedation." The vet carried x-rays in his other hand and turned to hang the films on the wall-mounted light box. Then he faced his clients to deliver the news.

"So, this is what we've got, guys." He pointed at the two black-and-white images of Jerry's rib cage and zeroed in on two faint white spots. "Honestly, it's not that bad. I thought that at this stage in his cancer, his lungs would have a lot more lesions like this, but he just has these two. See here? And here."

"What's not that bad?" Rene looked confused, and Jim thought he wasn't hearing things right. Did he just say their Jerry had cancer blobs growing in his lungs? If so, this was plenty bad.

"I'm really sorry. Let me start over." Dr. Mazzy circled the faint masses on the films with his finger. "These two spots here are metastases, the lung mets we discussed. From cancer."

The light box glare stung like an electric shock as the two fuzzy white blobs inside Jerry's lungs became crystal clear, taunting them from the wall. It was impossible to tell how long the monsters had been hiding out or how fast they were growing. Perhaps, if they had gotten more frequent radiographs, this wouldn't have come as such a surprise. After all, Jerry still wasn't showing any signs of the disease spreading. His vibrant, healthy body made it easy to forget he was technically sick. Maybe they had been in denial all along, but until that moment, he seemed like the same old dog he ever was, with one less leg.

"So, now what?" Jim asked the vet. "How bad is it?"

"I expected to see a much larger mass or lots more mets in both lungs. That's the normal progression with this disease. So, with only the two mets we can see here, and in just one lung, well...technically, it's not bad compared to others I've seen." The vet was doing his best to soften the blow of the bomb he'd just dropped.

The x-rays made it hard to gauge the actual size of the mets. But when the vet described them as "golf-ball-sized," the gravity of his illness progression became clear. He reminded them how a cancer cell's job is to replicate quickly, survive, and continue to multiply. At this rate, those mets could soon take over his lungs. Jerry would slowly suffocate to death if the tumors marched on unchecked. They sat in stunned silence, taking it all in.

"Can chemotherapy do anything for him now?" Rene surprised herself with the question she'd just blurted out. She and Jim had unanimously ruled out chemo just about a year earlier. But at this moment of truth, things were so different. Now, they knew what his future held and it didn't look good. Jerry was far beyond the six-month prognosis he had been given. He'd beaten the odds and showed none of the classic signs of slowing down. He was not lethargic. There was no deep, wet cough, and his breathing sounded fine. At least, it did to them. She wondered if a few shots of some expensive drug might help him enjoy more time. At that moment, she'd do anything to keep his momentum going.

"There may be treatments that can help, I really don't know for sure though." The vet seemed happy his clients were more open to managing the disease. "An oncologist can tell you more. I'm no cancer specialist, but I can write up a referral if you'd like."

Thinking back to Jerry's original veterinarian in Eureka who refused to collaborate with specialists, they appreciated his willingness to admit he didn't know.

Jim could see where this was going. "And if we don't do anything?"

"Well, when they get big enough, he won't be able to breathe. Euthanasia is usually next because labored breathing is very tiring for the dog. There's no telling how soon that could happen; not without an oncologist's opinion."

Jerry looked up at them with bright eyes. He was still the same old dog. All he wanted to do was get back outside, sniff the grass, and meet new people and dogs. The glowing black-and-white films on the wall didn't matter to him. Jim and Rene studied their oblivious hero, and after what seemed like an hour, made a silent pact while the vet waited for their answer.

Her raised eyebrows conveyed her thoughts to Jim. "We need to look at our options."

He simply nodded to her, thinking, *But we'll take time to decide what's next.* Then he broke the silence. "Okay, Doc, I think we'll take you up on that referral. We owe it to him to at least look into our options." The news still hadn't sunk in, and they were both eager to get out of there.

With the heartworm medication in one hand, Rene stared at the oncologist referral slip in her other. Jim guided her through the door so she wouldn't crash into it and Jerry guided them out into the sunshine wearing the canine version of a smile on his face. All were quite happy to get away from that place.

They walked Jerry to the truck and Jim hoisted him up into the back seat. He could see that nothing had changed in Jerry's happy eyes, but now, everything was different for the people he cared about. Jim and Rene felt so heavy from the burden of making a move to deal with Jerry's cancer. Both knew the time had come to get their heads out of the sand and do something about this awful disease.

＊　　＊　　＊

Later that night, a surreal scene played out in the darkest corners of Jim's mind. It felt straight out of some old Disney cartoon. A background of black and dark-green trees scrolled by, as if painted on acetate. The pattern repeatedly passed by as the three clueless characters trotted along the center of the screen. But there was no eerie soundtrack, just utter silence. Jim was alarmed by the dense forest canopy shrouding them in darkness. This was no dream; it was his rather vivid nightmare.

The three of them walked through the animated, two-dimensional forest. Rene's head comically bobbed forward as she strutted along, focused on something far ahead in the distance. Her gaze never moved or changed. Jim was much jumpier, his eyes scanning the woods as he checked out every shifting shadow. Jerry hopped along with his head held high, until his smile melted into a more serious sneer as he fell behind the pack.

Jim could feel the presence of something sinister. Then he saw it in the trees. Two glowing, red eyes belonging to a big, bad wolf started the terrifying chase, taunting and giving them a hard time as they tried to flee the dark scene. The devilish wolf leapt from behind, going from one tree to the next. Then he raced ahead, peeking around another tree, then disappearing, only to creep up from behind them again on tiptoes. Jim only caught a glimpse of the hairy stalker, but the vision was clear as day. The Big Bad Wolf was dirty and nasty, baring big, pointy teeth, drool dripping from his open jaws and with long, razor-sharp claws that could destroy prey with one fell swoop. The beast followed along, more menacing and threatening than before. Jim shivered as sweat fell from his brow. He couldn't turn back, and his feet felt like lead, making running impossible. The Big Bad Wolf was hot on their heels.

"Go on, guys, I got this," Jerry conveyed with impressive, wolf-like barks. Then he lunged and took off after the enemy. He barked and snarled, but the evil wolf persisted. Undeterred, Jerry ran like a sheepdog on the prairie and galloped big, sweeping runs around his flock. He barked fierce, teeth-snapping warnings again and again at the pair of red eyes glaring through the darkness.

"No, no. No…" Jim's murmurs got louder.

"Wake up!" Rene shoved him harder. "Wake up! You're having a bad dream."

"What?" Jim opened his eyes and saw Jerry standing at the side of the bed. "What's going on?" He felt disoriented as he lay on his back all sweaty and clammy. He had no idea where they were, and struggled to regain clarity. It was 3:00 a.m.

"You're all sweaty. Wanna talk about it?"

"No." The Fear, Uncertainty, and Doubt had returned.

Jim rolled back over on his side, only to see Jerry standing watch and staring at his boss as if to say, "I told you, it's all good."

The dream continued nagging at his thoughts on the following day. He had to purge it from his mind. So he did what felt most natural, and allowed Jerry to share his thoughts about the ordeal in the Tripawds blog:

— 181 —

Chasing rabbits, rabid wolves, whatever. As long as I get to run in my dreams. Let Jim think that the dream is a positive sign. That I will fight to the death to be happy together with my people. Why not? After all, I know they would do the same for me.

— 18 —

Living in the Now!

The comforting aroma of sizzling eggs and refried beans wafted through the kitchen while oil splatters popped out of the hot pan filled with homemade tamales. Rene's mom stood at the stove warming tortillas while her dad sat at the table reading the LA Times, ready to be served. Jim woke up feeling exhausted and without much of an appetite, but wasn't about to pass up his favorite breakfast. He forced a smile and greeted the folks. "Yum! Smells great in here." He poured himself a cup of just-brewed, strong coffee.

"Good morning, Jim; serve yourself!"

"Oh I will, thank you!" He took the plate from her hand, piled it high with tamales, one egg over easy, avocado, and fresh salsa. He sat down and smiled with thankful eyes, but feeling upbeat was hard.

"Morning," Rene's dad grumbled, then started rambling about current events as he handed Jim the front page. Living on the road, they rarely had the pleasure of diving into a local paper, but today wasn't the day for it. Jim just couldn't shake off the shock of his vivid nightmare. Or his worry over Jerry's state of health. The Big Bad Wolf had stolen his sleep, and hard news was the last thing he wanted to read. Rene didn't stick around for breakfast; she was already at her computer researching their treatment options.

"Here's the best part." Rene's dad smiled and handed Jim the comics.

"Perfect, thanks." Jim was a big fan of MUTTS, and that day in early March 2008 the strip's creator, Patrick McDonnell, seemed to know just what he needed to get through the day.

March 4, 2008

MUTTS © 2019 Patrick McDonnell

Ozzie sat working at his desk, wondering what time it was. His faithful dog, Earl, jumped up barking, "Now! Now! Now!"

Ozzie takes Earl for a walk and says, "Dogs always know what time it is."

Was it some kind of sign? A genuine grin spread across Jim's face as he looked around for Jerry. Blissfully unaware and content, the dog lay patiently several feet away on a rug, keeping one eye on the table and hoping for a taste of whatever it was that smelled so good. When he saw Jim staring intently, Jerry arose on those long, lean legs of his, stretched, and shook the sleepy kinks out of his body. Jim's eye contact could only mean one thing: food!

"Shh, don't tell Rene." He tore off a chunk of the thick flour tortilla and threw it across the room. Always eager for snacks, Jerry snapped his prize out of the air.

Jerry didn't need Mutts to tell him what he already knew. Every day was today, and the time was always Now. And right now, he wanted to know why they weren't out having some fun somewhere.

"We'll go play in just a bit, buddy."

Jerry heard that familiar old tone of empty promises in Jim's voice and walked away in search of Rene. Maybe she had some pan dulce for him. Not that she would ever give him any more of that Mexican sweet bread after learning that cancer feeds on sugar. But Jerry was on the hunt, and seemed keenly aware that his tactical pleading sometimes produced results.

When Rene declined the sweet treat he stood by her side, looking up at her as if to question why. Was it the thing she was staring at on the computer screen? He didn't know. After a moment, he gave up, went outside to the big avocado tree, and plopped down in the dirt with a sigh.

Jim took his last bite of tamale, then reached for a pair of scissors hanging next to the phone on the wall. Carefully and with precision, he cut the Mutts comic strip out of the paper. For the first time, Jerry's finite lifespan felt real. That little reminder to live in the now was perfect timing.

❧   ❧   ❧

Rene knew that if they were going to pursue treatment for Jerry's lung metastasis, doing it in a busy city like Los Angeles was not an option. Their home was on wheels, so why not get care in a prettier, more serene place that better suited them? In two weeks their new workamping job at a hot springs resort in the aptly named Truth or Consequences, New Mexico, was about to begin. They were heading that direction next week and as she surfed the Internet, she found a veterinary cancer care clinic just a couple hours north in Santa Fe. It had a board-certified veterinary oncologist on staff—a rarity in 2008— which guaranteed Jerry would have access to the newest cancer treatments. She picked up the phone and dialed.

In that instant, the stars aligned to make the sad situation more manageable. "Yes, I'll take that day," Rene told the receptionist on the phone as she booked the soonest appointment available. "We'll see you next week, thank you."

Jim walked in to show her the source of his resurrected happiness, knowing it would help her too. He looked down at the comic strip in his hand, which demanded: "Now! Now! Now!" The powerful simplicity of the three words made him smile as he placed the comic on Rene's keyboard. But she barely glanced down from her screen and hardly cracked a smile. Their travels had taken them far away from that awful time of Jerry's early recovery days, but now she felt overwhelmed, like they were starting all over again. Jim noticed her worried brow and tried to stay rational. There was not much they could do until they met with the oncologist, so he decided to follow Jerry's lead. Then, as if right on cue, Jerry walked up to the screen door and waited. It was time to consult with the CFO.

He left Rene to her research and went outside to make the most of the day ahead. He grabbed a dusty tennis ball and rolled it across the patio for Jerry. "Here ya go, buddy." Back and forth went the ball, skidding across the small, concrete yard. Jerry happily chased his prize but after just a few tosses was worn out enough for a nap in the warm, spring sunshine. He hopped up into the raised patio planter to cool off in the shade of the massive avocado tree. A small flock of chickens clucked at him from their coop, but Jerry didn't feel a need to regulate them. He was content. Jim turned to walk back inside when his cell phone rang.

"Hey, man! It's yer Big Dog!" They hadn't talked since the Austin to Boston walk kick-off party. Jim assumed his friend Luke was calling to ask for help with fundraising. He couldn't have been more wrong.

"You're going to love this, dude. Ya gotta call this person now. Grab a pen!" His enthusiastic tone grabbed Jim's attention. "Her name is Ellen; she's a producer with PBS."

"As in the Public Broadcasting Service? Huh?" Jim grabbed a pen from the table and notebook from Rene's bag, then started writing.

"You've heard of the show *Nature*, right?"

"Yeah...go on."

Luke was in his zone and unstoppable. "Good, look. They're shooting a show all about dogs, and cats too, and the bonds they share with their people. Crazy people like you and me, who do crazy things because they love their pets. Call her now! You have a great story. You need to share it."

"What about you?" Jim wondered why he was passing on the lead. "You're the one walking halfway across the country with your dogs; talk about a great story!"

"Yeah, she loved what I'm doing. But..." He paused. "I am walking for Malcolm, and he's dead. She wants someone who has a dog that's here, now. You have Jerry, man! I told her about your trip, and how you're doing it all for him. She wants to hear more. Go call her, dude!"

※　※　※

The conversation with Ellen was quick; she was for real. The New York City TV documentarian had many respected film credits to her name, including Emmy-award winning documentaries for HBO. Now she was working on a PBS *Nature* episode called *Why We Love Cats and Dogs*, and she wanted to include Jerry's story. Meeting Jim and Rene in Santa Fe the following week would not be a problem for her crew.

One phone call was all it took to get their minds away from Jerry's cancer developments. Instead of worrying about the future, they dreamed about how they might share his story with the entire PBS-watching world. It didn't even matter that they weren't going to get paid. Jerry would get to show the world that amputation isn't the terrible, depressing condition most people believe it is. Jerry would show the world how to live!

🐾 🐾 🐾

One week later, the wandering trio stood outside the Santa Fe veterinary clinic for a quick debriefing with the producer. Rene was glad Ellen spoke quickly. She'd had her eye on the time all morning, and being filmed was not her first priority. All she cared about was being on time for Jerry's first oncology appointment. With the crew assembled and cameras ready to roll, Jerry hopped through the clinic doors while Jim and Rene followed. All eyes turned to Jerry's paparazzi as an assistant circled the reception area to gather image release forms from clinic staff. The soundman appeared from behind and reached out with wireless microphones for Jim and Rene.

"Wait, doesn't Jerry get one?" Everyone laughed as Rene's attempt at comic relief lightened the mood.

They were all wired up for sound when a tall, slender woman in a white lab coat walked into the lobby. Here was the doctor who could help their Jerry, maybe even save his life. At the very least, she would help them understand what their options were for treating late-stage canine cancer.

"Well, this is a bit different," the vet said with a smile as she wrangled a microphone wire inside her long coat. "I'm guessing you're Jim and Rene, and this must be Jerry?"

Rene glanced around at the film crew. "Hah! How did you know?" She doubted the vet got requests every day to bring along a PBS film crew for an oncology consultation. Rene stretched her hand forward with a grin. "You must be Dr. Mullins?"

"Yes. And I've heard all about you, Mister Jerry G. Dawg," she said softly while kneeling to caress his soft ears. Jerry looked up with curiosity, and everyone smiled as the vet moved her hands gently along his body. This vet gave Jim and Rene a good feeling. She had obviously taken the time to read about Jerry before their appointment. There was no need for Rene to explain their unusual lifestyle. She felt like an old friend. "Follow me," she said while walking toward the back of the clinic. Everyone shuffled into the small exam room while the cameras started rolling.

"I've taken a look at Jerry's records. Thank you for sending them." She clipped the x-rays onto the exam room light box. Then she turned and jotted quick notes on a whiteboard mounted behind the door. After quizzing Jim and Rene about Jerry's current health, the vet began her talk.

"Our goal at this point is what we call Stable Disease," she said to Rene and Jim, who stared with attentive eyes. She must have sensed their confusion. "You're both aware that this cancer is not curable, right?" They nodded.

"We just need to keep it from growing or slow down its progress as much as possible—to keep the disease stable. Make sense?"

A moment of clarity lit up Jim's face. "Yes, great. How do we do that?" He knew they might not be able to make Jerry get better, but this hopeful news meant they could help keep him from getting any worse.

"I'm going to show you," she said in a knowledgeable and smart voice but with a warm bedside manner and bright smile that quickly put the nervous pet parents at ease. "There are various modalities for treating metastasis. And every dog is different. You'll never know what works until you give it a try."

The conversation turned more complex as she wrote down Jerry's options on the whiteboard:

Metronomics. Lung lobectomy. COX-2 Inhibitor. Doxycycline. Cyclophosphamide.

She put the cap on her dry-erase pen with an audible click, punctuating their options. "Basically, fighting cancer with different treatments is like throwing pasta at the wall to see if it's cooked."

Jerry looked up at his new friend and stared with curiosity. The vet noticed his unintentionally funny expression, then saw the blank stare on Rene's face. "You keep trying different things until you see what sticks." She grinned at them both and continued. "One thing you can try is Metronomic Chemotherapy treatments. This is low-dose chemotherapy; it is combined with antibiotics and a non-steroidal drug to reduce inflammation and any other side effects."

The cameraman zoomed in to capture the weight of the discussion as Rene reached into her bag for a tissue while Jim stared intently at the writing on the wall. "Chemo?" Jim choked on the word. "We won't be doing any chemotherapy. We already decided we wouldn't put him through all those vet visits and injections."

"Oh, no, sorry. I wasn't clear." Dr. Mullins tapped the whiteboard with her pen. "Cytoxan is a pill you can give him at home."

"At home?" Jim relaxed with a deep exhale. "Well, that's doable." A chemo treatment with minimal side effects, and in pill form? He was glad to see Rene offering a tentative nod.

The vet moved on to the next treatment. "Another option is surgery."

Surgery? Rene and Jim shot looks at each other. The vet could tell they didn't like that idea, but continued explaining every option available. "We could remove a lobe from his lung with the tumors; it's called a lobectomy. That part of the lung is damaged and not functioning anyway, so why not get rid of it? The goal is to prevent these existing lesions from growing any further." She returned to the light box and tapped the ghostly spots in Jerry's lungs. "But this would not guarantee additional mets wouldn't grow somewhere else."

They shook their heads no in unison without saying a word.

"So, his breathing right now is…" Rene hesitated, not exactly sure what she was trying to ask.

"Not compromised much at this stage." The vet finished the sentence. "Those few growths are relatively small now. When the mets do get bigger, dogs can comfortably live with much less lung capacity than people can."

Jim wondered if he was the only one who heard her say "when," not "if," and, "at this stage." The reality of his dog's terminal illness hit home hard, again. "Is there anything else we can do, along with that metro-whatever? Surgery seems so drastic."

Rene agreed, and she wondered if they were about to get the "Go home and make him comfortable" vet speech so typical for this disease. But what she heard next came as a hopeful surprise.

"Yes, there's also immunotherapy and nutraceuticals." Dr. Mullins was schooled in evidence-based Western medicine, but also comfortable recommending more natural remedies. "In fact, there's a new Chinese mushroom supplement we are studying. It helps boost a dog's immune system. I'm running a clinical trial on it, because we want more evidence that it helps the body get stronger and fight off cancer."

Rene and Jim weren't exactly sure what a clinical trial entailed, nor even what a nutraceutical was, but they did know that non-surgical treatment meant they could keep traveling with Jerry.

The vet went on to explain that as part of the trial, these magic mushroom capsules would be free. "All you have to do is file a few reports for me, and you can do that from anywhere." They both smiled. There was nothing more that needed to be said. The camera pulled back from their hopeful smiles as Jerry led them out of the exam room with his wide, swishy tail clearing a path.

*　　*　　*

"Okay, we found a great spot where we can go shoot. You ready?" Neither Jim nor Rene wanted to do much more on camera, but they weren't about to tell the producer no. Exhausted from the appointment, they felt obligated to see this through. Jim started removing his microphone, but the soundman stopped him. "You'll need to leave that on."

The producer's crew split up while Jim and Rene walked back to the RV. "I'm coming with you," the cameraman said as he opened the truck door and crawled into the back seat with Jerry. "Just pretend I'm not here."

Jim laughed as he spied the big camera lens obscuring the rearview mirror. "Nothing like being watched while you haul a ten-thousand-pound trailer through a tight parking lot," he muttered as the producer's car sped up ahead. He relaxed as the long road opened up before them, but felt awkward making up some idle "everyday conversation" with Rene at the cameraman's request. Thankfully, that didn't last long.

The cameraman's radio squawked and he asked them to pull over the next chance they had. "The boss has different plans." Once Jim found a large enough pull-out, the filmmaker grabbed all his gear and jumped out of the truck. "Follow us and stay as close as you can." He handed Rene another radio so they could communicate between the two vehicles as he headed to jump in the producer's car. Only a mile or so down the road, the radio silence broke. "Okay, we're gonna slow down. Stay close!"

"What is he doing?" Rene's jaw dropped as they watched the rear hatch of the SUV speeding in front of them open up with the car barely slowing down. The cameraman gripped a hand-hold inside the back of the van with one hand while leaning toward them and pointing his camera. "Is he filming us?" Rene laughed.

"Smile!" Jim kept pace directly behind the van at a comfortable 40 miles per hour. "This should be fun, as long as they don't hit the brakes." For a second Jim felt like an actor, but then remembered that Jerry was the real star in this show.

"Jerry! Sit up. Look!" Rene tried to wake up the sleepy hero, who couldn't care less about the commotion. Looking up at her with tired eyes, he sighed and nodded back off.

A pair of hands grabbed the cameraman while he reached up to close the back door bobbing in the wind, and the SUV sped up. The radio squawked again, but they couldn't decipher the instructions over the static. Jim quickly realized what was happening as the driver pulled into the opposite lane and slowed down. Once the SUV was driving alongside them, on the wrong side of the road, Jim held his speed and opened the rear window for Jerry. "C'mon, dawg...get up! Look who it is!" He used his best happy voice and laughed as the entire crew car called out and waved from the car speeding beside them.

"Jerrrrrrry! Hey, Jerry Dog! Look over here!" The crew's shouting continued as Jim noticed an oncoming car in the distance.

Rene joined the chorus. "Look, Jerry! Who's that? Look out the window!" She burst into laughter and reached back, urging the reluctant performer to do his job. He sat up slowly from his deep slumber, then raised his now grey-speckled muzzle to sniff the air. When he heard his new friends hooting and hollering at him from the other car, he panted joyfully and poked his head out the window to taste the air with his long, flapping tongue. Jim watched in the side mirror and grinned ear to ear as his sidekick and his appendage performed on cue.

"Yessssss!" the radio crackled, and Ellen held her clenched fists up in triumph as the SUV fell back to pull over behind the trailer, just as an oncoming car approached with horn blaring. Jerry vigorously shook his head, then laid back down. They had gotten the perfect shot.

The fresh air was a relief for everyone when they gathered at a mountaintop roadside rest area. Jerry found a patch of snow just a short stroll from the parking lot and flopped on his back in ecstasy, three legs sprawling in the air.

"Let's sit down over here and talk a bit first." The producer thought the scenery was perfect, and the afternoon sun was in their favor. She sat cross-legged in front of her subjects as they took a seat on a tattered beach towel Rene kept in the truck for cleaning Jerry. He lay softly with his head on Rene's lap as Jim rubbed the thick fur where his left leg used to be.

"Ready?" Ellen was looking at Jim but asking her crew, who gave her the thumbs up.

Feeling unsure about where to begin, Jim fell into his old marketing guy persona. "This is Jerry. He's the Tripawds spokesdog! When he lost a leg to cancer, we sold everything and bought an RV to travel the country together…" Then he blurted out phrases that sounded like a commercial for Jerry's blog.

"Cut." Ellen sighed out loud, then pulled her big, dark sunglasses from her face. She rubbed her eyes and turned to Rene. "How 'bout you just tell me your story? Tell me about your life with Jerry before you left." Then she looked at Jim and spoke in her sharp New Jersey accent. "Just be natural. Rene, let's start with you."

Jim loosened up as he listened to Rene while the big camera watched and the boom mic hovered overhead. He looked down at the big clumps of fur balling up in his hands and lightened his grip on Jerry, who was reveling in the gentle touch. "A lot of people thought we were nuts when we sold our business, and our house, and said we were gonna travel for a while. That just came naturally to us. But then others started asking, how far do you go for a dog?"

The producer smiled and continued questioning. An hour flew by as they filmed on that snowy mountain high above Santa Fe. The whole scene felt surreal to Rene and Jim, like they were telling someone else's story.

"He's not a kid. He's not human. But he means so much to us…" Rene's pause added the perfect touch of drama. "I can't picture our lives without him." Without meaning to, she had everyone on the verge of tears.

"Beautiful." The producer looked happy.

❈   ❈   ❈

The next day, Jerry was once again the star for a final afternoon of filming. They trailed him around the historic Santa Fe Plaza while an assistant followed, handing model release forms to anyone who wandered within the camera's view. They stopped at the entrance of the Cathedral Basilica of Saint Francis of Assisi, and to Rene and Jim, it felt like the universe had put them right where they needed to be. They looked up and smiled at the statue of the patron saint of animals, the man who cared for the sick and praised all God's creatures as equal. They weren't devout Catholics, but raised in the Church, they knew that each year the world pays homage to this saintly soul on October 4, the Feast of Saint Francis Day. The holy day was a long way off on that sunny afternoon, but the next time it rolled around, October 4 would take on a whole new meaning for them.

Later that evening, they relaxed at a lakeside campground Rene had chosen just outside of Santa Fe. It was nearly empty, almost as if they had the whole place to themselves. Just an hour earlier, the camera crew drove off into the sunset as warm shades of red, orange, and brown painted the historic pueblo of the Cochiti people. Happy to enjoy some solitude after the two-day paparazzi spree, Jim's emotions caught up with his spinning mind. They had just revealed their story to the world and now every decision they'd ever made about Jerry's cancer was going to be in the spotlight. Did they look like bad parents? Had they done the right thing leaving everything behind? Where the heck were they headed?

"Weren't we just in Los Angeles?" He handed Rene a cocktail. The longest week in their life together was now behind them. "Seems like a year ago."

"No kidding." Rene noticed he was visibly upset. "You okay?"

"Yeah. I'm just wiped out." He didn't want to talk about it. "I need a shower."

Jim finished his drink, grabbed a towel and a handful of quarters, and walked out to indulge in a long, hot shower at the campground's institutional-feeling restroom. Bare, bright bulbs threw an eerie fluorescent glare across the bathroom's steel sinks and mirrors. Alone in the fading daylight, he turned the light switch dial on the wall, walked into a shower stall, and dropped three quarters into a pay box. The quarters clattered, and the water timer's ticking echoed loudly as water flowed from the showerhead. A single fluorescent overhead light flickered like a scene from some bad horror film.

"BRRR!" The narrow jet stream of water came out fast and hard, and very cold. It wasn't warming up, and he wasn't about to keep feeding quarters to find out if it ever would. Jim lathered up in a frantic rage, but his three minutes were up before he rinsed. He added two more quarters and lowered his head back into the cold water. The cold stung his skin like needles, nudging him into a fit of heaving and sobbing. It was all too much—Jerry's metastasis, the oncology visit, the film crew, the long day of driving. Tears flowed from his eyes as all those fears and doubts came bubbling up once again.

"Get a hold of yourself!" Embarrassed by his annoyance at the minor inconvenience, he remembered how Jerry handled the Big Bad Wolf and tried to do the same. Embracing the cold water seemed like the way to go, but it didn't stop his sad cries from growing louder. Then, the lights went out with a loud click. "AAARRGH…"

Standing in the darkness, he folded his arms against the rough concrete wall, rested his head in his hands, and sobbed with loud, heavy heaves. The ice-cold water refreshed and numbed him until he could cry no more.

Soaking wet, exhausted, and cold, he turned the lights back on and looked at his reflection in the graffiti-marred steel mirror. Bloodshot red, swollen eyes stared back at him, and large goosebumps all over his body made him laugh at the insanity of it all.

Once dressed, he stepped out into the crisp evening air under a darkening indigo sky and silently prayed to Indian spirits of the Pueblo. "Please. Give me a sign, anything; tell me we're doing the right thing."

The spirits gladly obliged. On his way back to the trailer, he stopped to admire a large flowering cactus growing out of the rocky ground when a shiny glimmer caught his eye. A perfectly intact pint glass lay near the spiny plant. He bent down, turned it over, and smiled at the dancing silhouette of Kokopelli printed on the glass. Underneath it were the words "Rock Art Brewery, Morrisville, Vermont."

Kokopelli. The best-known of the Pueblo kachina spirits. The humpbacked flute player is a mythical Hopi symbol of fertility, replenishment, dance, and mischief. Was this prankster spirit playing with Jim now? How did a glass make it all the way from northern Vermont to the New Mexico desert? And how did he and Rene, for that matter? Why would a New England brewery have a logo depicting Kokopelli? Most importantly, he wondered, why didn't it break when it fell on the ground? None of it made any sense, until he recalled something even crazier.

A few months earlier, they had driven within fifteen minutes of that same brewery when they visited the Ben and Jerry's factory in Waterbury, Vermont. Somehow, that glass found its way across the country to this remote campground in the New Mexico mountains. Prank-loving Kokopelli appeared just when Jim needed him most. Clutching the glass, he understood the mysterious gift. In due time, the puzzle pieces of their crazy life would all fall into place. He couldn't see how or when it would happen, but at that moment, he intuitively felt that somehow, everything would work out exactly as it should.

BE MORE DOG

— 19 —

The Truth, and Consequences

Jerry, Jim, and Rene arrived at the hot springs resort, only to discover that their new campsite was far from luxurious. The RV park was a dusty gravel parking lot with an old, abandoned 1970s trailer that had seen better days. Just steps away from their door, remnants of a chain-link fence protected half-demolished buildings filled with trash and weeds. Every morning before sunrise, the town scavenger and his shopping cart filled with clanging cans made a pit stop at the dented garbage dumpsters across the alley, awakening everyone within earshot. Their new campsite wasn't glamorous, but the benefits made up for it.

The lazy waters of the Rio Grande River formed a gentle bend just across the street. Perched on a bluff above the gently flowing water was the aptly named Riverbend Hot Springs Resort, where they would work for a few months in exchange for the rustic accommodations and all the mineral water soaks they wanted.

The hot water sanctuary was the escape they needed, now more than ever. The constant din of Los Angeles, coupled with Jerry's latest diagnosis, had put them on edge. The job offer was a perfectly timed opportunity to bid farewell to Rene's teary-eyed mom. Their new home was Truth or Consequences, a hardscrabble New Mexico town that attracted free-spirit tourists who loved the bubbling hot springs coursing underneath it. The locals just called their rough, windy town "T or C."

Rene and Jim's work wasn't always easy, but when he was done cleaning the tubs and her office duties ended for the day, they had free access to the property's hand-built spring-fed stone spas overlooking the river. Maybe it was the love that the old hippie owners put into the place, or it could have been the high lithium content of the mineral water, but the ambiance instantly made guests feel relaxed, happy, and friendly. A little kooky, slightly spiritual and always kind, everyone who walked through the doors lived up to the stereotype of a Bohemian hot springs enthusiast. Rene and Jim felt right at home.

Dogs weren't allowed on the spa grounds, but Jerry was special. He had a way of getting people to bend their rules. In the quietest hours of the day, Jim and Rene would quietly escort him into one of the private tubs overlooking the river. The dog was no stranger to hot water. When they lived in Eureka, they always had a hot tub in their backyard, and one of his favorite games was licking the warm water off Jim's head while he soaked. "Hey, Jerry! Check it out!" Jim would take a big gulp of water, then slowly spit a stream toward Jerry. He never flinched. Instead, he just stuck out that big tongue to lap from his personal water fountain.

"Ha! Do that again!" Their special bonding session always made Rene giggle, but this time she felt a need to capture it on camera. The fun kept flowing. Jim spit a stream of water while Jerry happily lapped it up. Back and forth, from man to dog, they maintained the impromptu sharing game with a priceless act of love and cooperation. To anyone else, it was a guy spitting water at his dog, but to them, it perfectly captured their human-animal bond. Several months later, when the PBS producer saw the scene, she included it as the core message of her documentary.

Their work commitment only required them to work three days straight, followed by three days off. And although it bothered Rene to leave Jerry at home on those work days, he didn't really seem to mind. Home was just across the street, so every couple of hours, she found a way to alleviate her guilt by taking him for a potty walk and stretch. "But he's got cancer," she would say to the owner. "He shouldn't be left alone very long." He never complained.

One day during Jim's shift, he and Jerry were out for a short walk when they spotted a young man hobbling on crutches. A few people trailed alongside him as they gently held his elbows while he walked toward the spas. The man looked like a young army veteran with his short-cropped hair and khaki pants. His right leg was missing from the knee down, with that pant leg neatly creased and pinned up. He slowly made his way along the dirt path with an unhappy expression on his face. Jim sensed his anguish and thought a visit from Jerry might be therapeutic. But not this time.

Jim walked closer and let out the slack on Jerry's leash. The young man saw him, but his expression remained unchanged. Jerry wagged his tail and panted with excitement as he hopped around, trying valiantly to get some attention. Jim imagined his dog's motions were telling the new amputee, "You got this, man. If I can, so can you!"

The young vet hardly acknowledged the visitor, but his friend leaned over to stroke Jerry's fur. Of course he welcomed the praise, but this guy wasn't who he wanted to help. Jerry worked harder than ever to bring some comic relief, but even his friendly gestures couldn't win over this amputee. The guy hardly smiled and stayed quiet. He clearly wanted to be left alone to confront his demons.

Feeling awkward about the intrusion, Jim tugged on the leash, but noticed Jerry was already headed the other way. He knew when to say when. In his mind, Jim heard Jerry telling the young man, "That's okay, I understand. It's hard at first."

"You folks have a good day." Jim's greeting was met with silent nods as everyone went their separate ways. "Don't take it personally, buddy." Jim was speaking more to himself than Jerry. "You can't win 'em all over with that hop of yours. That guy just needs more time."

Jerry glanced up at Jim with a look that said, "Right, and he needs to be more dog."

❈   ❈   ❈

Riverbend ignited a spiritual fire within Jim. Not in a religious sort of way, but the calm, serene atmosphere and soothing waters helped him get more in tune with the life lessons Jerry was teaching them. The universe and Jerry seemed to be in cahoots, always conspiring to help him and Rene see the bigger picture about living happily no matter the circumstances. Ever since Jim's Big Bad Wolf dream, the oncology appointment, and his cold shower experience, his mind was more receptive to the higher powers that be. He welcomed whatever enlightenment they had to share. And lately, it seemed death was an integral part of their message. It started with the anniversary of his dad's passing. Then he met the kind and kooky matriarch who founded the resort. She had multiple sclerosis and reminded Jim of his mother, who had died from complications of the same disease just a few years earlier. Reminders of his own mortality were everywhere, including the shocking death of a friend who had introduced him to Rene. At any other time in his life, he would have found unhealthy ways to cope, but Riverbend's calm energy that surrounded him was perfect therapy when he needed it most.

Each day, Jim smiled as he walked past the courtyard's colorful murals and artwork depicting the earth goddess Gaia, the cosmos, and of course that prankster Kokopelli. Mystical sayings and wise proverbs adorned pennants strung among prayer flags that flapped in the desert wind. One in particular struck Jim's heartstrings so much that he wrote about it for Jerry's blog in a post titled, "Buying Time on an Emotional Budget."

He shared a photo of the flag imprinted with a quality of life lesson from Lao Tzu, author of the ancient Tao Te Ching. Writing in Jerry's voice, Jim discussed how the message might help others prepare for the loss of a beloved pet.

I have cancer.

I acknowledge the fact that it will take me someday. But this is by no means an excuse for complacency. And it is no reason to be sad. It is a fact of life and death. And it calls for celebration of every beautiful day...

Since I first got sick, my people have been preparing for the sad day when they will have to say goodbye. Yes, it will be unbearably hard on them. But they like to think it will be easier having had time to ready themselves emotionally. But exactly how does one prepare for such a dark reality?

I say listen to Lao Tzu. Understand the truth. Become tolerant. Welcome reality...

"If you don't realize the source, you stumble in confusion and sorrow.

Immersed in the wonder of the Tao, you can deal with whatever life brings you, and when death comes, you are ready."

— Lao Tzu

In between endless loads of laundry, pressure-washing the hot tubs, and managing the growing Tripawds community during their time off, Jim and Rene did their best to follow Jerry's lead and make the most of each day. They took daily walks along the river while crossing their fingers and hoping the combination of metronomics and new mushroom therapy was working. Jerry loved his new routine, but after hopping along for nearly 16 months, it became clear that even their short strolls may be a bit much for his body. Rene spotted the unusual limp as soon as it began. "We need to ask the oncologist about this." She was glad Jerry's follow-up appointment was just a few days away, when they would leave their trailer at the resort and make the three-hour drive north to Santa Fe.

❧ ❧ ❧

As soon as Rene tossed the old pup tent and sleeping bags into the middle of the RV, Jerry's eyes lit up. The gear smelled like good times, an era when he carried his own backpack and led everyone on the trail. For Rene, it was a bittersweet reminder that they may not have too many other opportunities to get closer to nature with Jerry. Determined to make an adventure out of the trip to the oncology clinic, she found a remote park where they could pitch a tent and have a campfire.

"Ya wanna go play in the dirt, buddy?" Jim smiled as Jerry pranced around the weathered nylon gear. His whole body went into a wag as soon as he heard his favorite question.

"Aww, look, he remembers. Smart boy!" They had shared many trips in that little tent, and Jerry's recollection of the woodsy scents made Rene so happy.

They were all ready to camp, but when they arrived in Santa Fe, it was time for the finer things in life. Jim rubbed Jerry's ear. "We'll go camping after this, OK? And no long hike, either. But tonight, we're living large!"

For the first time since moving into the RV, they checked into a hotel. The spacious room and white tile bathroom felt strange. "Look, a porcelain toilet!" Jim was easily amused by all the creature comforts.

"Don't get too used to it!" Rene giggled while jumping up and down on the bed as Jerry hopped around the room, giving his best impression of a scent hound.

The next morning, they grabbed their free pastry and coffee in the hotel lobby, then headed straight to the oncology clinic. Without the camera crew tagging along, things felt far more relaxed. The practice manager offered Jim and Rene a clinic tour while Jerry was in back getting his exam and x-rays. The clinic was as exceptional as any human medical facility. It had a state-of-the-art operating room, sparkling new recovery ward and current technology, like digital x-rays that would reveal the truth about Jerry's lung mets.

Dr. Mullins and Jerry joined the tour after his exam was finished. They stopped at a workstation where she pulled up his x-rays on a computer. Rene took photos for Jerry's blog as the vet gave them the news.

The happy vet zoomed in on the image. "I wouldn't say he's doing good."

Rene and Jim shot a sad look at each other.

The vet turned to them, smiling. "I'd say he's doing great!"

"Really?" they asked in unison.

"Remember, 'Stable Disease' is our goal." She pointed to the high-resolution scans of Jerry's lungs on the screen. "Normally, we don't expect to see an actual reduction in tumor growth at this point. But these have actually shrunk in size by ten percent. It's probably a good thing we got to the mets when we did. The treatment is doing its job."

The news was the best they could have hoped for. But Jim wasn't totally surprised. Jerry didn't act sick; he never looked miserable or uncomfortable—except for that random limp.

"Did you happen to take a look at his knee?" Rene hoped the vet could make sense of Jerry's limp. Could it be cancer in another bone? She had to know. Between the expensive diagnostic machines and the vet's trained eyes, they might be able to get the whole story.

"Yes, I sure did." With a couple clicks of her mouse, the vet brought up another x-ray and zoomed in on Jerry's cruciate ligament. "He does appear to have a partial cruciate tear. It's not major, and in his condition, I would not recommend surgery. You should be able to treat this with some confinement and hot/cold therapy. Just keep his walks to a minimum for a while."

Rene sounded audibly relieved. "Whew!"

"You hear that, buddy?" Jim rubbed Jerry's head. "You get to slack off!"

Joyful about the good news they got up, shook hands, and said goodbye to the oncologist. Her magic bag of tricks helped them have better days ahead with Jerry, like the one that waited just down the road.

✻ ✻ ✻

Twice a year, the Trinity Test Site opens to the public for tours of the testing grounds where the first A-bombs were exploded in the high New Mexico desert. To draw more tourists, on the same afternoon, the Very Large Array holds public tours of America's largest stellar antenna array. Both were on the way back to T or C, near the tiny village of Pie Town where they would camp out for the evening. Atomic testing, massive satellite dishes, and pie. What could be better to top off the week when Jerry got his clean bill of health?

With Jerry in the clear, they left Santa Fe and headed south to the bomb site. On any other day, there's hardly a soul near this barren stretch of remote desert, where a simple stone monument marks the first detonation of a nuclear weapon. But today it was filled with atomic tourists eager to learn about history.

"You'll find more radiation emitted from a pack of cigarettes than you will from the rocks here at Ground Zero." A man waved the wand of a Geiger counter over the pack of Marlboros when Jim and Rene stopped at an information table with a scattering of seemingly random items. Old dinnerware from the 1950s, a glow in the dark watch, and other radiation-laced goods were put there to prove his point as he waved the Geiger counter over them. When he did, it ticked faster than the ground on which they stood.

The loud ticking sound quickened, growing more frantic when he waved it over a banana. "See, even this is more radioactive! And we eat it!"

"Is that because of the potassium?" Jim was genuinely curious, but Rene could tell he was scheming about something.

"Yes! It is the potassium." The man smiled and nodded to Jim as he stooped to scoop up some of the shiny rocks and sand at his feet. He waved the wand over his palm filled with tiny stones. The frequency slowed a bit, but the counter kept ticking. "There is radiation everywhere, in everything. But even here, it is well within safe limits."

Jim looked at the guy testing the rocks, then watched children playing on the ground nearby. He picked up a few himself and studied their shiny surface. "Put that down!" Rene gave her best motherly scolding.

The man continued. "The rocks are shiny because during the explosion, tons of sand were blasted up into the air, where it melted, then fell back to the ground, cooling as glass."

Jim dropped the stones. "Can I ask you a favor?"

"Sure, ask anything." The man was used to answering questions, but would soon find out he was unprepared for this one.

A military band played festive music as Rene tried to listen to Jim explaining that Jerry was taking a chemotherapy pill. The man handed Jim the Geiger counter after hearing about Jerry's treatment. Rene watched and quickly figured out what he was up to.

"Hey. Grab the camera!" Jim slowly waved the wand back and forth across Jerry's back, and Rene hit the record button. The device didn't roar with ticking, and only spewed out a few random clicks, indicating the natural background radiation found in every mammal. It was nice knowing the truth. They were not living with a radioactive canine.

On their way out, Jerry posed for Ground Zero photos at a life-size replica of the Little Boy bomb. They were finishing touches for a silly video Jim later made, which featured sparkling effects scattered throughout Jerry's happy, hopping prance at the test site grounds. The title? "Atomic Dog," of course.

"Come on, we've gotta make it to the VLA!" Rene ordered Jim and Jerry back to the truck so they could make the one-hour drive before it closed for the day. Jerry slept in the truck during their hour-long tour of the radio-astronomy station where the movie *Contact* was filmed, and then they were off to Pie Town.

A year before, Rene had read about the famous Pie-O-Neer café, and always wanted to visit the wide spot in the road with the funky name. She already knew that there wasn't much to the town, other than a free campground and two small cafes that serve pie, naturally. But with a name like Pie Town, she knew it had to be good. Or at least she hoped. As the sun sank lower on the horizon, they hurried out of the VLA and down that lonely stretch of highway, better known by locals as Pieway 60.

By the time they arrived, warm sunset rays beamed on the weathered Native American Thunderbird sign that watches over the cafe. On a mission for pie, Jim and Jerry ran to the old wooden porch. "Uh oh." He knew it didn't look promising. The door was shut. The only car out front was a well-loved white Subaru with a license plate that simply read PIELADY.

Rene caught up and ran up the creaky wooden planks of the old, wind-worn building. One by one she peered inside each window while Jerry and Jim waited under the tattered pie-shaped sign that simply read PIES. Looking like lost, forlorn puppies, they finally spotted the "Closed" sign in the window.

"Well, damn! No pie for Jim tonight." Rene leaned over to give Jerry some water when a woman came to the door.

"Sorry, we're closed," she said through the window. She wore an apron speckled with flour. Her long, blonde-and-silver hair was tousled under her tie-dyed bandana. It was the end of another busy day at Pie-O-Neer Pies, and the Pie Lady was ready to go home.

"Awww…" Jim gave her his best sad face and turned his head down, intentionally looking at Jerry. "Sorry, buddy, we aren't going to eat tonight."

The Pie Lady smiled and opened the door. "Oh, geez. Come on in. But we can't allow dogs inside. Okay?" As she opened the door, she looked up and down the road for any onlookers. Pie Town was mostly deserted, with nothing but an old, abandoned gas station next door.

"Whoa! I didn't even notice he was missing a leg." Her smile lit up as she stooped to greet Jerry.

"Shhh…" Jim held his finger to his lips. "Don't tell him, he doesn't know."

"Ha! All right, come on, dog. I'm a sucker for animals. Just don't tell anyone." She held the door, looking up and down the street as all three of them entered.

Rene and Jim were so hungry they didn't even care what kind of pie was left over from the crowds, but the kitchen's lingering aroma told them anything would be delicious. The Pie Lady brought one slice of cherry pie and one apple to their table.

"Mind if I join you?" Exhausted from her twelve-hour shift, she put her feet up on an empty chair and enthusiastically quizzed her last customers of the day. "Where are you guys from?"

Rene and Jim looked at each other and giggled. "It's hard to say. And it's all this guy's fault," Jim offered. The Pie Lady patted Jerry on the head and listened attentively. They never had much of a story to tell before Jerry got sick. But now, they had a good one. People seemed to enjoy hearing about how a dog turned their life upside down for the better, and the Pie Lady of Pie Town was no exception. She was smitten by the three-legged guest and his giddy traveling people.

Jerry sat quietly at their feet, on his best behavior while wearing his red harness. He watched them enjoy the best pie they ever tasted, with one of the kindest people they had met since hitting the road.

"It's funny, really." The Pie Lady stared into her coffee cup, now nearly empty. "My mom used to give me a hard time whenever I'd bring home any boys she didn't approve of." She smiled, remembering how she thought her mom was crazy for suggesting they purchase the Pie-O-Neer together a few years before she passed away. "She would look at me with disapproval and shake her head. Then with her eyebrow raised up like this, she'd say, 'You don't have to bring home every three-legged dog you find!' And, here you are, Jerry." She reached down to caress his velvety ears.

The three laughed like old friends. "You can't make this stuff up!" The Pie Lady got up and took their empty plates. There was so much more they wanted to know about her own story—her mom, and the history of the Pie-O-Neer—but that would come in due time when they returned to Pie Town many times later during their travels. That little slice of heaven instantly felt like home.

"Thank you so much for letting us in. That was awesome." Rene led the way as Jim rubbed his belly and grabbed his two pie slices packed to go. The hot, glowing sun descended behind the big Thunderbird totem as the eastern sky darkened into twilight. Nearby, an old truck with a fading "For Sale" sign was the only other vehicle in this special corner of the universe. The remote stretch of road was empty for miles in each direction.

Before crossing the lonely two-lane Pieway to set up their campsite in the park, Jim and Rene turned to wave goodbye. From the old, weathered doorway, the Pie Lady watched her new friends walk away and hollered, "Watch out for traffic!"

— 20 —

Onward, and Upward

Southern New Mexico's earthy desert hues faded from the rearview mirror as the snowcapped peaks of the Sangre de Cristo Mountains grew tall on the horizon. The mountains weren't far. Now, it felt like home. The familiar scent of pine and crisp alpine air always made this wandering pack happy, and this summer, they would get plenty of it while working on a Colorado dude ranch.

Eager to flee the desert's warm spring temperatures, Jim steered their big, white trailer north along the remote highway. Today's destination was a free campsite Rene found in New Mexico's northern mountains. With a wave of his hand, he bid, "Adios!" to the hot weather and impatient drivers who hastily passed his slow-moving RV. "Even out here, people are always in such a hurry."

A passing car's tailwind filled the truck cab with a cool breeze. Rene nodded a silent yes. "As if they'll get where they're going any faster. Not."

She couldn't have picked a better parking spot for the night. Or maybe more, depending on how they liked it. One day while flipping through their road atlas, she spotted it. New Mexicans called it "Tres Piedras," but the gringos referred to it as Three Rocks. The number three had a magical aura these days, so the spot felt like a good omen. She glanced at Jim, then turned to watch Jerry happily stretching his head out the window. The laid-back morning scene was a far cry from their old life. The joy in Jerry and Jim's eyes melted her heart, and she smiled. "Anything with three in the name has got to be great, right?" Jim grinned in total agreement.

The highway narrowed, and he did his best to avoid steering them into a ditch. Jerry dutifully maintained his stance on the back seat, assessing the changed landscape. If his knee was still painful, he wasn't showing it. Were the lung tumors making it hard to breathe? Neither of them could tell.

The heartbreak of his lung metastasis still felt raw, but each time they looked at Jerry, they remembered their CFO was a dog who had already outlived his prognosis. He was still alive and happy. He did everything as before. He chased after sticks, obsessed over balls, and woke up excited each day. Even when life throws a curveball, Jerry was showing them that life is as good as you make it.

Back in Santa Fe, they vowed not to grieve for him a moment too soon. But they couldn't resist the human need to know the future. They quizzed Jerry's oncologist about what to expect with the metastasis, and she dutifully filled them in.

"You'll notice a deep cough first, most likely. It's kind of like a hacking sound. Sometimes it can be other things, but osteosarcoma usually progresses with lung tumors that impact breathing patterns."

Rene asked, "Can we do anything about it?"

"Sure, there are ways to help reduce inflammation that causes the symptoms. Prednisone and Albuterol, or an airway dilator, usually work for a while."

"A while? How long until he can't breathe anymore?" Jim was not yet fully practicing what he preached about living in the now. He and Rene were most concerned about Jerry's quality of life, and they wanted a timeline. The oncologist, meanwhile, already knew that in the business of cancer, a prognosis doesn't come on a set schedule or with any guarantees.

"Hard to say. It could be weeks, maybe months. You really can't predict it until you do another x-ray to see how things have developed." Dr. Mullins understood a parent's need to know and disliked sounding so tentative. But she spoke the truth. She had to. Nobody can ever say exactly how long a dog with cancer will survive.

Jim and Rene looked at each other, knowing that nothing more needed to be said. X-rays weren't in this dog's future. There were no veterinarians within an hour's drive of where they would spend the summer. More importantly, they promised Jerry there would be no more poking and prodding, no more surgeries. Even if the scans showed worsening disease, the only thing they would do with that information would be to keep him comfortable the best they could.

For as long as he had left, they would make the most of each day.

Exploring the mountains, swimming in lakes, hiking, relaxing, and letting Jerry set the pace. Someday, there would be plenty of time for tears. Now was not that time. Because Jerry wasn't thinking about lung mets. Instead, he stood tall and strong on that New Mexico mountain highway, nudging his long, skinny muzzle along the top of the cracked window and painting his tongue with the faint aroma of late-spring snow. His eyes were filled with the excitement of another adventure.

"Turn here!" Rene suddenly commanded and pointed to a dirt road.

"Huh. Where are you taking us?"

"Keep driving; you'll stop just around the corner." She was always so optimistic when leading them on a crazy hunt for free forest camping.

"Uh, before or after that big mud hole in the road?"

"Oh, just go around it, no problem!" She hoped her map was correct. "See? We're here!"

The approaching sunset cast golden beams on rocky boulders while Jim maneuvered the big, boxy vehicle into the middle of a grassy clearing. Unlike the confines of RV parks or campgrounds, no white lines told him where to park or which utilities to connect to. And there were no curious neighbors watching them get settled. In fact, there were no other campers anywhere, only remnant signs where previous occupants built fire pits in the most ideal parking spots. For Jim and Rene, Tres Piedras was as perfect as RV camping gets.

A year earlier, when they'd traded their weathered, old backpacks and bivouac tent for the RV, they assumed that remote campsites would be a thing of the past. But the longer they gypsied around, the more they discovered these gems. Their small RV gave them the best of both worlds: the wilderness they all loved, and all the comforts of home. Those sleepless nights spent in a tiny tent with a big, hairy dog were behind them, but the days of enjoying nature's untainted beauty were not.

The moment Jim turned the engine off, Jerry whimpered and waited for his command. Amputation took his leg, but it didn't steal his enthusiasm. Rene and Jim indulged him.

"Hey, Jerrrrrry! Wanna check it out?" Her high-pitched tone only meant one thing: playtime! Time to run laps around the bushy pinion pines. To dig in the soft earthy dirt, feast on deer poop, and greet errant rodents like long-lost friends. After spending the last few months cooped up in a gravel parking lot while Rene and Jim worked at Riverbend, this dog was ready to do what he wanted, when he wanted, for as long as he was able.

"Come on, Jerry, let's go!" Jim helped him down out of the truck. His three paws landed gently in the dirt and the grateful dog sped away in a cloud of dust, galloping in that funny, three-legged trot at full speed across the dry, grassy meadow. Bounding from tree to tree, he occasionally stopped to inhale some new and powerful scent undetectable to anyone but him. Nose to the ground, he circled a distant grove of trees, then turned back to check in with Jim. He was off-leash, but Rene and Jim never worried about their loyal shepherd, who never strayed far from the people he protected.

A minute into his mad dash, Jerry dug his one front leg into the ground and skidded to a hard stop. Through the dusty air, Rene could see him stumble a few paces forward, but he didn't fall. He regained his balance, stopped and stood rigid, as if on high alert. Those pointy twin satellite dish ears of his twitched side to side, then front to back as he tried making sense of a sound so distant that only he heard it.

"Hah! Maybe that Spirit Dog followed us." To Jim, it was entirely possible they were being chased by a ghost.

Two nights before, they were camped on a large property north of Santa Fe when a wolf-like dog mysteriously appeared at their open RV door. But as soon as Jim turned to greet their visitor, it left so quickly that none of them got a good look. He went outside and searched every direction across the wide-open field, but it had vanished. Perplexed, he even looked under the trailer. The Spirit Dog ghosted them and physically was nowhere to be found. But his presence was far from absent. Rene later recounted the unusual episode for Jerry in his Tripawds blog:

> While we were all sitting around like the calm submissive pack creatures we are, a beautiful big Husky dog suddenly appeared at our screen door without a sound. My people were as surprised as I was and didn't even have time to grab their camera before he disappeared. I, for one, was no longer calm.
>
> I admit it, I'm a whiner. And I wouldn't let up. This pup was out there somewhere, and I wanted to play! So, we went out to look. But this mystery dog was gone with the wind. Nowhere to be found. I

dutifully marked my territory all around the trailer and tried to calm down a bit. We went inside, and within minutes our visitor appeared again. Right at the door. Silent. Stoic.

Somewhere in the deep blue of his one white eye, ran the souls of all my canine brethren who have passed before. And then he was gone again. I spent the rest of the evening—and the next morning— standing watch. We never saw our mystery mutt again. And when we left, we saw the three dogs who supposedly lived nearby. None of which matched the description of our Spirit Dog.

Was the disappearing dog a reminder from the netherworld that Jerry's time was drawing near? If so, the timing was off. He was as happy as ever, and certainly wasn't thinking of spirit dogs or the condition of his lungs. Jerry quickly disregarded the odd noise in the forest. He. Just. Wanted. That. Stick. Jim indulged the obsessed dog, who patiently waited in the dwindling daylight.

Man and dog played fetch while Rene did her part to set up camp. She carefully placed their AstroTurf ground cover outside the door, wiped her hands on her jeans and declared. "Home sweet home!" Then she went into the RV, got their cell phone from her purse, and aimed it skyward. "We have a signal! Can you believe it?"

The backwoods campsite wasn't so far off the grid after all. Rene tapped the keypad and from outside the rig, Jim heard her leave a message. "Hey, Lee Ann, it's Rene and Jim. We're about an hour south of you in the mountains and gonna hang out here for a bit. We can't wait to meet you and Daisy! Call us when you get this, okay?"

Rene liked to say that all the coolest dogs have pointy ears, like Daisy. She was crazy about the new Tripawds member, a snow-white German shepherd who sported a pair of always-on ears that highlighted her muscular, angular profile. The strong, beautiful, twelve-year-old dog was now fighting the same cancer as Jerry.

Daisy's mom, Lee Ann, reached out to Tripawds in search of the support that other pet owners in her small farm town couldn't provide. She lived in the kind of rural setting where dogs get euthanized for illnesses like cancer. But Lee Ann was a city girl gone country, and she wanted to help Daisy fight it as long as she could. The connection with Tripawds seemed like destiny. After joining and comparing notes with Rene, the two women realized their dogs were going to the same oncology practice in Santa Fe. And when Rene realized that their route to Colorado would take them near Daisy's homestead, a real-time meet-up was inevitable. They talked about it for weeks, but shortly before the get-together, Lee Ann received the bad news that every Tripawd parent dreads: Daisy had lung tumors; lots of them. Rene cried almost as much as when Jerry's mets appeared, and assumed her new friend would cancel. But Lee Ann agreed to meet Jerry anyway. Like him, the tough old dog was feeling good and not ready to die.

The next day, their little flip phone rang with urgency. Rene answered, as usual. "Lee Ann! Hey, nice to hear your voice!"

"Hi, Rene." She sounded unsteady. Something was wrong. "Um, I just wanted to let you know…I had to let Daisy go yesterday."

"What?! Oh my gosh! I'm so sorry! Noooo…"

Through tears, she explained how she knew something was wrong. Over the last several days, her dog's behavior wasn't right. And just twenty-four hours before Rene and Jim landed at Tres Piedras, Lee Ann had driven Daisy two hours south to Santa Fe for x-rays, where she discovered cancer had spread throughout both lungs. The aggressive disease attacked Daisy less than a month after amputation surgery, multiplying so fast throughout her organs that even the vet was shocked. The dog was slowly suffocating. It was time to set her free.

As Lee Ann relayed the awful news, the hair on Rene's neck stood up when she realized they had passed each other on the highway the day before. Jim, Rene, and Jerry were northbound to their new spot right as Daisy and Lee Ann headed south, to eternity. Daisy and Jerry's spirits gently collided somewhere near the New Mexico state line.

"I'm so sorry, Lee Ann. There was no way you could have predicted it."

"Yeah. I understand, I guess. I'm not sure what to think. Except that I really need to meet Jerry."

"Are you sure? We don't want to intrude, really. It's totally okay if you want to be alone."

"That's the last thing I need right now. My husband is traveling. I need Jerry around. Please come visit, okay?"

The next morning, they packed up and vacated the campsite. Survivor's guilt weighed heavy on their minds as they headed north to Colorado. What made one dog die so quickly from the disease, and others not? Jerry's remarkable longevity was so unusual, especially for a dog who didn't go through traditional IV chemotherapy after his diagnosis. Why him? Jim and Rene wondered. There was no telling why. All they knew at that moment was that Jerry's gentle nature could be great medicine to the grieving mom. Less than two hours after hitching up, a highway sign directed them to the small farming town of Antonito.

"Hey, slow down! Here's our turn." Rene warned Jim just in time for him to make the sharp right turn. The swerving motion alerted Jerry, who stood up and strained his head out the window to investigate the low, flat landscape. After a long, dusty mile on a country road, they came upon the small, white farmhouse where Lee Ann waited on the porch.

"Jerry!" Lee Ann called out in a happy voice as the RV came to a stop in her wide driveway. Through red eyes, she smiled and walked up to pet his long snout poking through the open window. "Oh, sweetie, you don't know how much I needed to see you."

Rene hugged Lee Ann like an old friend. She listened intently and said little to the grieving woman, knowing that one day, she would need the same kind of support. But Jim was at a loss for words. He was uncomfortable with the stranger's raw grief. It was one thing to console members in the Tripawds discussion forums from the safe space behind his keyboard and screen, but face-to-face support made him feel awkward. Most of the afternoon was spent in silence, but Jerry knew just what to do. He gave Lee Ann all the love she needed, and then some.

— 21 —

Ranch Life

"Every day is a great day."

Long ago, someone had scratched that phrase onto the dirty, cracked windowpane. Today, Jim stood in the big metal barn at Vickers Ranch and wondered who. The air was chilly inside, but by 7:30 a.m., bright sunlight beamed through the words, warming up the cavernous workshop. Random containers of used motor oil or brown paint lay scattered among rusty old tools, dirty shop rags, and a disassembled weed-eater nobody had bothered to fix. Hydraulic oil, hayseed, sawdust, and dried elk blood splatters decorated the sturdy workbench holding one hundred years of hardworking history. A pile of chains lay alongside a small gas can with a big bolt stuck in the spout as a stopper. Jim lifted the container to read another message, this one carved into the eight-inch-thick tabletop: "Keep Area Clean!"

"I think I'm gonna like it here," he said to his new boss while looking around. The shop had everything anyone might ever need to do just about anything—drill press, large metal cut-off wheel, grinder, gas welding tanks, and bins and boxes with nuts and bolts of every possible size. A dusty, cockeyed deer head with a torn ear watched over the shop, precariously hanging on by thick layers of cobwebs. Next door, a smaller shop housed all the woodworking tools for the self-contained operation. Jim smiled. He felt right at home.

"Good!" Larry Vickers was a man of few words.

     ❀   ❀   ❀

Three months earlier, while Jim and Rene were still back on the farm in Florida with Jerry, they contacted Larry after reading his ad for summer workampers. Seasonal help was nothing new to his family. Larry's dad, Perk, helped homestead the large property in the mountains south of Lake City, Colorado, with his father and brothers during the late nineteenth century. One hundred years later, the Help Wanted online advertisement read:

> *Friendly couple needed for hard work with long hours and low pay on working guest ranch. Enjoy world-class fishing at your backdoor on your day off.*

Jim and Rene enjoyed the humor in the ad and didn't notice how the ad said day, not days. One day off. That meant they would both work six long days a week, with all hours paid. The wording of the ad was no joke! It sounded intimidating, but Jim thought working on a ranch and spending summer in the mountains seemed like a dream come true. He was a country boy at heart, and getting away from sitting at his computer so much sounded like food for his soul. Plus, he knew Jerry would probably love it. Since the Vickers already had several ranch dogs who roamed at large, he would fit right in.

"You sound great. When can you be here?" Larry was strictly business on that first phone call.

Jim explained it would be a couple months before they would even be in Colorado, let alone ready to start working. More job details would be nice to know. "What kind of work will we be doing?"

"Oh, well…we have all sorts of work waiting for you!" The old rancher was clearly happy to have two helpers lined up for the upcoming busy summer. "And we'll find something for your wife to do."

Jim could practically hear the old guy grinning on the other end of the line. It was clear they weren't gonna get much more detail or any sort of written work contract from this good old boy.

"We could be there June first." Rene had her calendar open, along with a long list of questions they never had the chance to ask.

"Good."

Very few words, indeed.

❀ ❀ ❀

That first week at Vickers Ranch, Jim was looking to make a good impression. He tidied up the big shop the best he could and cleared off a section of the workbench for his next project, gathering various salvaged parts for the exploded weed-eater. He then swept the shop floor and grabbed the hose attached to a large air compressor to blow cobwebs and debris off all the shelves. He soon realized the place would never have any real semblance of order until summer's end. And if they returned the following year, it would likely be one big mess all over again. Little did he know at the time that for the next eight years, this would be his first task of the season.

Surrounded by a cloud of dust and covered in grime after the first summer's cleaning, Jim stood in the big open entry and admired his work. Then he spotted an old man rolling toward him in a rickety, beat-up golf cart.

"Who are you?" Like son, like father. Ninety-five-year-old Perk Vickers was direct and to the point. Later, the family joked how he referred to the workampers as "the hired help," and rarely remembered their names. The stocky, old rancher didn't get his hands dirty anymore, but he still took pride in playing the role of supervisor to newcomers.

"Hey there, you must be Perk. I'm Jim, how ya doin' today?"

"Great, great, what?" With the stub of an unlit cigar in his hand, he fiddled with trying to put the cart into reverse.

Jim raised his voice a few decibels. "I said, how ya doin' today?"

"Just great. Every day is a great day!"

❃   ❃   ❃

Across the yard, Rene was learning her own tasks in the main building. While Jim worked outside in the fresh air, she carried out her role inside an old ranch house converted into the office and laundry room. Families wouldn't start arriving for at least another month, so she had a chance to settle in. Come mid-summer, Rene would barely have time for lunch while washing endless loads of linens from guests staying in the dozen hand-built log cabins dotting the riverfront. In between taking phone calls, booking horse rides, and overseeing Jeep rentals, she would always have something to do. But for now, it was time to sweep, dust, and get the office in order. Just like the workshop, it was left in disarray over the winter. After teaching herself the reservation software, she organized the front desk, donned big, orange rubber gloves, grabbed a bucket of Pine-Sol cleaner, and got down on her hands and knees to start spring cleaning of the cabins.

"Does your mother know you went to college to do this?" Larry's wife, Paulette, burst into the wood-paneled living room wearing her usual vibrant smile. The tall, fit woman was also wearing orange gloves, and from the moment she got on the floor to help scrub, Rene knew she would like working for her.

Manual labor felt good to both of them. It had been almost a month since leaving their last job at Riverbend, and most of those days were spent driving or sitting behind their computers. With one cabin cleaned, Rene wore a silly grin as she returned to the office to hang the morning laundry on the clotheslines to dry. The white cotton sheets billowed in the breeze against the clear, blue sky, giving her a crisp, wet slap on the cheek as she tried to hang them with precision. To nobody in particular she declared, "Yep, I went to college to do this, and it's great!" then fought her way out of the rows of soggy linens. Across the yard, she spotted Jim struggling to back a weathered silver flatbed Ford into the metal barn. The old truck leaked more steering fluid than anyone could ever keep putting into it, which made turning around and backing up a long, tedious chore.

Over the sound of the big Ford engine, he yelled out to her, "Great day, eh?"

"Always!"

※　※　※

"Hi, Rene!" Paulette pulled up on her big, yellow Yamaha four-wheeler. Accompanying her in the large steel basket on the back sat a grey-muzzled, black-and-white sheepdog. She raised her voice over the ATV's engine. "Have you seen Larry?"

"I haven't seen him since he was showing Jim around the shop yesterday." Rene pulled the last of the clean, dry linens off the line and placed them in a basket. Then she looked at her watch. She still needed to fold the sheets and run the pillowcases through the 1950s Mangle ironing machine.

"You two go grab some lunch. We'll see you later!" Paulette turned around and spied Larry heading up the hill to their house on his own red quad, with a shovel and pistol strapped to the front rack. "Looks like Larry wants his lunch too."

Rene stopped her before she sped off. "Wait! Who's this?" She immediately fell in love with Boone, the oldest of the ranch's free-roaming herding dogs. He was such a kind-hearted old soul, and she needed a dog fix. She caressed Boone's long muzzle while he quietly licked her arm. Boone didn't run with the pack so much anymore, but even at nine years old, he still got around pretty good. Osteoarthritis made his gait more of a waddle, but just like old Perk Vickers, the dog took pride in his job of keeping the younger pups in check.

Paulette drove away and a minute later, Jim pulled up to the office. He was driving Old Blue, a beat-up, early 1980s model Jeep with a cracked windshield folded forward, no doors, and no top. The old workhorse could go anywhere, and quickly became his favorite ranch vehicle. "Let's go! Lunchtime."

Rene put the "Closed for Lunch" sign on the door. She hopped into the open-air auto and hung on for the short, bumpy ride across the flat railroad car bridge that led to their campsite. She desperately wanted to see Jerry, who stayed home in the RV until they figured out their new daily routine. Emotionally, it was toughest on Rene. Back when Jerry was Chief Fun Officer of their marketing company, he never left their side. At the Florida farm, he followed them around most days. And at the hot springs resort, he was always within earshot during their three-day workweek. They had assumed Jerry could be with at least one of them most days on the ranch as well. But now they could see how this may not be practical. Ranch days were unpredictable and long. On any given day they could jump from one task to another, sometimes more than a mile apart on the mountain property. Although Jerry was still in good shape for a dog living with metastatic cancer, all that hopping around would be too much for him. Rene felt terrible for leaving him alone, but Jerry seemed content lounging around the rig all day.

Clearly, she was the one with separation anxiety, not him. "Aww… hey, bubba. I missed you so much!" Jerry stood in the doorway looking down at her. Through watery eyes, she reached up and scratched his scruff. "I'm so sorry."

He shook the sleep out of his eyes with an expression that seemed to say, "Sorry for what?"

"Come on, buddy, Let's get some air." Jim grabbed Jerry's harness handle and helped him hop down the steep RV steps. "Make some sandwiches, we'll be right back." Jim reminded Rene they only had an hour for lunch. Their spot for the summer was nestled in the woods, across the river and away from the pack of unleashed miniature collies and Shetland sheepdogs who reigned over the property. Back here was the perfect place for Jerry to roam and walk off-leash.

He was good with all dogs, especially ranch dogs who tried to put him in his place the day he arrived. They yapped at him and herded at his heels, but the ever tolerant and patient Jerry brushed off their tactics. He seemed to accept their attitude, then ignored it for the rest of the summer. On quiet days when Rene brought him by the office, he and old Boone would sit quietly together on the back porch, watching the young dogs run around the laundry lines. Like two elderly men getting together for coffee, they sat in silence, content enough to simply be.

After the short walk, Jim stopped to let Jerry roll in the tall grass. "You gotta get used to this new routine, buddy." Jerry lingered on the ground, casually covering himself with some invisible scent. "We'll be back for lunch every day, and just wait…we'll take you to the upper ranch and go fishing a bunch this summer. Maybe we'll even get in a camping trip!" Jerry looked up, then tilted his head at the word camping.

They ate faster than they should have, then prepared to head back for the rest of the workday. Rene frowned as she turned to leave Jerry, who was already sprawled on the couch, ready for a nap. "We'll be back before you know it. I promise." She bent down to cup his face in her hands, then smothered him with kisses. "I'm gonna miss you, baby." As she walked out, her uncertain voice left Jerry wondering why she was so upset.

She had yet to learn that dogs don't perceive the passage of time the way their people do. While some canines can't stand to see the pack split up for even a moment, most will patiently wait for their return without eating the couch. Jerry was one of them. From the time he was a pup, he was confident being on his own, always trusting his people would return, just as promised. Each time they did, he greeted them with exuberant tail wags and happy smiles.

Everyone adapted to the new routine. Jerry relished in his new role as Chief Couch Potato, and the ranch work kept Jim happy. Meanwhile, Rene enjoyed meeting all the guests and did her best to stop worrying about Jerry being home all afternoon. In some small, sad way, she knew it was preparing her for life without him. The reality of his terminal condition was getting real.

❀   ❀   ❀

"Oh. My. God. Look at this!" One evening after another long day in the office, Rene was replying to Tripawds forum posts. She turned her laptop so Jim could see the picture someone had shared. "We have to write about this."

"Ha! Cool." The photo was of a bottle of wine. A black-and-white dog on the label was missing a front leg. Above three gold paw icons was the name in big letters: Three Legged Red. "We have to get some of that."

The gears in Jim's marketing mind started spinning. He did some quick research to learn that the red table wine from Dunham Cellars was named after a dog rescued by one of the winery's founders. The dog had been in a fight, and when found, his right front leg was injured so severely it had to be amputated. With only three legs, two of them on the port side, the vintner named his puppy "Port," since he was an avid sailor. From that moment, Jim was determined to get a bottle of that wine.

"Let's pitch them on doing a review. I like wine, but free wine is even better!" He helped Rene draft an email to Dunham Cellars, explaining their passion for three-legged dogs and red wine. Within a week, the FedEx man delivered a large package addressed to Jerry Nelson.

"Whoa. They sent us a magnum!" Jim ripped open the carton and held up the big bottle of Three Legged Red. Jerry inspected the packaging, wondering what the big deal was all about. "This is cause for a celebration!"

"Yeah, we should put together something special for the review." Rene grabbed the bumper sticker and wine catalog Dunham sent and sat down. "Why not produce a short promo video? We can do a live wine tasting!"

"Right, because we are such aficionados," Jim joked. He knew his wine from a previous life in the restaurant world, but also knew he was no expert. "We'll talk about its body and bouquet while sitting in our RV."

"No, that's boring! Let's take that camping trip we keep talking about." Now Rene's mind started going, calculating details of what could be their last camp-out with Jerry. "Who knows if we'll get another chance." Her joy went to sadness in an instant as she looked at Jerry.

Jim knew exactly what she meant. "We've got 2,500 acres to

explore here. We could take Old Blue and camp out at Vickers Lake."

Rene added, "The Perseids meteor shower peaks on Wednesday night. We can leave after work and spend Thursday fishing."

"Paul did say we could have that day off. I'll ask if we can take the Jeep." The Vickers had taken in Jim and Rene as family. He knew they wouldn't say no.

❀   ❀   ❀

Shades of pink streaked across the darkening sky as Rene set up the camera. She perched it on a tripod to frame the two of them next to their little backpacking tent with Jerry laying down on his Barney blanket and Old Blue in the background. A grove of tall aspen trees towered above as they peered out over Vickers Lake, the largest of many fishing holes on the vast upper ranch that the family dredged out of the landscape many years before. The sun had not quite set, but the light was growing faint.

"We only have time for one take, so we'd better get this right." Jim hit the record button and ran to Rene and Jerry to kick off the four-minute video. She giggled while sampling the wine and tried to sound like a connoisseur. Meanwhile, Jerry appeared perfectly content with all the cheese and crackers getting stuffed in his face to keep him from running off and attacking the fallen tree branch taunting him just a few feet away.

"Cheers! Here's to Jerry, and Port, and Tripawds everywhere!" Rene raised her glass to the camera.

"What do you think, Jerry?" Jim held his glass out, figuring he could play up the cornball factor, rather than trying to impress with his limited wine knowledge. Jerry sniffed the bouquet but was not amused.

"Well, it doesn't matter what he thinks, cuz you shouldn't give it to your dog anyway!"

Rene sipped the wine from her plastic cup. "I know absolutely nothing about wine tasting or the proper terminology to use, but this is really good!"

After a few more off-the-cuff comments, with plenty of cheese and crackers, Jim nodded to Rene and then to the camera.

"We love it." She took her cue and got up to stop the recording.

The air was cool and skies clear, being so high in the mountains. Night was falling fast, but not before a bright-blue streak flashed across the sky. The temperature continued to fall, and an hour passed before they saw another meteor. Jim gave Rene a hard time about the big show that wasn't happening. "Hundreds of meteors per hour, eh?"

"It's not supposed to get really good until two or three." She looked at her watch; it was eight o'clock. Then she prepared the sleeping bags and crawled into the tent. "I'm gonna set my alarm."

"Well, I know I won't make it! Waking up once a day is enough for me." He stoked the fire and added another log. Jerry was curled up in the dirt to stay warm until the flames grew, but soon spied Rene getting comfy and decided to join her. "Oh great, you're not even gonna keep me company either?" He patted the dust off Jerry's rump as he hopped toward the tent.

All alone under the stars, Jim poured another cup of wine as another bright shooting star swooshed across the sky. Then he made a wish, whispering to himself, "I just want more time with Jerry."

He sat up by himself until the fire dwindled down to a single lonely flame dancing on the embers. With no moon and the fire sputtering out, darkness surrounded him. Then the cold crept in. He buttoned up his big wool shirt. The same one he wore on those first long hiking trips with Jerry. It was a magnet for dog fur, and he pulled a few hairs off it, rolling them together between his fingers.

The fire finally went out and he raked the coals for extra safety. Slowly fading away, their soft, red glow grew dimmer by the minute. Just a few feet behind him, Rene and Jerry slept soundly, but oddly enough, he felt utterly alone. Starry reflections danced on the still lake water, but the dense forest all around him seemed to be hiding something. He knew there was nothing to fear, but a shiver grabbed him by the spine. Something silent and brooding. Deep down, that big bad wolf in the back of his head was about to bring him to the verge of tears. He couldn't smother the fire fast enough.

❧   ❧   ❧

"Jerry and I are going fishing," he announced to Rene one morning on his day off. It was early September, and Jim had not yet fished all the lakes on the upper ranch. He grabbed his favorite fishing hat, put his gear in the back of Old Blue, and helped Jerry hop up into the rear where he'd placed an old saddle blanket to keep him comfortable.

"Have fun!" She was happy to see her boys go off and enjoy the day together. "Catch us some dinner."

Jim heard there were some record-setting lunkers in Joe Bob Lake, a small irrigation reservoir the Vickers dug in a big, open meadow. Getting there on the narrow dirt road was like driving up a mountain bike trail. Many years earlier, old Perk had carved a narrow swath through the aspens and over a rock field. Decades of spring snow runoff eroded the path, which made a bumpy ride for anyone willing to get there.

Jerry bounced along in the back of Old Blue. "Almost there, buddy!"

Jim steered the old Jeep through another tight bend, then crested a hill overlooking the small lake. He was glad to see that none of the ranch guests were fishing Joe Bob that day. "We got the place to ourselves!" After the rough ride, Jerry didn't wait for Jim's help to get out. He hopped from the front seat and stumbled as he leaped down to the ground, quickly recovering, but not before Jim saw him fall. "You okay?"

Jerry ignored him and wandered off to a nearby small patch of wildflowers. While Jim gathered his gear, the sun beat down on his back. "Come, sit here in the shade, Jerry!" Jim yelled from the shoreline. But Jerry seemed content to plop down in the flowers instead of seeking shade or running around to investigate the area. Jim stopped to take in the beautiful scenery and capture a mental snapshot before assembling his vintage fly rod, a keepsake from his father.

"You gonna stay there, eh?" He couldn't bring himself to disturb Jerry, who was sprawled out soaking up the sun. Instead, he walked around the pond to fish the far side. Old Blue sat on the slope at the other side, its reflection rippling in the water. Swaths of gold and orange painted the endless aspen groves while a few wispy, white clouds skirted the distant mountaintops. He inhaled deeply and filled his lungs with gratitude. Whatever fears he had been feeling about Jerry's health were far away. He cast his line and peered across the lake, watching the fly float on the surface. Jerry lay peacefully among the flowers. It was just another great day at the ranch.

"Fish on!"

The hard strike bent his pole, but the big fish quickly got away. A moment after the commotion, he noticed Jerry was up and about. He started to grin when he saw Jerry spinning in circles, nipping at his back legs. Then he realized something was wrong. He reeled in his line as fast as he could. "What's the matter, buddy?"

Their eyes connected from across the lake. A second later, Jerry fell to the ground and nipped ferociously at his hind end. Jim dropped his pole and sprinted back, panic setting in. The fear had returned. "What is it, dude?"

When a cloud of yellow jackets swarmed him, too, he got his answer. "Oh no! Get up, Jerry!" He grabbed his harness handle and dragged him toward the water, away from the swarm of angry insects. "Ow! Crap!" Jim felt the sting of another one as he swatted to keep the bloodthirsty pests away. He maneuvered Jerry out into the water just far enough to give a good shove, pushing him out into deeper water. The trick worked. Jerry dog-paddled a few strokes, then turned and swam to shore. A few surviving yellow jackets flew away and resumed their business inside the hive Jerry had disturbed.

"Come on, let's go home." Jim hoisted his tired, soaked dog back into Old Blue. Exhausted, wet, and uncertain about what had happened, Jerry plopped down on the blanket with confusion in his eyes. Jim retrieved his fly rod, hugging the shoreline to avoid any bees, then piloted Old Blue back down the mountain. Halfway down the bumpy road, he stepped on the brake pedal to slow down. Instead, it gave way to a sickening thud as it hit the floor. On the trail's steepest slope, the brakeless old Jeep careened toward an aspen grove. He stomped on the clutch, struggling to downshift. The aspens got closer. At the last second, Jim managed to pop the clutch and shove Old Blue into first gear then finally, low four-wheel drive. Shaken and weary, they crept all the way down the mountain as if passengers on some creepy old Disney ride.

※　※　※

"You're home early. You catch our dinner already?" Her question trailed off as she looked into the Jeep and noticed Jim's wet pant legs, along with the flushed look on his face. "What, did you fall in?" Then she spotted Jerry, who was all wet, looking sad and in no hurry to get up. "Oh my God! What happened to you two?"

"Long story." Between the dark lurking sense he'd felt on the night of the Perseids, the swarm of angry bees, and the close call on his wild ride down the mountain, he felt as if the signs added up to an end to their idyllic ranch life. After enjoying a blissful summer of ignorance regarding Jerry's declining condition, Jim was once again starting to fear and doubt the uncertain road ahead of them. He really didn't feel like talking about what he knew was a deeper meaning behind these recent events. Instead, Jim denied his sixth sense and crammed it down deep inside his soul. The essential details were all he could manage to share.

"Bees!? Oh, poor baby, you okay?" She fawned over Jerry, who stood up to soak in her attention.

"Hey, I got stung too!" Jim smirked as he helped Jerry out of the Jeep. They both watched as he hopped a few steps over to the mat in front of the RV and plopped down.

"Poor guy, he looks terrible."

"I know."

   ❀   ❀   ❀

Jerry's stamina went downhill over the next few days. His tolerance for walks became much shorter, and his breathing more labored. He developed a persistent cough that sounded nothing like the light, shallow rasp of the allergy scare back in Utah more than a year before. This was a much deeper, moist-sounding hack. Neither Rene nor Jim could say it aloud, but it appeared that the cancer had caught up to him. Quietly, they each wondered when Jerry's time might come. With weeks of work left on the ranch, the logistics of death weighed heavy on Jim's mind.

"What are we going to do if the time comes…you know, while we're still here?" He doubted there was even a vet in the small mountain town, and the nearest decent-sized city was an hour away. "What if we need to rush him somewhere. What if he…"

"I don't want to think about that right now." She didn't want to discuss it. At all. Flustered, Rene reminded Jim to take his own advice. "Why don't you practice what you preach?"

Jim had a favorite reply to Tripawds members who frequently asked the big What-If questions: "Forget What and tell If to take a hike!"

   ❀   ❀   ❀

Within a week, Jerry proved they were both worrying too much. He was back to himself, happy and alert after the bee stings healed. Concerned over his health and with no way to tell if his lung metastasis had worsened, all they could do was live the latest version of his new normal. So instead of making the long walk across the bridge to his favorite swimming spot in the fishing pond near the office, they would load him up in the truck to drive him there. It always sent Jerry into a happy frenzy as he wondered if they were headed somewhere new and exciting.

Twenty-one months after his amputation, he was still swimming and smiling. There was no better time to celebrate by making a new video for his fans. On a cloudy afternoon, they drove to the nearby San Cristobal reservoir, a large glacial lake with long stretches of sandy beach. Sitting before the camera and tossing sticks into the lake, Rene and Jim took turns explaining Jerry's current condition for his fans as he splashed out to retrieve his prize.

She began with a big smile as Jim threw the first stick. "We're here celebrating Jerry's twenty-first ampuversary!" Someone had coined the term in the Tripawds forums months before, and now everyone in the community understood its significance. Jerry swam back with the stick in his mouth, his head bobbing in the water a bit more than usual even though he was wearing his bright-yellow life jacket.

"It's great to see him run and play like that, knowing his condition." Jim threw another stick, not tossing them as far as he used to. "It's been twenty-one months since his amputation, and they only gave him four, so we have every reason to celebrate."

"It's pretty amazing." Rene focused on the positive. "Every time I watch him swim, I'm just so inspired by him."

"Any regrets?" Jim threw one more stick.

"Absolutely none."

They were at a loss for words. Pushing aside what they knew was really going on inside the body of their three-legged hero, they provided an honest update without revealing too much detail. That wasn't the last movie they made with Jerry. But years later, it received a comment from a woman whose shepherd mix was diagnosed with osteosarcoma, just like Jerry. The dog was going in for amputation surgery the next day, and she was looking for hope and inspiration, just like Jim and Rene were doing when they came across Moose on YouTube. But this time, they were able to help a worried pet parent by sending her to the amputation support resources on the Tripawds website.

❄ ❄ ❄

"He's just not eating; he's looking weak. We need to do something." Rene was in deep research mode about cancer cachexia (muscle wasting) when she discovered that Jerry's oncologist had relocated from Santa Fe to Denver, a convenient first stop after leaving the ranch in a couple weeks.

"We are. We're doing it." Jim looked forward to seeing Dr. Mullins again. "Look at him; he's still happy and getting around pretty well…" The rest of his thoughts silently floated through his mind. "…for a dog on borrowed time."

Unable to discuss it further, he left the RV to walk with Jerry. He needed fresh air more than his dog. In the cool, late afternoon, Jim slowed his stride to walk alongside Jerry. Still active and able to walk for several minutes, even on half his lung capacity, Jerry hopped over to the pasture with a wildly flapping tongue and big, goofy grin, then plopped down in the tall grass. Jim grabbed a nearby stick to entice Jerry into a quick game of tug, and he happily took the bait without even getting up. As he gnawed and shook the stick still clutched in Jim's hands, Jim made another promise to his CFO.

"You just tell us when, boss, okay?" His voice cracked as he choked back tears, knowing how Jerry hated to see them upset. "I'll never let you suffer. I promise. And we'll never let you lose your dignity. You just give us a sign when you've had enough. You gotta let us know, okay?"

Jim looked deeply into his beautiful dog's eyes. "I promise you, my friend, no suffering."

❄ ❄ ❄

Jim and Rene both enjoyed their time on the ranch, enough to promise they would return the following summer. But they were ready to move on. Rene had already made an appointment with the oncologist at her new Denver clinic. The visit felt so far away.

They relocated next to the big metal shop a couple days before their departure. Jim took advantage of the shop's facilities to make

— 228 —

sure the truck and trailer were both ready, a critical task after sitting still for a few months. Rene used the opportunity to wash the rig, after giving Jerry a much-needed bath—dreading the whole time that it would likely be his last. Walking toward the trailer with a bucket in her hands, she dragged a hose behind her. Jerry hopped up behind her and grabbed the snaky rubber, just like all those times he'd attacked the pesky kelp on his favorite beach back home. "Hey, look who's helping!"

Jim smiled and replied, "Yeah, he's feeling pretty good today." Every day they wondered what kind of day was waiting for Jerry. This was another good one. Then Jim heard the rickety golf cart come around the corner and skid into an abrupt stop in the shop.

"How ya doin', Perk?" Rene had learned to greet the old man with a shout, rather than repeat herself.

"It's another great day." A frustrated look drew across his weathered face. Perk had cornered himself once again. Jim reached down and flipped the reverse lever for the old man, who lightly tapped the drive pedal and started rolling backward. "Thanks. What's your name?"

Jim didn't bother with an answer. The funny old man was already on his way. He caught a glimpse of that cracked window on the shady side of the shop and smiled at the saying: Every day is a great day.

Two days later, the truck, trailer, and dog were all serviced and sparkling clean. Everyone was antsy. It was time to go. They piled into the Dodge, and as Jim pulled away from the red-roofed ranch house, he was glad to feel the wheels rolling again. From the rearview mirror, he studied Jerry looking out the window as they drove past the fishing pond and his favorite swimming spot. Then he pointed the truck north toward Denver and sped up.

— 22 —

On the Road Again

Time doesn't slow down for anyone. Not even dogs with cancer. The fluttering aspen leaves proclaimed the end of summer with an eye-popping debut of bright gold, orange, and red tones of fall, but Jerry's pack couldn't stick around for the finale. They broke camp for a quick return to the real world in Denver. Filled with heartache and sadness as Jerry's stamina declined, Rene found comfort in writing for Jerry's blog. That September of 2008, she shared a brutally honest description of his current state:

> I just don't feel like myself lately. My head says, "Play! Play! Play!" But whenever I get excited and try to run around, my energy level drops, really fast. If I move around a lot, I'll let out a heavy, deep cough/choke, and sometimes it takes me a second to recover from it. I've had "the cough" for a while now, but it seems to be worse lately.

She tried not to let cancer get the best of her, but fear flooded her heart whenever she imagined Jerry's future. Each morning right after awakening, she wondered what kind of dog would greet her. Would Jerry be perky and sitting up in bed, waiting for his morning walk? Or would he lay there? Sleepy. Lethargic. *Dying.* The uncertainty brought back roller-coaster emotions from the early days of his amputation recovery.

His winning streak was almost over, and she knew it, but she wasn't about to let cancer steal one moment of the remaining time they had together while Jerry still enjoyed a good quality of life. He got up each day and went on a short walk to check his pee-mail. He ate, drank, and wagged his tail whenever a stranger approached. And he still shook his Barney dolls as vigorously as ever. He may have been getting slower, but the sparkle in his eye was still there. Each day, she tried to push her worries aside to enjoy his company without fear getting in the way.

They hoped Jerry would see his tenth birthday in October, but it seemed nature had other plans. Symptoms of metastasis, like the coughing and unpredictable hacks, taunted them with audible reminders of his condition. Sorrow and dread floated in and out of their thoughts, but they never missed a chance to try something new that might help him feel better, like the prized elk meat the Vickers family gifted him.

Before leaving the ranch, Jerry had run to the door the day Rene came home with the little square package wrapped in butcher paper. "Hey, look what I have here!" Rene did her best to get him excited as she put the raw meat in a bowl. The pungent, gamey scent got Jerry's appetite up, and he began taking small nibbles of his special dinner. "Yeah, that's it! Eat up, you silly dog." She was happy to see him eating again.

But today, the meat had no appeal. He appeared to only eat enough to please her while she eagerly watched through watery eyes. "Oh, Jerry, don't you like it, baby?" He always loved unusual meats. But now, he stopped and stared at the offering. After one last gentle nibble, he looked up and pleaded as if to say, "No more, Mom, okay? I'm not really hungry."

Jim walked over and put his arm around his heartbroken wife. "You wouldn't want to eat with someone watching you either. Let him be." The last thing that sensitive dog needed was for her to be upset. Jim reminded her how someday, she could cry. But not now. He had wiped the tear streaming down her face and fought off his own emotions. "At least he ate something. It's still a good day, see?"

*　　*　　*

Jerry's return to Kenosha Pass was perfect timing. It was autumn, and Tripawd Calpurnia's sled dog team had begun their fall training season. Jim and Rene couldn't resist stopping to see the team once more with Jerry, knowing it would likely be their last chance. Blazing orange aspens towered in the distance and warm afternoon sunlight beamed down on them in the parking lot. It was cold outside, but the sunshine felt warm on their faces. This was a day they hadn't been entirely sure would happen.

Their friends were the only other visitors, a rag-tag team of retired Iditarod racers and grey-muzzled huskies. They yipped and howled in unison as soon as they spotted Jerry. The sound of Calpurnia's bark floated above the others, indicating she was especially excited to see her old friend.

Instantly drawn to one another after months of being apart, the dogs softly nudged muzzles and pranced while inspecting butts and bellies. When they'd first met a year prior, Rene and Jim assumed that the mutual attraction had something to do with them both being front-leg Tripawds, but now they knew better. These dogs just got along. They liked each other's energy; it was that simple. Unlike dogs, humans always overthink things.

"Jerry! How are you, my friend?" Calpurnia's mom, TC, ran toward them, and Jerry responded with equal enthusiasm. She smelled heavenly to him, like a furry bouquet watered with the slobber of twenty-four different dogs. Jerry hopped over to greet his friend with ease, then leaned on her legs and looked up with adoring eyes. The mushing dog mom was his kind of people.

"Jerry, you want to go with us? We're going to do a short run with the, ahem, mature dogs," she said while making air quotes with her fingers. She turned to Rene and pleaded, "Can he come with us? Pleeeeease."

Sadness filled Rene's eyes, and she couldn't find the words to say no.

Jim stepped in to prevent more tears. "He would if we let him, but he's not up to it. You guys go on your run, and we'll stay here with Jerry."

She had coped with cancer in her own dogs and didn't want to pry. "I totally get it, you guys. He'll be running with us in spirit today!"

The carefully orchestrated chaos of excited sled dogs was primed for the run. When the last husky was clipped into the line, TC lifted Calpurnia away from Jerry and gently placed her in the ATV's rear gear box. The old gal's missing limb had caught up with her too, and she now led the pack from her cushioned chariot.

"Where you off to now, Jerry?" TC asked, fully expecting an answer from him.

Rene jumped in on his behalf. "We're going to Yellowstone, right, Jer?" She bent over to scratch his rump, which sent him into his happy three-pawed dance. "After we go see his oncologist, that is."

"Oh, cool. My sister lives right outside the park. You'd love her; she's a gypsy, just like you guys. Lives in Florida all winter and Montana in summer."

"I remember you mentioning that. In fact, I was going to ask you something about her." Rene dreaded the question, but it had to

— 233 —

be asked. Her smile faded into a serious expression. "She has dogs, right?" Rene knew she did, and TC nodded. "Do you think I could get her vet's name and number?"

"Of course, I'll send her an email. Why? What's going on?"

Tears pooled in Rene's downcast eyes. It was time to come clean about Jerry's condition. The inevitable end was just around the bend. Talking about his decline with anyone but Jim made it official.

"Jerry's not doing so good. We're not sure how much longer he can go on. If your sister likes her vet, we'll feel better if we need to make *that* call when we're there."

"Say no more." This mom to two dozen rescue huskies knew the rest of the story and reached out to hug Rene. She had nurtured many dogs from puppyhood to their final breath. The heartache of living through those final days felt all too familiar.

"I'll get the number for you. I know she loves her vet." TC reached down to rub Jerry's scruff. "And you didn't hear that, right, buddy? You still have some roads to travel!"

Jerry paid no attention to the discussion. He was more interested in what his friend was doing so far from his reach. Rene lifted her glasses and wiped away tears with the back of her sleeve as Calpurnia's team sped away on the dusty trail.

※　※　※

Hard-backed seats lined the walls of the sterile veterinary clinic, with its shiny floors and brisk air-conditioning. There was no comfy lounge furniture or soft carpet for the patients to lay on, like at the New Mexico clinic where Jerry first met his oncologist. She now cared for her patients in Denver, at a rather institutional, big-city specialty hospital for pets with major medical issues. Palpable anxiety lingered in the lobby while Jim and Rene waited for Jerry to return from his x-rays.

Almost every day before their arrival, Jerry woke up eager to explore whatever the day brought. He still didn't resemble an animal weakened from cancer, but for the last couple of weeks, he sometimes let out an ominous, deep cough that stirred them from their sleep. While lying in the darkness waiting for the fit to subside, Rene and Jim both silently concluded that things weren't good.

A clipboard-wielding assistant entered the lobby. "Jim and Rene? Come with me, please." They got up, and the nurse led them into a small exam room where Jerry waited. As they entered, they noticed Dr. Mullins following them, her broad smile of recognition breaking through the somber atmosphere. Then she spoke with a tone that put everyone at ease.

She had a knack for knowing how to deliver bad news. In the world of veterinary oncology, it was inevitable, and she had lots of practice. Always respectful of her client's fragile emotions, she offered a prognosis with a balance of hope and reality. Today, she would do that for Jerry's people.

The three humans gathered around a monitor where a monochrome image of Jerry's rib cage filled the screen. It wasn't immediately clear what Jim and Rene were supposed to be looking at, but the moment the vet pointed out a bright-white, ghostly shadow that almost completely covered Jerry's right lung, they knew. Tears cascaded down Rene's face while Jerry gently nudged the back of her legs. He seemed to sense it was time to get comfortable and made himself at home by lying on the cool floor. Jim cleared his throat in a half-hearted attempt to hold back his tears.

"That one lung tumor we've been watching has grown considerably. You can see how it's consumed much of the right lung here. He's basically operating on only one right now. That's why he gets tired so easily," the oncologist explained while circling the image with her pencil eraser. "He won't eat because the tumor has grown big enough to irritate the airway, which is causing the coughing fits."

Rene and Jim paused and looked down at their beautiful, oblivious dog. He found the courage to speak first. "Is there anything we can do? To shrink the tumors? Other than surgery that is."

The oncologist stood up from her chair, then knelt to Jerry's level. She found strength while petting his soft fur as Jim and Rene slowly absorbed the news. Then she leaned over, placing her stethoscope bell on Jerry's chest to listen to his breathing. A textbook case of osteosarcoma lung metastasis progression filled her ears. "I wish I had better news. But the cancer cells are reproducing faster than chemotherapy can control them."

"So, now what? Is there anything we can do?" Jim needed to know when Jerry's time would come and prayed it wasn't that day.

"Oh, yes! You can do something." The doctor provided the most encouraging advice she could offer. "You can do things that keep him comfortable and eating. There is a medication that can stimulate his appetite, and one that might help him breathe easier. None of it will get rid of his symptoms completely, but he may get some more quality time with you guys."

More time. Jerry had been living on borrowed time for the last twenty-two months. It was inevitable that the cancer would take over his body, but the dog seemed as happy and joyful as ever, even with half of his breathing capacity stolen by the disease. His walks were only a few minutes long, and he didn't eat much these days, but he simply appeared to be an older, mellower version of himself as a senior dog.

They looked at the blissful dog resting at their feet and knew he wasn't ready to go that day. Jim pressed for more facts from the vet. "Give us your best guess, please."

"It could be a couple weeks…maybe a month. That's usually how it goes at this point." She had seen hundreds of osteosarcoma cases, each developing almost identically to this one. "The mets will keep growing. Keep in mind, though, he's not in pain. He will just become more uncomfortable…more quickly now, as it gets harder to breathe." She didn't sugarcoat the message, but did soften the blow to their hearts. "Jerry has already beaten all the odds against him. We just don't know for sure exactly how long he has."

She stood after delivering the reality check, along with a little hope for two heartbroken people. "Just keep him rested, give him lots of love, do the things he enjoys, and don't let him overdo it. I'll give you some medication to help with his appetite and breathing issues. Oh, and you can also stop the metronomics; those pills are no longer working."

Good news and bad, Jim thought. Cutting so many pills out of his routine would be nice. Jerry looked up and studied their expressions as if wondering what all the fuss was about. He saw Jim staring into space and Rene's eyes filling with water, then slowly stood and moved over to lean on the kind doctor's leg before lying back down at her feet. A radiant smile spread across her face as she leaned over to caress his soft fur. "Oh, Jerry, you know how to make us all feel better."

🐾   🐾   🐾

Long before Jerry got cancer, a visit to Yellowstone with him was always on their bucket list. They didn't care much for the trip to Denver, but at least they were now within a reasonable driving distance for getting to the national park. That evening after dinner, Rene grabbed her giant road atlas and sat at the table. Route planning always helped her feel hopeful. She thumbed through the pages, found Wyoming, and pointed at the big, green spot in the western half of the state. "Look! We're going there. Jerry and Barney have to see Old Faithful together!"

Jim relished the happier tone in her voice. "Darn right! And we're going to cross the Continental Divide...again! Did you hear that, Jer? Let's get outta this city and head back to the mountains." Jerry looked up from his bed with perky ears and a bright expression filling his eyes. Their excited voices told him more good times were coming.

Leaving Denver couldn't come fast enough. The next day, Jim steered the rig north on the interstate through a slow-moving traffic mob. They had just finished a short tour of a neighboring city to the north, Fort Collins, Colorado. The college town had been on their radar ever since spotting it in one of those best places to live lists. Everything they read about it was accurate. It had a cute downtown with thriving independent businesses. Bike trails everywhere. A large university. And the stunning Rockies for the town's backdrop.

Always the first to get excited when expectations match reality, Rene was the first to speak her mind about what they saw. To her, Fort Collins seemed like the kind of place where they could settle down. "Real estate is doable here! Bet we could find some acreage just outside of town. I like it. Don't you?"

Jim didn't answer, and held steadfast in his usual role as the careful skeptic. Rene didn't expect him to agree right away, she knew that wasn't his style. Instead of waiting for an answer, she glanced over her shoulder and turned her attention to Jerry, something she did even more than usual these days. He napped peacefully in the back seat on his Barney blanket, head carefully propped on a pillow. A sense of relief filled her heart as she watched his rib cage softly rising and falling without a stutter. The new medications were working. Just days ago, even a simple rollover would launch a sudden coughing fit bursting with deep, wet hacks. But not anymore. At that moment, he was breathing normally and resting comfortably. It was the greatest gift of the day.

She wondered, if Jerry could talk, when would he say he was done fighting? He couldn't use English to tell them, so instead, it was their responsibility to read his signals, to understand when it was time to take that last walk together. From the earliest days of his diagnosis,

Jim and Rene knew they had to prepare for the inevitable and create boundaries to deal with the progressive disease. First, they agreed that "quality of life" for Jerry meant they wouldn't put him through IV chemotherapy sessions or force him to take dozens of supplements. Next, they agreed that incontinence or paralysis would steal his quality of life. And now, they both felt a commitment to save Jerry from further medical intervention, aside from medications to ensure his comfort. They understood these final steps were simply a Band-Aid, and that they would not save him from the tumors destroying his lungs. If Jerry's remaining days were to be good ones, there would be no more vet visits or surgeries or chemo pills for him. Just whatever helped him breathe a bit better and prevent any pain. Whatever time Jerry had left in a capable body was going to be spent on his terms, doing what he loved most.

＊　＊　＊

Their cell phone rang just as they passed the last exit to Fort Collins. It was Luke Robinson, their crazy dog friend who was hiking from Austin to Boston to raise canine cancer awareness. He must have seen their Tripawds blog news about Jerry's lung metastasis. Rene hesitated to pick up, knowing that he was probably calling to offer suggestions for fighting it.

"Hey, Rene. I saw the blog. I'm really sorry. It sucks."

"Yeah. It does."

"Where are you guys now? Anywhere fun?"

When she told him they had just left Fort Collins, he nearly shouted, "What? Did you go to CSU for Jerry? That's great! The vet school there is awesome!"

"No, we didn't." She didn't care to get into details about their Denver visit.

"Why? Don't you know?" Luke grew animated, as he tends to do whenever discussing cancer care. "Colorado State is the best place for treating osteo. You have to go back. Turn around! They can help Jerry beat this."

Rene sighed. Her gut feeling was right. "We already left. We're headed to Yellowstone now."

"Look, I know people there. I can get you guys into a clinical trial.

You want me to make some calls for you?" Luke's passion to fight dog cancer was stronger than ever. He just genuinely wanted to help Jerry win the cancer battle.

Rene didn't know how to tell him they were just going to keep driving. They had drawn the line. In desperation, she pressed the phone's speaker button and held the device out to Jim. "Tell him," she whispered.

"Hey, Luke, Jim here. We're not going back; we can't do that."

"Really? Aw, man, c'mon. Why not?" He sounded disappointed.

"It would only be for us, not Jerry." Jim couldn't quite get his point across without becoming emotional. "It's all about quality of life now, not quantity. We just met with his oncologist, and we don't have much time left. We're gonna go enjoy it together."

"Are you sure? I've seen dogs get more time when vets said they wouldn't!" Luke's passion and persistence would eventually serve him well in the canine cancer research world, but not today in Jim and Rene's situation. They stayed with their decision.

"Yeah, we're sure. We're going to Yellowstone." Jim appreciated the offer of help but wanted to wrap up the call. "But thank you for the offer; that's really nice of you to call."

"No problem, man, I understand." The discussion ended as delicately as it could, and they hung up. Then, within seconds, Rene was overcome with guilt. Maybe they should go back, she thought. Perhaps Luke's call was a sign that there was some scientific breakthrough that could save Jerry's life. What if there was something that could give him more time and they had just passed up their one chance?

She dug deep to find the words, "Turn around!" But instead, she did her best to Be More Dog. She took a deep breath and looked at the road in front of them. Traffic had subsided; two lanes stretched to the blue horizon, bordered by rolling hills and green pastures. She contemplated the big picture. They had to follow their gut instinct. They could go on and give Jerry the time of his life at Yellowstone. Or they could turn around, check him into an institution, and potentially rob him of any great days he had left. For this wandering pack, it was a natural choice. She said nothing, and Jim kept his hands on the wheel.

❋ ❋ ❋

Traveling north on rural Highway 287 toward Wyoming, they remained silent for about an hour as the prairie gently rolled into the rocky foothills of northern Colorado. All the hay had been harvested, and an earthy aroma of cut grass filled the fall air as they passed through a small, red rock canyon. A sign pointing toward Red Feather Lakes appeared on the shoulder.

"Red Feather Lakes. That sounds pretty. How come we're not going there?" Jim was surprised Rene hadn't mentioned it. He felt like they were missing out on something as he passed a quaint little market called The Forks.

"Because we wanted to see Fort Collins." Rene had no intention of stopping so soon. "And it's still a couple days to Yellowstone."

The towering peaks of the Mummy Range lay to the west, dappled in shades of purple and blue as sunset slowly fell to the horizon. Jim yearned to see those mountains up close.

"I like the sound of it. Put it on the list," Jim said. "We need to come back and check out this area again someday."

"Sure. What do you think, Jerry?" She looked back for an opinion from their copilot.

Jerry rose and gingerly nudged his head through the truck's open window to catch a whiff of his surroundings. This air was not sterile or medicated, nor institutional in any way. The air here tasted so good, like being back on the ranch. Clearly, there was a lot to love here, making this one more great day in the life Jerry lived.

— 23 —

Keeping Promises

Deep in the heart of the Jackson Hole valley, groves of deciduous giants tower over the banks of the Gros Ventre River watershed. The ancient sentinels stand tall in the shadows of the Teton Range, where a canopy of thick cottonwood trees and skinny aspens protect overeager campers settling down for the chilly fall night. Jerry's pack joined them, and as Jim jockeyed the RV into one of the last campsites available, he felt an immense sense of relief when he spotted an open patch of sky that would let their satellite internet system connect to cyberspace. Satisfied with his parking finesse, he took his hands off the wheel, cut the engine, and deeply inhaled. They made it.

He didn't need to look over his shoulder to sense Jerry approved of their temporary home. A steady stream of happy, hot, panting breath billowing over his neck said it all.

"Thank you, Jerry." There he was, talking to his dog again. And he desperately wished Jerry could talk back.

Several hours on the road left him weary from commandeering the large vehicle. There were no hoses or cords to connect at this primitive campground, so instead of tackling his usual camp duties, Jim relaxed with Jerry on his big Barney blanket while Rene prepared dinner. It felt good to be off-grid in the woods again.

"We owe this all to you, buddy."

After nearly ten years at each other's side and almost two roaming the country, he was confident they could communicate pretty well. Jerry had no command of the English language, but the dog's emotions conveyed a more profound message than any words. From moment to moment, whatever wild turn their life had taken, Jerry intuitively delivered the exact energy Jim and Rene needed to feel grounded.

But cancer had a way of distorting their non-verbal communication. Deep into the worst and probably final phase of Jerry's disease, Jim felt he was losing the ability to read his dog. Was Jerry feeling okay with the new medication? Or, was he ready for a set of wings? Tossing aside everything he believed about being fully present in life's everyday moments, all Jim wanted was to know what was going on in that dog's brain.

As if to prod Jerry into speaking, Jim gently rubbed his index finger knuckle into his dog's giant ear flap. Deeply, blissfully, Jerry moaned his approval. But he voiced no words. And gave no answers.

The brilliant amber sun sank behind the Tetons, and Jim got lost in his own thoughts recalling the memories from their previous life. Jerry's head lay peacefully on his lap, relishing the attention. Never in his wildest dreams did he think they would still be living in the RV and enjoying bucket list places most people wait decades to explore. While he was lost in his thoughts, kids ran wild around the cottonwoods and played at one end of the park, while deer grazed on the remnants of summer grass at the other. The campground chatter didn't bother him the way it might have in the past. This new way of being was better than anything he could have imagined.

Jerry sought more affection and rolled onto his back for a full-body belly rub. Limbs stretched end to end, long and lean, he raised his one remaining front leg and pointed it straight into the air like a conductor's baton. Jim laughed when he read into Jerry's request and slapped that giant paw with a high five. Oh yeah. They still understood each other.

He continued the ear-rub ecstasy while Jerry's eyes gently closed, his giant, lazy tongue lolling outside his lax jaws. Today, Jim's fear couldn't overshadow the moment. The Big Bad Wolf was not lurking in the forest; everything was as it should be. He owned it. For the last two years, he felt confident they had given Jerry everything they promised when cancer came calling. Gone were the constant worries about deadlines and loans and career pressures. Today, he sat in silence, content to just absorb himself in the space between thinking and doing. When he stared into Jerry's eyes, he could swear Jerry said, "Thank you."

"I promised you we would go to the beach again if you made it to the Atlantic, didn't I?" Jim smiled when he recalled Jerry barking at the buried beach rocks on the Acadia shoreline. It was one momentous milestone they didn't expect to see.

"And remember my promise that we could swim in the ocean if you made it to Florida?"

Jerry's eyes remained lightly closed, but his ears twitched. He sensed he was being spoken to and looked up at Jim as if to reply, "Yeah, we've had a pretty good run here."

Jim continued. "You know what? I'll always keep my promises to you, buddy. You just gotta keep one for me, okay?"

Then he stopped and stared deep into his once-in-a-lifetime dog's eyes.

"You're gonna tell me when you're done, right, buddy?"

A soft voice in his head quietly replied. "Oh, you know I will."

※   ※   ※

"Isn't that just too cute?" Rene opened the screen door and softly stepped outside to join the moment of appreciation. But not before she grabbed the camera. She had taken more photos than ever the past couple of weeks, desperate to capture what she knew were Jerry's final days, slipping right through their fingers.

"Hey, Jerry! Look up, baby, over here! You too, Jim."

She lightly tiptoed around while cradling the camera in her hands. Aware he was being watched, Jerry sat up as if to pose while audible clicks of photo after photo floated through the gentle evening breeze. He looked regal, sitting elegant and proud on his purple Barney blanket, surrounded by the warm colors of autumn.

"Somebody has a birthday coming up!" Rene said to Jerry in her high-pitched sing-song voice. Continuously aware that their good fortune couldn't last forever, her prayers for more time together seemed to have been answered—at least today. In just a few days, Jerry would turn ten years old, a remarkable accomplishment for a dog who at age eight was given six months to live. *So much for that prognosis*, she thought. "You showed them, didn't you, buddy?"

This was the week they would celebrate his big day, with a homemade chicken liver cake topped with cottage cheese frosting and carrot stick candles. She scratched between Jerry's ears and said to Jim, "Let's go check out Jackson tomorrow and get some groceries, okay?"

She beamed in the evening sun, her mood so elevated that Jim decided to spare her the heartache of knowing what he was thinking. Under his breath, he begged Jerry to be honest. "You gonna make it, buddy?"

Focused and alert, Jerry stared into Jim's eyes and with all his heart, promised that he would.

❄ ❄ ❄

The rustic enclave of Jackson, Wyoming, was an excellent place to kick off the birthday celebration. It was the first time they could relax in a week. Jerry appeared to be feeling better since starting his new medications, which lightened their mood. He breathed easier thanks to a bronchial airway spray and the small dose of Prednisone that filled his body with puppy-like energy. Being close to the only vet clinic for a hundred miles in either direction was also comforting.

Unfortunately, the medication came with another set of issues. Any slightest exertion gave Jerry a ravenous thirst, causing him to drink water all day, and night. And although he seemed to have more vitality than before, any sudden movements or noise excited him with jumpy, nervous energy. They noticed the questionable side effects, but small bursts of Jerry's old personality shone through again, filling them with hope for a better quality of life. Then, when Jerry gathered enough energy to run around after squirrels, they thought he'd turned a corner. But two days before his tenth birthday, the dog ran too fast for his own good, collapsing after a few strides while pursuing his pests. The rodents taunted him from afar while he lay on the ground trying to catch his breath. Jerry's steroid-fueled recovery was not what it seemed.

The next day as they got ready to go to town, Jim saw Jerry bolt to the door. "Wait! Hold on, Jerry!" The overly excited dog barreled across the RV before Jim could help him outside. The screen door accidentally blew open when his muzzle nudged it, and Jerry made a mad dash to freedom. When Jim reached for the harness handle, his hand slipped and missed. Jerry leaped out of the RV, touched the first step with his one front paw, totally missed the other two steps, then face-planted onto the dirt.

"JERRY!" Rene's tearful cry echoed across the campground.

If she had seen it through Jim's eyes, she would have yelled even louder. From where she stood, she only saw a blur of brown fur as he tumbled out the door and down the steps. But Jim saw Jerry's body land in the dirt, hitting hard and knocking the wind out of him.

She hastily ran down the steps, but Jerry had already staggered to his feet to relieve himself. Thirstier than usual because of the

Prednisone, he ran outside not because of excitement for their trip to town, but so he wouldn't pee in the house. His tumble came as a surprise, but it was more painful for Jim and Rene. He shook it off almost as soon as his business was done. When it was, he walked over to the RV and peered in as if to say, "OK, I'm ready!" But Rene and Jim were not. Now, there would be no trip to Jackson for his birthday cake supplies. "Come here, buddy." Jim could see Jerry looked a little out of sorts after the fall and sat down with him on the leaf-covered ground.

Rene watched him pat Jerry's body with all the affection in his soul while steady tears streamed down her face. Her heart ached harder than she could ever remember. She knew what was coming and wiped her eyes with her shirt sleeve. "I think we need to go see that vet."

"I'm not so sure." In the heat of the moment, Jim's instinct disagreed, but he immediately second-guessed himself. He wanted to keep his promise to Jerry. The trio sat in silence on the ground while falling aspen leaves fell to earth around them. They watched Jerry's breathing, searching for some kind of clue that his time was at hand. But Jerry only wondered why they weren't leaving yet.

One by one, minutes floated off into the breeze until sixty came and went. Finally, they reached a wordless agreement. Looking into each other's eyes, they knew it was time. Rene called the Jackson vet clinic from inside the RV so Jerry wouldn't hear her tearful request. Outside, Jim helped Jerry into the truck and had an odd sense that his 75-pound body felt heavier than usual. It took a little more effort than usual for him to stride up onto the bench seat, but Jerry wasn't bothered by the struggle. He was just happy to get out for a trip to wherever.

❋   ❋   ❋

"This just doesn't feel right." Jim watched from the front row of clinic parking spots and could see that the practice was busy. Behind the glass front door inside the small waiting room, a dozen people sat patiently, waiting to see the busy vet. He glanced up into the rearview mirror and smiled back at Jerry, who was sitting up and looking back at him, curious, alert, and seemingly happy. Jim's mind was made up. No, it wasn't time after all. Not yet.

They talked about it, and Rene agreed. "Let me just go check it out. We might need them again if we stick around here." She walked inside, and Jim saw her get in line with other clients. Overcome by her own heartache, she couldn't help feeling as if her animal should be moved to the front of the line. He was, after all, the traveling miracle dog now dying before her eyes.

"New client? Here. Fill out these forms. It's gonna be a while before we can see you." The receptionist didn't even give Rene a chance to explain why she was there before announcing: "Next!" And she didn't even notice when Rene put down the clipboard and walked out of the busy lobby and back to the truck.

Jim examined her expression with hopeful eyes.

"You're right. Let's go. This isn't the place for us." When it was his time, she knew that Jerry deserved a much more dignified send-off than this noisy, impersonal clinic could ever provide.

They found a grocery store, and Jim waited in the truck while Rene ran inside to pick up a box of carrot cake mix, cottage cheese, and a couple big steaks. Jerry had no idea the party favors were for him. He rested peacefully in the back seat, maybe a bit too at ease. Jim reached around and gently placed his hand on Jerry's soft chest. Awakened by the light touch, Jerry lifted his head with a glance that said, "What?"

Leaving that vet clinic was the best thing they ever did. They meandered through town and took the long way back to the campground on a less-traveled road through the eastern section of the park. Lost in their indecisiveness about Jerry's quality of life, they arrived at Jenny Lake and got out to admire the crystal-clear waters from a scenic overlook with a hiking trail. Neither needed to say it: Jerry had to stay in the truck.

Thirty minutes later, they returned to find Jerry resting his head out the sliding back window, gazing at the scenery and probably wondering why he was left behind. Jim noticed the look of quiet confusion on Jerry's face and recalled a question he'd been asking himself for quite some time now. "How do I want to remember him? Is that it?"

He couldn't bear the thought of letting Jerry go without honoring the dog's need to be in nature, not just looking at it. "Cheer up, buddy! I promise we'll go for a walk." He knew it wouldn't be a long one, but even a few minutes of including Jerry in the sightseeing would lighten up the day for all of them. And he always kept his promises.

They drove on to Jackson Lake, where a small herd of wild bison feasted in the grasslands. Jim slowed his heavy truck and rolled down

Jerry's window so he could inhale the wild, musky scents. As expected, Jerry stuck his head out to assess the herd. Staying true to his humble personality, he never once barked at the gentle giants.

As they paused beneath the timeless peaks of the Teton Range, the wily creatures reminded Jim of their important place in the lives of native peoples. He explained to Rene that when he was a young child, he learned that those who believe in spirit animal totems also believe buffalo are a reminder that you will always be looked after and provided for. And right now, they were looking after Jerry, who quietly communed with the stoic symbols of prayer, gratitude, and praise for all the gifts of the universe. They silently stared out into the prairie, knowing that this remaining time with their copilot was indeed a great gift from the spirits.

Before heading back to the campground, Jim pulled over at another pretty spot beneath the giant peaks. He stopped the engine and stepped outside, then noticed a guitar pick on the ground. He tucked the thin plastic trinket in his pocket, not thinking much of it other than he always enjoyed finding little treasures.

Jerry sat up and eagerly waited for his walk to begin. He had no problem waiting for Jim to help him down out of the truck. Once his paws touched the earth, they didn't walk far at all, but Jerry appeared to enjoy every step, nonetheless. He stopped every couple feet to sniff the grass, gobble up elk poop bonbons, and gnaw on a large, woody branch. He may not have been very fast, but he was still pretty strong, and loved nature's chew toys.

"Ohhhh! You wanna play?" Jim picked up one end of the long branch and walked alongside Jerry, who led the way. With the sun high in the afternoon sky and the Teton Range as a backdrop, the enchanting fall scene unfolded while Rene connected their camera to a tripod.

Jerry gripped one end of the stick tightly in his jaws while Jim and Rene held on tight to the other. They pretended to pull back hard in the gentle tug-of-war game. *Click.*

"Get it, Jerry!" Rene giggled. *Click.*

"All yours, buddy!" Jim released his end, relishing in Jerry's ecstasy at the new prize. *Click.*

Framed by the snow-capped peaks, surrounded by aspens with golden leaves flickering in the breeze, the photo does not show that they are just a few yards away from their truck. And it also doesn't show cancer's ugly, internal destruction. In truth, and despite the disease's progress, the photo shows how Jerry was living with the disease, not dying from it. The happy dog and his humans found a work-around to the lung metastasis challenge. They were making the most of every single day, without worrying about the next one.

Jim was never more sure about the answer to his unspoken question. "This is how I want to remember Jerry."

"Happy birthday to you, happy birthday, dear Jer-ree…"

❀   ❀   ❀

October first arrived, and the pack was jubilant. Jim and Rene sang an off-key tribute, and even Jerry joined in with a loud bark. Perhaps he was singing along, but he was probably just demanding a piece of his carrot cake. His appetite was back and stronger than ever, thanks to a bigger dose of Prednisone to manage his symptoms.

Everything felt so right that later in the evening, Rene published a birthday post for his fans, along with a glamour shot of him majestically posed beneath aspen trees shrouded in fall colors.

There's a reason I've been hangin' in there…Today is my birthday. I am now 10 years old! With plenty of reason to celebrate. For starters, I'm getting a big steak for dinner and carrot cake for dessert. My people also gave me a new pill. It's supposed to help me breathe easier. I suppose it did, but the side effects make my heart race, so I'm panting like crazy. Or maybe I'm just excited about my special birthday dinner.

Dozens of encouraging comments floated in immediately after. All of Jerry's friends were closely following his progress and cheered him on. Lalla's mom, Eisen, Zeus, other Tripawds members, and even complete strangers wrote to congratulate Jerry on beating the odds. Again.

❀   ❀   ❀

The short drive to Yellowstone took them through some of the most stunning Rockies scenery yet. But Jerry missed most of it. Recuperating from his big celebration, he slept the whole way. But the minute the truck engine quieted, he sat up with curiosity about his new location.

Even during the waning weeks of fall, the Yellowstone campground buzzed with vacationing families in rental RVs, all competing for the last open campsites. Rene and Jim were lucky to get one at all. They didn't get to choose their spot, which was obscured by a thick pine tree canopy. Any other campers would have adored the woodsy ambiance, but not these two. Rene fretted as Jim maneuvered the RV in a struggle to find open sky for a satellite Internet link to the heavens. Now more than ever, they felt a calling to stay connected and share Jerry's status with the world.

He programmed the dish to connect with their assigned satellite, but it failed. Then, Jim noticed an opening in the trees overhead and decided to try one last thing before surrendering. He got back into the truck and moved the trailer three feet in reverse, then went inside to monitor the electronics. From the doorway, he declared, "If that doesn't do it, we'll just live with it. Or, without it, I guess."

Rene could hear the frustration in his voice. "But Jerry has to post his new video! Aww, I hope it works." She was eager to get online, but was more concerned about the campground's lack of cell phone service. She looked around their new surroundings to assess the situation. The bathrooms were nearby, and a well-used phone booth stood about fifty feet away.

The mechanical whir of the dish rising and falling echoed throughout the campground. Rene watched it try to connect and prepared to live without the Internet for a few days. She vowed if they couldn't get online, she wouldn't let it get her down. After all, Jerry was comfortable, the scenery was pretty, and the world-famous Madison and Firehole rivers converged within earshot.

Those three feet Jim moved were just enough. "Wait for it…" He looked at Rene from the open RV door, pointed up to the dish, and cocked his head. No sound of spinning gears. The antenna mount stopped moving. He opened the modem cabinet, saw they were online, and gave Rene a thumbs up.

"Yay! You hear that, Jerry?" Conscious that he was being spoken to, Jerry awakened from his afternoon nap and lifted his head from the Barney blanket. His look questioned her, as if expecting a treat or an afternoon walk. But he didn't rise up, clearly too tired for any fun.

While Jerry rested on his blanket, they checked their email. One stood out: "Good Montana Vet," read the subject line. Calpurnia's mom had sent the name of her sister's vet clinic just outside the park.

Rene studied the name, and while she hated to think about making the dreaded phone call to a vet she didn't know, having a reference helped her feel more in control of an out-of-control disease.

Jim rushed to upload another video before sunset. The short clip showed Jerry close up, catching popcorn as Rene tossed one kernel after another to the eager, hungry dog. In his blog, she wrote:

> *The other day, when my people were gonna take me to the local vet, I was feeling so good that we decided to go enjoy life instead. We went to check out more of Grand Teton National Park and took lots of pictures. I even played a bit and chewed on some sticks. But, boy, did that tire me out!*

> *When we got back, I had fun catching popcorn with gusto and gulping it down...All this from a dog who, a few weeks ago, wouldn't eat a thing.*

> *Today? Eh, not feeling so hot. Maybe I'm just hungover from my birthday party last night. Such is life on the emotional roller coaster that is cancer in dogs. But what does that matter when every day is a great day?*

— 24 —

Knowing When to Say When

Just beyond the turn for Big Sky, Montana, time seemed to slow down. With no other traffic on the two-lane highway, the pine-green valley floor opened up on the horizon, and brilliant-blue heavens reached as far as they could see. At once, they understood why it's called "Big Sky Country."

Jim drove faster than usual without the trailer attached, but he was in no hurry to get to this destination. In two hours they would arrive in McAllister, Montana, where a small country veterinarian was waiting.

Just one hour earlier, Rene made the call. The one they never wanted to make; the one that every pet parent hopes to avoid. Since that teary conversation, she and Jim had hardly said more than a few words to each other. The scenery on the way to the clinic was breathtaking, but that's not what had them speechless. None of their friends, family, or anyone in the Tripawds community knew that the hardest day of their lives had begun.

※　※　※

"Morning, Jerry!" Rene chirped when she awoke at seven. She noticed he wasn't up and moving around yet, which was unusual. When she walked downstairs to the living room, she could see why. Jerry looked up at her from his bed. With questioning eyes, he lay on his side atop a damp, dark wet spot and whimpered.

"Oh, nooo...Jerry, baby, I'm so sorry!" Their eyes met, and she burst into tears. Jerry didn't move to get up out of the urine. He just looked up at her with his big, pointy ears pinned flat and sad alongside his head.

Everyone who has ever loved a dog hopes to escape that responsibility. The one in which they must put their own grief aside and find the courage to allow a pain-free, peaceful end of life for the dog who gave heart and soul to the pack with no strings attached. But today, it was Rene and Jim's turn. When she saw him lying in his wet bed, stabbing pain shot through her heart. There was no escaping their moment of truth. Jerry's body had betrayed him. More indignities were sure to follow. And no words were needed to say what needed to be done.

For the last few weeks, Jim secretly hoped Jerry might just pass peacefully in his sleep. He wondered if that was why Rene cried out that morning, and paused for a moment. But when he heard her try to lift Jerry, he quickly dressed and stepped out to find she had collapsed over him, tears pouring over Jerry's gentle, weakened body.

"It's time, this is it. This is it," Rene repeated several times. Her eyes were scrunched shut as she tried to stop herself from making Jerry feel worse. The words faded in and out between heavy sobs and heaves.

"Okay, I hear you." And he did. But he wasn't ready. What pet parent ever is? Like all the others, he had so much he wanted to say, to argue for more time together, to keep on fighting. But two years ago he'd made a promise to his dog, and he wasn't going back. The time had come to stay true to his word as he leaned down in silence to help Jerry to his feet.

※　　※　　※

Over the last few weeks, Jerry's stamina had weakened before their eyes. Jim and Rene both knew it, but neither could admit that Jerry was quickly approaching the final quality-of-life indicator that would tell them he was ready to surrender his mortality. Long ago, when they were handed his diagnosis, Jim and Rene decided that the day Jerry couldn't stand up to eliminate, it was the day that he was done. They frequently mulled it over in their minds.

"When he stops eating, then we'll know." Then they remembered Jerry was never a really big eater.

"What about when his tail stops wagging?" Vets would say, maybe. But canine behaviorists debunked tail-wagging as nothing more than a neurological reflex.

Once they put themselves in Jerry's place, his last quality-of-life indicator finally came to them. "He would never be happy if he were so weak he couldn't pee on his own," Jim offered. And Rene agreed. Other than his first night at home on the day they adopted him, Jerry never had another indoor accident. Could the dog who lived for the outdoors ever be happy if he needed help for simple tasks like going potty? Never, they said.

It was settled. Incontinence was the sign. Had they not agreed on it ahead of time, Jerry's final day may have been even more difficult than it already was. Rene composed herself, and Jim tenderly helped Jerry down the RV steps, smiling as he watched him hop along and stop to smell the morning dew. Was that the behavior of a dog standing at death's door? He couldn't be 100 percent sure, but if today wasn't the right time, then when? Waiting might prolong the inevitable for another couple weeks. But at what cost to his dignity? And who would they be waiting for? Jim knew that between Jerry's fall down the steps just one day earlier and last night's bed-wetting, they had all the proof they needed. If anything, he realized he was glad Jerry stopped to sniff the fresh morning scents. Even now, that was his dog, always stopping to smell the roses and enjoying every moment in time. That is how he wanted to remember him.

Jim reached down for Jerry's harness handle and gently hoisted him back up the steps into the trailer. He tossed together a breakfast of ground bison and scrambled eggs, something that would have brought Jerry running just weeks earlier, but not today. He wasn't hungry. Nobody was.

"We need to do something about his bed," Rene said under her breath as she grabbed her coin purse and headed out the door. She was going to call the veterinarian's number she got from Calpurnia's mom.

Jim intuitively knew that "we" was meant for him. "I'll take care of it." While Jerry lay on the couch, he bent down and slipped off the handmade cover Rene had made two years earlier, then placed it in a trash bag. He had a feeling that once things quieted down, she would want to save the sentimental cover, decorated with comical dogs driving cars and covered in fur. But the foam was already starting to stink; it had to go. He watched Rene walk away toward the phone booth nearby, then headed for the dumpster by the restrooms in the other direction.

"Great..." He folded the wet foam, but it still wouldn't fit through the small bear-proof opening. He shook his head and choked back more tears. After ripping it up and forcing the pieces into the metal trash box, Jim glanced over his shoulder to see Rene still on the phone with her back to him. Good; he didn't want her watching this. By the time he was done, his hands smelled like pee. But he didn't care; it was Jerry's pee. He held his hands to his nose and started to sob.

         ❋   ❋   ❋

The events of Friday, October 3, 2008, were not unexpected, but the challenge of coordinating Jerry's passing in a strange place only added to their grief and stress. Rene stood at the only payphone in the Yellowstone campground, installed at a time when cellular service didn't even exist. She reached inside her front pocket for a scrap of paper with the local vet's phone number. Wiping away the stinging stream of tears spilling down her face, she knew if she didn't make that call now, she would be filled with regret later.

A kind female voice answered, "Hello, Meadow Creek Veterinary Clinic," and the terrible words quickly tumbled out of Rene's mouth. "Hi, I have a dog with cancer who needs to be put to sleep today."

"Oh, I see. I'm sorry. What exactly is going on?"

She took a deep breath, then blurted out their complicated life story in under a minute: passing through the area in their RV...the amputation...end-stage osteosarcoma metastasis...labored breathing... lack of appetite...incontinence. Somehow, she remembered enough clinical aspects of his diagnosis to sound coherent and aware of the irreversible decision. She dropped the name of Jerry's oncologist and offered a phone number, but the vet nurse could tell she was managing the situation as good as anyone could, given the circumstances. She listened patiently with sympathy and understanding.

"No, we won't need to do x-rays again, I believe you. Of course, you can bring him in today. Whenever you can get here."

Rene hung up the phone, held her face in her hands, and cried. There was no turning back now. Campfire smoke mixed with the aroma of frying bacon and eggs lingered in the air as other campers began stirring, getting ready for a day filled with fishing and sightseeing. By the time she walked back to the RV, Jim had Jerry cleaned up and ready for his final truck ride.

"Can they see us today?"

"Yes. Let's go."

❈   ❈   ❈

Nothing more needed to be discussed. Jim loaded Jerry up into the back seat onto his Barney blanket. They drove in silence along Highway 287 for more than an hour before realizing it was another leg of the same highway they'd traveled when Luke begged them to take Jerry to the Colorado State University vet hospital for a last-ditch attempt to treat his cancer. If their driving that road was any kind of sign from the universe, they didn't care to discuss it. Instead, they spent the morning lost in their own thoughts, trying to accept the heartbreaking moment.

In Montana, the peaceful two-lane highway meanders alongside the Madison River for a scenic ride through forests and meadows. On any other day, they might have stopped for a photo, but not this one. Jim drove in silence, and with intent, as if stopping the truck might make them back out of the decision. Once they approached the vet clinic's rural property perched at the crest of a hill with stunning 360-degree views of snow-capped mountains, they instantly knew that if Jerry's departure had to happen today, there could be no better place. Serene and filled with songs of happy birds flitting about, wispy cloud strands drifted across the endless sky toward distant, snowy peaks. Big sky country indeed.

Jim shut off the engine and reached over the seat to check on Jerry. For the first time ever, their faithful traveling companion was not already sitting up to sniff the air of unfamiliar surroundings.

"Remember, we're doing this for Jerry." Rene hesitated and fiddled with her purse, prolonging the inevitable as long as she could.

"I know." Jim fought back the tears and unsnapped his seat belt. The unclicking lured Jerry into a sit; slower, and with somewhat of a struggle. "You go in and check it out, I'll get him."

"Great. Thanks." She pulled the truck door handle and let herself out. Her feet felt mired in concrete as she walked up the dirt path to the clinic door. Before turning the knob to open it, she recalled the reminder Jim drilled into her head whenever she outwardly wept over Jerry's cancer: "There will be plenty of time for tears later."

A middle-aged receptionist with kind eyes and a gentle voice greeted her at the counter. Rene took a deep breath and started explaining Jerry's story again. "I don't know if I spoke to you earlier, but..." The receptionist immediately knew who Rene was and why she was there, but allowed her to continue. She needed to get the words out, to remind her and everyone within earshot that she wasn't asking them to put him down without good reason. Luckily, she was the only client in the lobby.

"Go ahead and fill this out now; you won't want to later." The woman reached over the counter and handed Rene a clipboard with paperwork. The questions were important, but daunting: "Do you want a mass cremation? A private cremation? Are you keeping the cremains?"

Just outside the window, Jim helped Jerry out of the truck. Only now it seemed Jerry didn't need much help. From the moment he left the truck, his body firmed up with a strength that was totally missing the last few days. He didn't want assistance; he went straight to investigate the dogs in boarding kennels out back. Jerry hopped over, forcing a smile on Jim's face and causing him to second-guess the decision. But when Jerry hopped only a few feet before stopping from exhaustion, he knew this was the right time.

      🐾   🐾   🐾

"This must be Jerry," said the tall, sturdy woman in the white coat with the name "Dr. Cashman, DVM" embroidered on the front pocket. She smiled and knelt down alongside the traveling dog. Genuinely interested in her patient's story and how they ended up in McAllister, she was in no rush to get though this introduction. During their conversation, she gently ran her hands along Jerry's body, gave a gentle exam, and finally validated Rene and Jim's decision. Slowly and with simple words, she took time to explain what was about to happen.

"I find it goes best when people are prepared for what to expect."

"Thank you." Her compassionate tone told them they had picked the right vet.

"We'll use two injections. One to sedate, and then a second drug, which is responsible for the end." She chose her words carefully, and gently suggested that they allow her to use a catheter for the injections. The vet hesitated before explaining the extra fee involved. "Dogs who have been on steroids typically have collapsed veins that are hard to locate. A catheter will make the injection go a little smoother and be less stressful for everyone."

"I don't care about the cost." Jim was grateful she told them this and quickly accepted her advice.

"Some people prefer to do this outside, too. We can do that if you like."

"Yes, please." On such a beautiful fall day, Rene was glad they wouldn't be saying goodbye on a steel table under fluorescent lights. "Thank you for that."

"What will happen with his body?" Jim wanted to know every detail.

"Well, being Friday, we will need to keep him in a freezer until Monday, when we can coordinate the cremation." The rural vet had witnessed the harsh end to many ranch dogs in her time and seemed happy to hear such concern for a patient's aftercare.

"I'd like to help with that." Jim felt a bit stunned by his own words.

"Moving his body?" The vet's eyes widened.

"Yes, please." He was determined to help Jerry through to the very end. He owed it to his CFO.

"That's fine, but just so you know, we will be using a trash bag. Some people are uncomfortable with that."

"I understand."

"And depending on when he last ate, it may also get a little messy..." The kind vet described what can happen when all of the muscles relax, without getting into unnecessary specifics.

"I understand." Jim appreciated the details and stood firm, but he was ready to get this done before his confidence disintegrated. "I'm gonna take Jerry outside."

Then the vet kindly asked Rene if she had taken care of all the paperwork and costs before the deed was done. That way, they could just leave after saying goodbye.

"It's all handled, thank you."

❀　❀　❀

"You won't be needing this anymore, buddy." Jim unclipped the leash and removed Jerry's harness, then pulled his collar over his head. Seeing him naked and smiling, with his fluffy fur shining in the sun, was a beautiful sight. This was how Jim wanted to remember his CFO.

Moments passed while he got lost in thought until the barks of excited dogs in the boarding kennels stirred Jerry to stand. Gingerly walking on wobbly legs, he hopped over to say hello through the chain-link fence. Nose to nose without any aggression, the dogs communicated something Rene and Jim would never understand. Jerry turned to look at Jim and Rene, then plopped down on the sweet-smelling grass without returning.

"Wait." Rene was walking outside with the vet's nurse but quickly turned back toward the truck. A moment later she returned with Jerry's Barney blanket and spread it out. Jim had already grabbed the small Barney doll from under the seat in the truck and a large pack of liver treats that was still half-full. She brought a few more of Jerry's favorite toys. His big, green, floppy frog, and Hoppy the three-legged dog.

"Hey, Jerry, come!" Rene called, but he just looked up into the sky, with the dogs barking behind him and the sunshine lighting up his smile.

"Want a treat?" Jim shook the bag of treats. "Come on, dawg, get with the program…" The dog wasn't budging.

"Okay, buddy, I get it." Jim went to Jerry's side, slid his hands underneath his belly, and helped him up. Jerry slowly hopped back to lay on the blanket alongside his toys, Jim, and Rene. He sniffed the treats, which Rene started feeding him by the handful. While Jim kneeled over him to stroke those velvety ears, a vet tech quietly laid out tools, including a pair of clippers and two syringes filled with liquid, one clear, one blue.

"You sure you want to help afterward?" Rene couldn't believe Jim had offered. "Remember what the vet said about it being messy?"

"I don't care. Look at him. I owe him." Surrounded by his favorite people and toys, Jerry was happy. A peaceful passing, surrounded by epic scenery and everlasting devotion is what every living being deserves. This was the least they could do for their once-in-a-lifetime dog.

❈   ❈   ❈

"Are you ready?" It was the kind of question for which there is no right answer. Neither Jim nor Rene would ever be ready for this moment. But if they backed down, nature would find a way to decide for them, and it wouldn't be as pretty as this.

"Ready as we'll ever be." Staring into Jerry's eyes, Jim gently said his final goodbyes. "I love you, dawg."

"I love you, Jerry; I love you so much!" Rene blurted out louder than she wanted to, but she just couldn't stop crying. She heaved with shallow breaths and buried her face in his fur. She wanted so much to remember his scent, what his fur felt like, what it meant to have him by her side "You're going to be okay, baby. Lala is waiting."

"Thank you, boss." Jim rubbed Jerry's ears.

They gently caressed him for the last time, then Jim looked up at the vet, who understood the wordless gesture.

❀   ❀   ❀

In a matter of seconds, cancer's pain was purged from Jerry's life. His body was loose and light. He was finally free. No more altered gait, no more sore neck muscles, no more arthritic hips. His beautiful, eternal spirit was released from the broken body that could no longer contain it. Jim tenderly ran his fingertips over Jerry's eyes to close them, then gently placed his head back on the blanket. Rene sobbed uncontrollably, and the kennel dogs remained unusually quiet.

❀   ❀   ❀

"We'll give you some time here." Lost in their grief, neither noticed that the tech had already removed the catheter and cleaned up around Jerry. The vet quietly got up and followed closely behind her assistant. "Take as long as you need, just come get us when you're ready."

Rene lay her head on Jerry's chest as she had done so many times before. But the dog she adored was gone, his lungs devoid of movement and sound. They sat alongside their CFO in silence, stunned at their place in time. Twenty minutes passed before either found the strength to stand. Then, Jim rose first. He had one last promise to keep and scooped up Jerry in his arms. The weight of his dog's limp body caught him by surprise, and when Jerry's head slumped to one side, he almost collapsed in a fit of angst. Barely able to see through tears, Rene followed behind and opened the clinic's back door while urine dribbled down Jim's arm.

The vet was waiting inside. "We can take care of it from here."

She meant well, but Jim needed to see this through. "That's okay. I need to do this."

He followed her into a dimly lit exam room where she had a large, black bag opened on the table. Together, they carefully tucked Jerry's body inside, then Jim picked him back up. The weight felt foreign; nothing like the dog he carried before.

He followed the vet out into the clinic's storage room, lit only by streaks of sunlight shining through small garage door windows. She stopped at a big, white chest freezer and opened the lid. Thankfully, it was empty. Treating Jerry's body with the utmost tenderness, he bent over to reach inside and softly lay his best friend to rest.

Without a word, she closed the lid on the freezer—and that ten-year chapter of Jim's life.

"Thank you." He wiped his eyes.

"No, thank you. Jerry was lucky to have you." She handed him a tissue. "We'll be in touch next week about his remains, okay?"

"Sure."

❀   ❀   ❀

Rene waited in the driver's seat until Jim returned. "I'll drive. You drove us here."

"Thanks." Jim sat back and rested his head against the window as she slowly returned to Yellowstone on the meandering road. Dazed, queasy, and exhausted halfway through the ride, an unexpected gut instinct compelled him to sit up and look out the window. What he saw, nobody would have believed. Not even himself, at first.

Jerry was running alongside them. Real as the road under their wheels, Jerry bounded up like a deer and leaped through the woods with all four legs. He wore a big, happy grin, his long tongue wildly flapping in the wind. It was a ghostly figure, but there was nothing eerie about it. Jim glanced at Rene, who didn't see anything but the road through her red, puffy eyes. He turned to look outside at his spirit dog as he ran faster and higher up into the trees. Slowly, softly, Jerry's form faded as he rose above the horizon into the sky.

Rene sensed Jim's surprising burst of energy. "What's up?"

"Oh, nothing…I'll tell you later." He stared into the heavens and grinned as the last celestial sign of Jerry's spirit floated away.

— 25 —

Signs

Now it was time for the tears. Lots of them. They cried themselves to sleep in each other's arms at night, and every morning, they woke up feeling lost and uncertain. There was no need to rise early to feed Jerry or spend time walking him, or perform any of the loving routines that held their days together like the framework of a house for the last ten years. Instead, they awakened without an alarm, brewed coffee, and sat staring out the window into the campground while happy vacationing families stirred about, preparing to start their day.

"Jerry would want us to check out the geysers. We came here for him." Jim closed the window shade to hide the dumpster containing Jerry's bed.

"Yeah, I guess." Rene didn't have the energy to argue.

"So we need to get out and go do something. The CFO wouldn't want us to sit around and be sad."

Tears flowed freely down her face, landing on the kitchen table. She knew Jim was right, but couldn't stomach the idea of touring Yellowstone, pretending to be one of those cheery tourists just outside their door. "Maybe later."

❀   ❀   ❀

Yellowstone's majestic peaks and sprawling valleys would soothe their souls any other time in life, but today it couldn't pull them out of their grief. Jim finally convinced Rene to get outside and drive around, so they dutifully drove around the park, stopped at various geysers, and completed their solemn tour at Old Faithful to watch the show. It was the right way to honor Jerry, but the joyful ambiance surrounding them felt foreign and superficial.

Jim tried to keep them moving. "Done. Got the t-shirt. Let's go check out the inn. Okay?"

"I'm not hungry."

"Me neither. Let's find the bar, we need to toast Jerry."

She was totally up for that.

In pursuit of their only real ambition for the afternoon, they looked up in awe at the historic Old Faithful Inn's expansive entry and massive, four-sided stone fireplace centerpiece. The monumental chimney towers far above, rising past each floor with its own wooden walkway that overlooks the lobby below. They casually walked the halls while admiring the impressive log-built structure, and read up on the history of the park. Over at the bar, they spotted a small table in the corner that invited them to sit down for a while. Why not? they figured. No dog was waiting in the truck or back at home. They had all the time in the world to linger.

Rene handed Jim the long, leather-bound wine list. "Just pick one. I don't want anything strong. Just wine."

He carefully studied the heavy binder and grinned for the first time in two days. "Ha! I know what we're having." He handed the tablet across the table; she read the top line and returned the smile. It was Three Legged Red by Dunham Cellars.

They sipped quietly while thinking about Jerry's gentle nudge from afar. Both understood that there are no coincidences. Jerry put them exactly where they were supposed to be, at a moment when they needed to see past their broken hearts. He was always around.

※   ※   ※

Grief-stricken and disoriented without their copilot, the finality of Jerry's physical loss hit them hardest four days later. It was time to leave Yellowstone and retrieve his ashes from the friendly crematorium owner. She met them at a Montana truck stop and handed them the only physical evidence of the dog who stole their hearts: a two-pound tin of ashes gently stored in a burgundy velvet bag.

"That's it?" Jim stared at the box Rene held on her lap in the truck.

"I guess so." The finality was too much to bear. She cried all the way to the state line.

For nearly the first time since they were married, it was just the two of them. Unsteady and often on the brink of crying, they drove out of the vast prairie lands and into the Idaho mountains. During their brief, quiet highway conversations, they agreed it wasn't time for any major decisions. All they could agree on was to keep on keepin' on in their search for Jerry's final resting spot. The website would continue, of course. Tripawds was now their life's work. A helpline to others who understood, or who wanted to understand more. It was a community that brought them new friends across the country, shared experiences, both sad and happy. Now it meant so much more. It was Jerry's legacy, and their only therapy. But how would they run it without him as their constant reminder to live in the now?

Somewhere in the freezing mountains of northern Idaho, they got their answer.

❃   ❃   ❃

Nowhere near ready to rejoin civilization, their unusual life gave them the luxury of hiding out as long as they wanted. For now, it was at a national forest campground. Perched high in the mountains where hard October freezes are a way of life, it was easy to understand why campers had abandoned the free spot. The morning air was so cold outside that even inside their off-grid home they exhaled clouds of condensation, fogging up the windows and obscuring any faint rays of sunshine poking through the pines.

It was exactly one week after Jerry passed, and they were drowning in the deepest depression of their lives. Desperate for a way out, they set out for a long walk in the woods, something they hadn't done since Jerry's trail hiking days. The trailhead parking lot was empty, and as they approached the trail in silence, sorrow smothered the joy Rene would have felt at any other time out in nature.

"Jerry would have loved this," she said while walking through the gate. Jim didn't feel a need to reply to the obvious.

Her conscience battled over whether or not this was the right thing to do. It felt wrong to seek a reprieve from grief so soon after Jerry's death. But she also knew it was exactly what the CFO would have ordered. Silently, she wrestled with her emotions while Jim forged ahead on the steep mountain trail.

For more than an hour, they climbed up through the dense tree cover until they reached the snow line. Through the trees, a broad valley beckoned with hazy sunlight, compelling them to step out of the forest for a look. They said nothing while admiring hints of fall clinging onto distant mountain peaks. Just inches away, small drops of dew dripped from pine branches, capturing the entire natural world in a tiny bubble. A bluebird singing a happy morning melody stopped for a moment as they approached, then flittered off to catch up with friends.

"I get it now." She hadn't spoken for at least a mile. A hint of wonder filled her voice.

"What's that?"

"It's Jerry. He's everywhere."

She explained how she felt his presence in the surroundings. In the sunlight hitting the big cedar trees. And in the sound of water trickling in a nearby stream. Jim agreed, and also understood how that sweet, beautiful, and loving dog shed the baggage of a temporary, fragile package. No longer restricted to a physical being they could touch and see, he was now a formless spirit adding his own unique beauty to everything on this earth that they held dear.

On that cold October morning, they found the peace they had been looking for all along.

❈   ❈   ❈

After a few moments of tolerating the cold, they turned around and headed back to camp. Halfway home, three distinctive, deep, dog barks interrupted their quiet descent. The chorus of happy calls originated from the lookout above, but nobody had passed them on the narrow trail below.

"Uh…that's not coyotes," Rene said to Jim as they stood in place to listen. A symphony of continuous barks played from deep in the forest; sounds that seemed to come directly from the joyful hearts of happy dogs in the wild. They smiled, remembering how much Jerry loved hiking. But almost as soon as the barks started, they stopped and faded into the forest forever.

Rene and Jim remained frozen, unsure of what to do next. Looking into each other's eyes, they simply smiled and said nothing. Their Jerry was close. He wasn't going anywhere.

❈   ❈   ❈

The cold, damp weather of the northwest soon became unbearable, so they pointed the RV south for winter, visiting a few Tripawds members along the way. Interacting with Jerry's online friends in person was a helpful distraction from their overwhelming grief, and a reminder of the vital work that remained on his website. But as they headed down the Oregon coast on Highway 101, a constant October drizzle drained them physically and emotionally. The mildew slowly forming inside the RV windowsills didn't help.

"I'm done visiting people for a while. Can we just find a quiet place to hide out for a few days?" Jim struggled to emerge from his sorrow.

"Way ahead of you." Rene had already done her homework. "There's supposed to be some good boondocking spots along the Rogue River. Go about another fifteen minutes south, then turn left after the bridge."

"Turn left, you got it." He willingly followed her instructions while unpredictable rays of sunlight tried in vain to poke through the thick marine layer.

"This must be the spot." Jim studied the road as they crossed the river, slowing to a crawl as he approached a sign at the other end of the bridge.

"Uh, yeah, sure looks like it. Check it out!" Rene reached down for the camera, then aimed it out the window. The sign read: "Jerry's Flats Rd."

🐾   🐾   🐾

Heavy mist hovered in the tall redwoods while uninterrupted sounds of a wide, shallow river cascaded down the rocks and filled the air with nature's white noise. The environment felt so familiar to Jim. As a college kid, his dad fished that same river while taking short breaks from caregiving for his sick wife. Jim looked after his mother then, and now here he was, camping on the same gravel bar where his dad once sought refuge from the emotional burdens of an incurable disease.

After setting up camp they walked along the bank, high-stepping on rocks and pebbles of all sizes, admiring the varied shapes and colors blanketing the shore.

"Ha!" Jim stopped in his tracks and bent over to pick up a treasure.

Rene admired how he routinely spotted things on the ground that her nearsighted eyes always missed. "What?"

"Remember the guitar pick I found on that last walk we took with Jerry by the Tetons?" He looked down and pointed. On the ground was another pick, the exact same color and size as the one he found on that final walk. He grabbed it, held it out in his palm, and looked all around. "What are the chances?"

"I'm telling you, he's everywhere." She felt grateful for this little reassurance to her grieving husband, then grabbed his hand as they walked back to the RV.

*   *   *

Another teary night spent in each other's arms passed, and the next day, they walked the other direction along the river. Once more, Jim stopped to look at something on the ground.

"You won't believe this." He looked up at her, smiling.

She moved closer to see what got his attention. A flat, smooth river rock lay at his feet. Penciled on the gray surface were the words "Grandma & Jerry."

It took only a moment for them to realize who "Grandma" was. One of Jerry's favorite tasks as CFO was visiting Jim's mom after she moved into the nursing home. Nothing made him more excited than the words, "Wanna go see Grandma?" Jim picked up the rock for them to admire it. Then he tenderly put it back on the sandy impression where it lay. "Yeah. Just like you said, he's everywhere."

— 26 —

Walking the Talk

Without a dog to pull them away from the overwhelming work ahead, Jim and Rene got down to business. Their meandering search for a path into the future took a back seat to endless hours glued to their computers, fingers ferociously typing to bring in money through freelance design and writing jobs. Four months later, Jerry's fifteen minutes of fame set them free from the drudgery.

The PBS show aired on a cold February night. There was no fanfare within the Tripawds community, for it was still quite a small pack back then, before the age of social media. Jim and Rene did not hold a big gathering with real-world friends, either. It was just the two of them watching quietly from their campsite underneath the starry skies of southern New Mexico. With Jerry's favorite stuffed dog in her lap and a box of tissues on the table, tears flowed freely when Jerry came alive in the one-hour *Nature* documentary about the bond between people and pets. Gobsmacked from reliving their time with the film crew and seeing flashback videos of Jerry's entire life, they watched in awe as his story weaved the three-part documentary together.

Looking into the camera with those big, soulful eyes, Jerry spoke deep into the hearts of all who watched. He seemed to say, "It's okay, guys, see? I don't care about cancer. I'm still having fun; I am still me."

Then the credits rolled. Reality hit. Jerry was not sitting at their side anymore. But after witnessing how the audience reacted to the show, Jim and Rene felt reassured that his legacy would continue. Viewers left so many heartfelt, positive comments on the PBS website that it crashed within an hour of airtime.

Their devotion to his Tripawds community was renewed, along with their search for the property they always wanted to give him.

❁   ❁   ❁

"Look familiar?" The majestic, snow-capped peaks of the Colorado Rockies glimmered in the distance as they turned west toward Red Feather Lakes. Off they went along the narrow, winding road into the secluded wilderness for a closer look at the breathtaking landscape they had bypassed two times before while traveling with Jerry. *Third time's a charm*, Jim thought. Six miles past where the pavement ended, he slowly maneuvered the RV down a steep hill and parked in front of a small, vacant cabin.

Jerry would have loved it there. Green pastures and farmland gently rolled up to the foothills of the Mummy Range, where a priced-to-sell property waited for their offer. The five-acre mountaintop retreat their realtor found held almost all the features on their wish list. Tall, healthy pine trees rose high over aromatic sagebrush blanketing the rocky land. Aspen and pines obscured several dramatic rock outcroppings with large granite boulders covered in burnt-orange and day-glow-green lichens. In the shadow of Rocky Mountain National Park, it was a paradise for eager day hikers to explore and happy dogs to romp. It was that place they had always dreamed about.

"You think Jerry would approve?" Rene needed to be sure it was meant for them.

"I know he would!" Jim bounded off a mound of rocks and down a slope of sagebrush, just as he would have done with Jerry in the lead. He bent down to retrieve a small treasure and called out to her. "See? He'd love it!" Then he waved a small deer leg bone with the hoof still attached. "This is Jerry's Acres. His name is all over it!"

— EPILOGUE —

How to Be More Dog

Learning to Be More Dog is a lifelong process. Rene and Jim discovered that understanding the concept is one thing, but living it every single day through life's daily challenges is the hard part. Having a dog curled up at your feet makes it harder to ignore. The ability they have to help us be more present and aware is best taught by spiritual guidance master and *A New Earth* author, Eckhart Tolle. Animals' primordial nature, he writes, is what keeps them living in the now. In a 2019 episode of Oprah Winfrey's *SuperSoul Conversations*, he explains:

"The dog lives in a state of consciousness prior to the arrival of thought."

When a dog looks at you, he is not thinking about the kind of person you are, says Tolle. The dog does not judge people or events. He is simply Being—living in the moment and accepting life for what it is.

Tolle adds, "In some ways, dogs are more connected with Being than humans are."

This is why, for many people, most dogs—and yes, many cats too—fulfill the role of a spiritual guide. They help ground their humans and make them more present. They protect them from Fear, Uncertainty, and Doubt. They are Guardians of Being, says Tolle.

For Jim and Rene, Jerry G. Dawg never became the intimidating guard dog they thought they wanted, but he was the spiritual guardian and guide they needed throughout their long, strange trip together—and beyond. He protected them from the anxiety of life's most challenging moments. He taught them how to simply Be.

❧ ❧ ❧

In the summer of 2009, the book *Guardians of Being* was first published and found its way into Jim and Rene's hands. Filled with Eckhart Tolle's spiritual wisdom and illustrated by comic artist Patrick McDonnell, of the MUTTS comics fame, the book beautifully integrates two of their favorite topics: spirituality and dogs. The moment Jim gently cracked the book's spine, he randomly landed on the page that serves as the core of the little book with the big message. He grinned upon seeing that same 2008 MUTTS strip he had clipped out of the newspaper the morning after they learned of Jerry's lung metastasis. The one featuring Earl, the terrier, and his human, Ozzie: Buried in piles of paperwork at his desk, Ozzie asks himself, "Gee, I wonder what time it is?"

To which Earl the Dog repeatedly yaps, "Now! Now! Now!"

In the next frame, Earl is happy to finally be out walking with his human, who concludes, "Dogs always know what time it is."

❖   ❖   ❖

Shortly after settling in at Jerry's Acres that summer, Rene learned that McDonnell was hosting a book signing in nearby Denver. At last, they had a chance to thank the famous illustrator for creating the strip that lightened the mood of a very difficult time in their life. Every morning since then, they'd studied his comic taped inside their bathroom medicine cabinet. It had meant so much to them during their journey with Jerry over the last couple years, and remained a daily reminder of lessons learned from their own spiritual guardian.

In the comfortable downstairs meeting room of the Tattered Cover bookstore, McDonnell spoke about his work to an intimate audience of enthusiastic fans. The down-to-earth New Jersey artist sketched on a giant pad, chatted about working with Tolle, and his passionate devotion to giving animals a voice in the world. When his talk was over and the crowd thinned out, Jim and Rene stayed.

"Patrick, I just want to tell you how much your work has meant to us," Jim blurted out. He quickly explained the comic strip they studied daily, and asked if they could record a quick interview. As he spoke, a look of astonishment appeared on McDonnell's face.

"Heyyyy…I know who you guys are!"

"You do? How?" Overcome with surprise, they couldn't believe what they were hearing.

"The PBS show. My wife and I were in love with that show; watching it, we just thought yours was an amazing story," Patrick explained while Rene recorded video. "Then when you mentioned that strip with the 'Now, Now, Now,' we both got little chills."

Wide-eyed and elated at the serendipitous encounter, Rene and Jim beamed with ear-to-ear smiles. Many roads after they first discovered the strip, Jerry's spirit pulled them all together, in the right place at the right time.

An extended conversation ensued about the Tripawds community Jerry inspired. Days later, an email from the kind-hearted artist appeared in Jim's inbox. "I want to send you something; where can I FedEx it?" the artist asked.

Later that week, a package arrived at Jerry's Acres. The note inside simply said, "I thought you guys should have this." It was the original, hand-drawn illustration of McDonnell's three-panel "NOW! NOW! NOW!" comic strip, with an inscription that read: "In honor of Jerry."

❋　❋　❋

Still in awe of their new mountain home, Jim and Rene sat side by side on the wooden patio deck, looking into the wilderness and smiling. Each had their work spread out in front of them, but neither could focus. Billowing, white clouds sailed across the clear, blue sky while sweetly scented breezes of wild sage and pine floated in the air. Aspen trees budded with spring's first foliage, hiding the fact that in a few short months, deep snow would bury that deck and blanket the property. But not before they winterized the small cabin and headed south again, snowbirds in search of the never-ending summer.

"We really need to share our story," Jim said later that night while looking over digital maps on their travel blog. Amazed at all the places they had been so far, he scrolled through the dozens of Tripawds blog posts he and Rene had written in Jerry's voice. Lost in reflection of their brief time together, he wondered, "But where do we begin?"

He startled Rene with the sudden suggestion. She vaguely understood what he meant—the overall journey, both internal and external, needed to be told. "Okay then, let's tell everyone what Jerry taught us. How he got us here today." She got up from her floor cushion and walked inside to retrieve the old, leather-bound journal they occasionally filled with random hopes, dreams, and plans. She returned and sat back down, opening the book to the first blank page.

"So, what exactly did he teach us?"

Jim nodded as she grabbed a pen and began writing Jerry's lessons in her notebook.

Every day is a great day, no matter what adversity life throws your way.

Enjoy life. Live each day to the fullest. Using nothing more than happy howls, wild tail wags, and determined intention in his eyes, Jerry understood this and taught them that every moment is a gift.

Don't let adversity defeat you. Instead, embrace life's challenges to make the most of what's ahead.

Roll with the punches and adapt to enjoy those things you can do, right now. The moment Jerry hopped out of the veterinary clinic after his amputation surgery, he never looked back with anger, sadness, or regret. With every step, he moved forward into new experiences with all the enthusiasm in his grateful heart.

Balance the yin with the yang. Life inevitably throws "bad" things our way, but these are momentary and, by opening our eyes, we can see they are balanced with all the "good" in our lives.

Welcome balance into your life to stay grounded to this intention through thick and thin. When Jerry lured Rene and Jim away from an anxious workday for a quick game of soccer—or keep-away—he pulled them out of weighty mind-sets to remind them that a full life was about so much more than making money or meeting deadlines.

Take time to stop and smell the roses.

Always pause to observe the world around you; there is magic you might miss. Each time Jerry sniffed the grass, peed over another dog's mark, or studied whatever caught his attention, he showed how easy it is to find immense joy in any surrounding, whether it's around the neighborhood or the country.

Be open to loving everybody.

Do your best to find the good in everyone and everything. Jerry was the kind of dog who never held judgment. He greeted every living being with wide-eyed enthusiasm and acceptance.

Memories of their old neighborhood grump, Steve, filled Jim's mind while Rene wrote this lesson, the man's rough voice echoing like it was yesterday. "C'mon, dawg, get with the program..."

Rather than be sad after reflecting on so many memories of Jerry, Rene closed the notebook that night and smiled, vowing to live by the lessons their CFO taught them.

They would spend many summers writing notes in that journal before getting with the program to finish this book. Life got in the way as they continued to work hard and perfect Jerry's tale. Then, after one particularly stressful workday, his most important lesson struck a chord deep inside them both:

Be More Dog.

Accept life for what it is, and people for who they are. Be tolerant and determined to live a happy life. Embrace the day without expectations and give thanks for the chance to be part of it. This was how Jerry lived; this is his legacy.

Could another dog ever fill those big paw prints of his? Perhaps, someday, another might try. But that is another story altogether, and one best told from the beginning.

BE MORE DOG

— ACKNOWLEDGMENTS —

With Gratitude.

We are, and will always be, eternally grateful to Jerry for choosing us to be his parents. Our heart-and-soul dog saved us from the insanity of the rat race, showed us how to make the most of every day, and changed our lives for the better. Jerry, we hope we have evolved into the people you thought we were.

We also want to give a big 3-paws-up and special thanks to:

Every single pet parent who has ever joined and participated in the Tripawds community. By taking time to share your story, you give hope to others when they need it most.

Joel and Ross, who shared that short video of their amazing three-legged Great Dane, Moose. Without seeing your crazy gopher hunter, none of this may have ever happened.

Martha Lowe and Ralph Kanz, two amazing pet parents as wild about three-legged, pointy-eared dogs as we are. Tripawds could not do what it does without your help.

That vet tech who suggested we get another opinion about Jerry's persistent limp.

Dr. Marie Mullins, Jeannette Kelly, and her Santa Fe Veterinary Cancer Care clinic team. You gifted us so much more quality time with our Chief Fun Officer.

Every veterinarian who examined Jerry, and all those we have met and interviewed over the years. You are doing life-saving work! Thank you for allowing us to share it with our community.

Dr. Jennifer Cashman and Joanne at the Meadow Creek Veterinary Clinic in McAllister, Montana. You helped us give Jerry a fear-free, unforgettable send-off under those big, blue skies. We are forever grateful.

Big Dog Luke Robinson, for his efforts in the fight against canine cancer, and for introducing us to Ellen Goosenberg Kent, who beautifully illustrated Jerry's story in her excellent PBS documentary. And many thanks to all the "Why We Love Cats and Dogs" viewers who shared their own pet parent love stories with us.

TC Wait, Calpurnia's mom, for your compassion and understanding in our time of need.

Patrick McDonnell, for connecting us to the essence of a dog's nature, for believing in Jerry's story, and graciously offering to help us tell it.

Good ol' Perk Vickers, who put into words for us what Jerry was trying to say all along, that every day is a great day.

Sandra Haven and Lee Ann Wolff, two fellow nomads, Tripawd dog moms, and excellent editors. You understand the gifts of three-legged animals like no other wordsmiths could.

Lena West, for believing in the Tripawds mission. Through her generosity, wisdom, and support, Jerry's little blog has blossomed into the helpful resource it is today.

And last, but in no way least, thank YOU, dear reader, for taking time from your busy life to read about the lessons of our once-in-a-lifetime dog. We hope someday you will share your dog or cat's story too! We are grateful for your support and would be thrilled if you left a review on Amazon, and shared your thoughts with the hashtag #bemoredog on your favorite social media channels. Please send us a link to your review at **https://bemoredog.net/reviews** and we'll give you a special gift.

With all our heart and soul,

— Rene Agredano and Jim Nelson

— RESOURCES —

Purchase "Be More Dog" books, e-books, apparel, and gifts at:
https://bemoredog.net

Find Tripawds community pet amputation resources at:
https://tripawds.com

Share assistance programs and support the Tripawds Foundation at:
https://tripawds.org

Jim and Rene's travels continue at:
https://liveworkdream.com

HELP FOR THREE LEGGED DOGS AND CATS

Download pet amputation recovery and care handbooks at:
https://downloads.tripawds.com/store

Jerry with his pack atop Engineer Pass, Colorado—September 2, 2008

Be More Dog Apparel and Gifts

Find t-shirts, stickers, and more at
https://bemoredog.net/shop

Get Free Bonus Material

Leave book review for free gift at
https://bemoredog.net/reviews